SIMON & SCHUSTER

New York

London

Toronto

Sydney

Tokyo

Singapore

COP
TO
CALL GIRL
BY
NORMA JEAN
ALMODOVAR

SIMON & SCHUSTER
Simon & Schuster Building
Rockefeller Center
1230 Avenue of the Americas
New York, New York 10020

Designed by Liney Li
Manufactured in the United States of America

1   3   5   7   9   10   8   6   4   2

Library of Congress Cataloging-in-Publication Data

Almodovar, Norma Jean.
    Cop to call girl : why I left the LAPD to make an honest living as a Beverly Hills
prostitute / by Norma Jean Almodovar.
    p.   cm.
    1. Almodovar, Norma Jean. 2. Prostitutes—California—Los Angeles—Biography. 3.
Policewoman—California—Los Angeles—Biography. 4. Police corruption—California—
Los Angeles. I. Title.
HQ145.C2A45   1993
306.74'2'092—dc20
[B]   93-20149
                                                                                CIP
ISBN: 0-671-79425-6

This book is dedicated to my love, my friend,
Victor,
without whom I wouldn't have made it.
Thank you, my darling.

*Names and identifying characteristics
of certain individuals portrayed
in this book have been changed.
In addition, although many quoted statements
are based on court or other records,
some others reflect my own
best recollection or reconstruction
of conversations.*

CONTENTS

◇

CONTENTS

COP TO CALL GIRL

PROLOGUE

THE MORNING AFTER my wedding was cool, rainy, and bleak as I drove the three of us downtown to the courthouse. The brand-new clothes that had been approved for my incarceration were packed in two plastic garbage bags. On the sides I had written in crayon GUCCI PRISON SPECIAL, a last, weak attempt at humor.

I was wearing a pair of faded jeans and a simple oversized white sweatshirt. My long red hair was pulled into two braids that stuck straight out from either side of my head. My face was scrubbed and pale—one of the few times in my life when I wore no makeup in public. My infamous long, manicured fingernails were now pathetically bare, bitten stubs, hangnails and all. I looked about twelve years old.

The judge was a few minutes late. I sat in the back row of his courtroom, holding my mother's hand and with my husband Victor beside me. My "designer" luggage sat on the floor by the bailiff. No reporters today; besides the three of us and my attorney, the courtroom was empty. A far cry from the circus that had been the trial.

Maybe it was because it was September and ratings month, or maybe it was because the accused was a call girl, but the media was fascinated with my trial. It also didn't hurt their ratings that for ten years I had been a member of the Los Angeles Police Department and was writing a book about police corruption.

The lurid headlines in the *Daily News* and the *Los Angeles Times* brought throngs of gawkers to the courtroom every day. The TV people arrived early to set up their cameras. Even the hallway was filled with camera crews that hadn't made it in time to secure a spot in the courtroom.

The charge was one count of pandering, a felony in California with a mandatory three- to six-year prison term on the first offense. (Despite its being mandatory, very few people actually go to prison—most get probation.) Usually the charge of pandering is brought only against a madam or a pimp, and I was neither, so both the media and seasoned court watchers were positive I would be acquitted. Victor and I weren't so sure.

The L.A.P.D. had gone to a great deal of trouble to set up a sting operation to arrest me and confiscate my unfinished manuscript. It seemed they were determined to stop me from writing this book. I would not put anything past them, even making certain that I spent some time in prison to teach me the lesson that no one breaks the code of silence.

When the judge arrived, my case was the first order of business. He read his decision without once looking at me; he mumbled a few brief words and remanded me to custody for ninety days. I was being sent to state prison for a 12.03.03, a psychiatric evaluation, to determine if I posed a threat to society. The results of the study were to be the basis for determining my final sentence.

The bailiff allowed me to say my good-byes before putting the handcuffs on me. Victor and I kissed long and hard, as newlyweds would, and I gave my mother a last hug. Poor Mom. It was very difficult for her. She had flown all the way from New York to California to watch her oldest daughter be sent to prison.

The clock on the wall of Division 32, Superior Court of California, County of Los Angeles, read 9:23 on that morning, November 21, 1984. As the solid oak door closed behind me, the vision of the clock burned into my memory forever. It was the last clock I saw for quite a while.

1. THE GARDEN OF EDEN

Once upon a winter's day
I set off in search of play.
To California I came
To seek my fortune and my fame.

Along the way I lost my cherry
To the man I had to marry.
Lost my cherry, lost my mind,
Left my innocence behind.

Praised the Lord and learned to screw,
Asked the sisters what to do.
When they found out what I had done—
I married till I was twenty-one.

Left the church and Al behind,
Finally found some peace of mind.
Short-lived peace was not for me—
I joined good old L.A.P.D.

"EXCUSE ME, OFFICER, could you tell me where room three forty-two is?"
I coughed nervously as I tried to get the attention of the tall, good-looking
policeman standing in front of the academy. My first day, and I was
scared out of my wits by all the ominous-looking uniformed officers
milling around the grounds of the old naval hospital on Elysian Park
Road. The Police Training Center nearby was filled to capacity, so the
dilapidated medical buildings abandoned by the armed forces served as
temporary training facilities for class number 235 of 1972.

"Say, you're cute. You a new traffic officer?" he said, smiling, but
it didn't relieve my jitters. "Look, I'll take you upstairs to your class-
room. What's your name, babe?"

"Uh, no. That's okay. If you just tell me where it is, I'll find it
myself." I hated to sound stuck-up, but my husband warned me about the
onslaught of advances I might get if I took this job.

"It's the third floor, to your left. Take the elevator over by the statue of Admiral Byrd." He stuck out his hand. "I'm Sergeant Paul Lewin."

I extended my own and smiled shyly. "Thanks. I'm Norma Jean. Oh, and I'm sorry I didn't know you were a sergeant. I don't know how to tell that yet. I hope I didn't offend you." I looked into his big brown eyes and saw I had made my first friend.

"Good luck, Norma Jean. I'm sure the department will be very lucky to have someone as pretty as you out there giving tickets."

Room 342 was a large, reconstructed hospital ward, and it still smelled of antiseptic and old wars. It had a makeshift platform with a podium at the back of the room, and odds and ends of chairs and tables in neat rows. A blackboard against the back wall was filled with unintelligible words, numbers, and diagrams. The city's insignia hung proudly in the center of the board, but somebody had written FUCK YOU in the middle.

The room was filled with an odd assortment of humanity. Seventy-five people, mostly men, had made it from the waiting list for the job of traffic officer. They had been rescued from the terror of the unknown—a job in the private sector—and were all glad to be there.

I felt lucky to be one of only six women considered worthy of hiring; these women were unlikely candidates for this job. Besides myself, a newly remodeled wallflower, complete with contact lenses and red hair, there was a tall, lean, tan, young blonde with a leathery outdoors face; a short, middle-aged Italian woman with a gap between her teeth and with a body that looked as though it had borne many children; two young black ladies who might have been lion tamers; and a Hispanic-looking woman about my age with long blondish hair.

The men and women were standing around in groups of twos and threes. I figured my best bet was to make friends with the Hispanic-looking female, who was talking a mile a minute to one of the young men.

I took a deep breath, walked over to her, waited for her to finish a sentence, and introduced myself: "Hi, I'm Norma Jean. I guess we will be training together."

"I'm Sylvia Carter." She smiled enthusiastically and held out her hand. "It looks as if we're going to have a very interesting couple of months. Did you see all the brass hanging around this place? I sure am going to have a good time!" The young man she had been talking to scratched his head and walked away.

Sylvia took my arm and steered me toward a couple of empty chairs in the middle of the room. "Let's sit together, Norma Jean. I have a feeling we are going to be good friends."

"Great," I said. "I hope we get assigned to the same place when we get out of here."

"Can I have your attention, please?" a tall, dark-haired woman in her late forties with a very military looking outfit stood at the podium. "If you will all take seats, we will begin. I'm Traffic Supervisor Vilma Gerny, and I'll be giving you your class schedules. Please take one of these forms and pass the rest down your row as I call out your name. Almodovar, Norma J."

"Here," I said in a high squeaky voice, my trademark throughout my police career. I reached for the form and smiled as I heard several whistles from the males in the class. It wasn't long ago that I had been the class wallflower in high school. It felt good to be appreciated.

"That will be enough! Please remember that you have been hired by the Los Angeles Police Department, and from now on you will exhibit behavior becoming to traffic officers. As far as the public is concerned, you represent the whole police department. They do not care that you are civilians and not sworn police officers. You will be held accountable for your actions as if you were."

"Old biddy bitch," said a male voice from the back of the room. The men all laughed. The women in the class tittered behind their hands.

Supervisor Gerny gave us a look that could kill. Then she tried to smile. "I realize it's your first day and you are not familiar with department policies, but you will be!"

I smiled at Sylvia. "Was that a statement or a threat?" I whispered.

Supervisor Gerny completed the roll call. There were a couple of clowns in the group. One of them, a dumb-looking young man with a strange haircut, emitted a loud fart during the introduction. The men applauded, and he thanked them. I made a mental note never to sit near him.

During training we were taught how to write citations and how to use the police radio. We had classes in traffic safety, traffic directing, and motorcycle riding. Most of the technical stuff was boring, the lectures were tedious, and the instructors lacked teaching skills. But one of the more fascinating lectures was on ethical conduct and police corruption. I was genuinely puzzled by this concept—surely the L.A.P.D. didn't have *that* problem!

Sylvia and I were becoming good friends. We sat together during the lectures and spent our lunch at the police academy itself. I learned more about the police department during those lunches than in all my training classes. Sylvia's brother-in-law was a sergeant in the Van Nuys Division, and her soon-to-be ex-husband was a motor cop. She said she intended to marry another cop, a captain, at least, before her career was over. "It's very exciting to be married to a cop," she gushed one afternoon after motorcycle training class. "They are sooo macho!" There was no argument from me. They sure looked macho, and many were really good looking! I felt like a kid in a candy store!

Even though I was hit upon a lot during training, I turned them all down. My marriage was unhappy, but although I wasn't sure I was ready to leave my husband, Sylvia's entrance in my life made me consider my options once again.

Two and a half years earlier, seven months out of high school, I was bored, freezing, and barely making a living after moving to New York City from my hometown of Binghamton in upstate New York. On a particularly bitterly cold day in January 1970, I made up my mind to take a two-week vacation in California. And who knew, maybe I'd stay there!

My father's sister Rusty, who lived in Newport Beach, invited me to stay with her. I also had a place to stay in Los Angeles if I wanted, with my Puerto Rican friend Lou whom I'd met at the Christian summer camp I'd attended as a teenager. She had come to California a year earlier and was involved in some sort of religious group.

My oldest brother Doug lent me a hundred dollars and warned me to behave, as big brothers are apt to do. Aunt Rusty met me at the airport in Los Angeles, and we drove to the vacation home she and her husband owned in Palm Springs. She was gabby and friendly and made me feel welcome. When I was a child, I had little occasion to get to know my father's side of the family. Listening to her talk, I decided that Aunt Rusty was definitely more interesting than my mother's sisters.

Later in the week we returned to her home in Newport Beach. By this time I had fallen in love with California—the weather, the palm trees, the smell of gardenias in the evening air, and the ocean, which crashed against the rocks on the bluffs far below her home.

Trying not to be a nuisance, I spent most of my time sitting in the rattan swing on the porch, watching the tide, and writing letters to my mother and friends in New York.

One Saturday my friend Lou called and asked if I was ready to join her and the "brothers and sisters" in Los Angeles. I really wasn't ready to leave the paradise of my aunt's home, but I had promised Lou I would visit her and see what this church stuff was all about. On Sunday, Lou and some of the "sisters" came to pick me up.

Lou's friends were all very attentive during our two-hour ride to Los Angeles. They sang hymns and praised the Lord and called me sister. But their doting soon became stifling, and by the time we arrived at the place where the unmarried sisters lived, I had a splitting headache.

An assorted group of Asian, Hispanic, and Caucasian women, most in their early to late twenties, gathered to hug me and welcome me to the church. Their faces were bright, sweet, and smiling, clean, freshly scrubbed, without a trace of makeup. Most were wearing white head scarves and had their long hair pulled back from their faces. No matter what I said they responded with "praise the Lord." Behind fixed smiles their vacant eyes stared back at me.

One woman showed me to my bedroom, which was on the third floor, and I was assigned a bunk bed, two drawers in a large antique wooden dresser, and a small closet space that, unknown to me at the time, closely resembled the living area I would have years later in a very different place.

The meeting hall was across the street in an unpretentious one-story building with no sign, no pulpit, no platform, and no pews. Rows of metal chairs were set up in a circle around the room, and more smiling faces enthusiastically greeted the visitors and handed out the evening's music sheets.

There was no organized service. The meeting went on for hours; it was all spontaneous singing, testifying, and lots of loud acclamations. No one seemed to want to leave except me, and I couldn't because I couldn't get back in the sisters' house without a key. I didn't know any of the hymns, and I certainly wasn't planning to stand up and testify, so I fidgeted uncomfortably in the chair until one of the elders closed the meeting with a prayer.

Lou had to stay around for a while, and she insisted I stand at the back of the meeting hall and listen to the declarations of faith from the newly converted. All I wanted to do was return to the house, take a bath, and go to sleep. Finally the meeting hall cleared of all the happy believers, and we, too, left.

The next morning I was awakened very early by the head sister, Madeleine, and invited to join the prayer group for breakfast. It was more prayer than breakfast, and a mini-version of the evening meeting. I thought it would never end. Lou had several job interviews that day, so

I was left with Madeleine, whose duty was to make certain I was not left alone for a single moment. I soon learned the church considered thinking the devil's tool, and it was the church members' mission to prevent potential converts from spending time alone. From sun up to sun down I was inundated with church dogma and was never allowed to be by myself, even to go to the bathroom.

Friday night—two days before my scheduled return to New York—I had such a severe headache that I couldn't even stand up or move my head. The pain was so intense I became sick to my stomach. After getting an ice pack and some aspirin, Lou and Madeleine convinced me that my headache was a sign from the Lord—they said I was being stubborn and should call on the Lord to be saved.

The pressure was too much. They wore me down. I gave in to their pleas and that evening had a "born again" experience, for the second time in my life. Perhaps the encounter I had as a child didn't take. Like magic the headache disappeared. The brothers and sisters rejoiced when I testified at the meeting that night and was accepted.

I called my mother in New York to tell her the good news—her errant daughter had come back to the fold, finally accepting the beliefs she herself had embraced years ago. I also told her I was not returning to New York. Mother was not overjoyed to hear I was staying in California, but I explained that the sisters persuaded me to stay and share my newfound salvation with others. They claimed the church was the only safe environment. Hallelujah! If that is what the brothers and sisters felt, then of course I must stay.

With the help of a sister I found a job as an insurance rate adjuster at Continental Insurance. It was close to the church, and we were able to "fellowship" for lunch every day.

Life seemed idyllic. I didn't have to worry about making decisions; they were made for me by the elders. The elders knew what was best for all of us because they spent long hours in prayer; God gave them the answers. I was such a good little sister, I never questioned anything they said or did.

Then into my Garden of Eden the "ugly snake of sex" reared its evil head. Lou's cousin Al arrived from New York, fresh out of the air force. He was a big hunk of a guy, tall, dark, and dangerously handsome. I was instantly attracted to him, and he seemed to like me, even though I was a size sixteen.

We began supervised dating, having coffee together with the other brothers and sisters after the evening meetings. A month after meeting Al I moved out of the bungalow and into an apartment with three other single sisters. The apartment manager and his wife were also in the church and gave the sisters a special rental rate.

One night Al and I went up to the roof of the building to talk. We began kissing and petting up a storm. One thing led to another, and the next thing I knew he was unbuttoning my jeans, and his large, hairy hand made its way between my legs. As he kissed me he masturbated me to orgasm. After I recovered, I reached for his penis and pulled it out of his pants. Breathlessly, Al asked me to take it in my mouth. With eagerness I began moving my mouth up and down over it until finally he let out a loud cry. This was the first time I had experienced an orgasm with a man, and it felt good. For the moment I forgot about sin and guilt, but the sound of my roommates calling brought me crashing back to reality.

We continued to see each other and tried not to give in to our growing passion. The only thing it could lead to was intercourse, and we couldn't do that. Not without marrying. My mother tried to instill the concept that sex was reserved for marriage, and the local church parroted her beliefs. While Al and I had not yet had intercourse, I knew in my heart I would if he asked me.

I was confused and ashamed of the intensity of my sexual feelings toward him. I needed to talk with someone who might help me sort them out. I went to Carol, a sister with whom I had a growing spiritual relationship; she was totally devoted to the church and to her husband. I foolishly confided the details of my rooftop liaison to her. We prayed for God's guidance.

A week later Al approached me after an evening meeting. He looked sad and asked, "Honey, who did you tell about us?"

Puzzled, I shook my head and looked at him. "Why do you want to know?"

"The elders came to me before the meeting tonight and said we would have to get married immediately or leave the church. They want an answer tomorrow."

I had been betrayed by Carol. Al was unusually quiet. "Honey, what do you want to do? If you want to leave the church, I understand . . . but if you want to, I will marry you. I love you, Norma Jean." He tenderly brushed a lock of hair from my eyes.

We decided to get married. Saturday morning Al and I went downtown to city hall, stood before a judge who stamped our certificate after the perfunctory, obligatory mumbo jumbo, "And I now pronounce you husband and wife." No notice in my hometown paper that little Norma Jean Wright had gotten married!

After the ceremony we returned to our respective apartments. We had no honeymoon, and it was a while before we could afford an apartment of our own. When we finally saved enough money for the first and last months' rent, we found a little one-bedroom apartment in the same neighborhood where most of the brothers and sisters lived. The night we moved in, we consummated our relationship with actual intercourse. It was quite a letdown. The spontaneity was gone, and so was the passion we felt for each other before my betrayal.

I was still so shy and unhappy with my overweight body that I did not allow Al to leave any lights on. When I had to run into the bathroom, I grabbed the sheet to cover my nakedness. It was a long time before he ever got to see his wife without clothes.

The only thing Al and I had in common was the church, and it was not very long after we were married that I began to doubt my commitment. The tenets of the church were not really what I believed at all, but I felt too pressured by the other members to examine my beliefs. Gradually I stopped going to the meetings. It took Al a little longer to quit, but eventually we both left the church and moved into a charming little apartment in the San Fernando Valley.

Al had a job in construction, but when he was in the air force, he had worked in security, and now he thought he wanted to join the Los Angeles Police Department. He sent for an application.

Meanwhile, I had gotten pregnant. I was raised to believe that all adult women *had* to have babies to complete their lives. I wanted the baby. Al did not. He threatened to leave me if I did not have an abortion.

After the abortion I was unmotivated to return to my new job as a clerk for the Pacific Bell Telephone Company. I stayed at home and moped. When the application forms for the job of traffic officer came, Al decided he was happy with construction after all, so I filled them out and sent them in. After two years on a waiting list, the reply arrived. I took the civil service exam and was hired in 1972.

By then my marriage had become unbearable. We had no sex life. Al was the one with the headaches when I was in the mood. Still overweight, I felt unattractive, unloved, and rejected when he told me he was too tired to make love.

Al didn't want me to work. His Latino mind-set said that was the man's role. But I was bored. The apartment was too small to keep me busy cleaning, and I didn't have many friends, so I was alone most of the time. To fill the lonely hours I taught myself how to make clay dolls, a hobby that became a secondary income for many years.

When my sixteen-year-old sister came to live with us for a while, I had someone with me when Al wasn't home. There was only five years' difference between us, but I became a doting "mother." When she registered at the local high school in the fall, I got involved with the P.T.A.

My mother had surgery in October and needed my sister to take care of her. Since I wasn't working, I volunteered to go instead so that my sister could stay in school. It was the first time I had been away from Al. I missed him so much, I called every day. One night when I called he was very drunk and was crying.

"Sweetheart, last night . . . I got your sister drunk, and I fucked her. Listen, I know I'm a no-good bum. I'm sorry." He sounded so pathetic. I'd been gone only a week!

Angry and confused, I flew back to L.A. the next afternoon. Al was at work and my sister was in school when I arrived. I paced through the apartment and cried for hours. When they finally came home, I had made up my mind. If our marriage was going to work, my sister had to go.

The next day I put her on a Greyhound bus for New York. For many years we didn't talk, but eventually we made up. I guess I always knew it wasn't her fault. Now we are as close as sisters can be.

Al was a different story. I thought I could forgive him, but I couldn't. Our marriage was on shaky ground, and I didn't need much coaxing to leave. I thought if I lost weight, dyed my hair, and started wearing makeup, he would find me more attractive. I went on a stringent diet and became a redhead. As I took control of my life, I felt better about myself and cared less and less about what Al thought. When I married him, I believed I would never find another man who would love me. But if what we had was love, I could do without it.

By the time I entered the academy, I was down to a size seven from a size sixteen. I felt sexy and ready for whatever new ideas and experiences my friend Sylvia would share with me.

2. SHATTERED DREAMS

When all of our dreams have been shattered
And we're lost like a little child,
When all of our heroes have scattered,
And the hills of glory grown wild

Those dreams so many years woven,
Those heroes, so tall and so true,
Those hills once so glorious a haven,
The skies that are no longer blue

Who, and what will replace them?
And how shall we mend our heart?
And how shall we find our way back home?
And when do we get to start?

"NORMA JEAN, you really should meet my brother-in-law, Jerry. He's a sergeant in Van Nuys, and he is separated from his wife. I think you'd really like him." Sylvia took a sip of iced tea. She and I were having lunch at the academy restaurant, ogling the passing parade of handsome hunks in their starched blue uniforms.

"What about my husband, Sylvia? How am I going to get out of the house?" I had already told her that I was thinking of leaving Al as soon as we completed training and I had a steady paycheck.

"Just tell him you're going out with the girls. We women need a night out, too! I'll even call him and talk to him if you want, okay?"

"Sure, Sylvia, if you think it would help."

Before we returned to class she called Jerry to introduce us over the phone. He sounded nice enough, but what did I know about dating cops?

I agreed to meet him one night after class. He worked until eleven, so we arranged that I would go to his apartment and we would go out for a drink when he got home from work.

Meanwhile, I called Al from the academy and told him Sylvia and I were going out. It wasn't as difficult to deceive him as I thought it would be.

Jerry lived in an apartment over the garage of a house he and his estranged wife owned and rented to another cop. The key was under the mat, and I let myself in. The place was exactly what I imagined a typical bachelor pad would be: very little furniture but lots of crates filled with books, clothes, and police paraphernalia.

Sitting on a box, I nervously tapped my fingers on the coffee table. Sylvia told me he was thirty-five; I was only twenty-one. He's old, I thought.

By the time Jerry got home, around ten-thirty, I had fallen asleep on the box. Sylvia was right. He was very good-looking and also very charming.

We went to a cop hangout bar in Glendale. Jerry kept me amused with his police anecdotes and made me feel very comfortable. When the bar closed he took my hand gently and looked into my eyes. "Will you get mad at me if I say I want to go to bed with you, Norma Jean?" At least he was direct. I was still too inexperienced and shy to come right out and say what I wanted, so I mumbled a reply.

Instead of going back to his apartment, he rented a motel room. He explained that he didn't want to make love in his messy apartment. He didn't need to explain; I just wanted to get laid.

The lights were off and Jerry was under the covers when I shyly came out of the bathroom. Even though I had lost weight, I was not comfortable with my body.

He switched off the TV with the remote control, kissed me, and laughed. "What took you so long? For a minute I thought you might have made your escape out the bathroom window!"

My body was tense, and I shivered as he pulled me close. "Hey, hey, calm down, honey. I'm not going to bite you. You're scared to death, aren't you?" He kissed my forehead tenderly. "We're going to have to do something about that!"

He sensed I had needs I couldn't vocalize. When he thought I was ready, he entered me, gently thrusting back and forth. He was very well endowed, and he knew what to do with it, although he didn't do it nearly long enough to bring me to orgasm. After he climaxed, he held me tenderly, caressing me. "Your skin is so soft, Norma Jean. You are so pretty. Will I get to see you again?" He kissed me gently. I was crying quietly.

"Hey, what's the matter? Did I do something to hurt you?"

"No, no, Jerry. Nothing like that. It's just that you are the second man I have ever made love to, and, well, it was very nice, and . . ."

"Didn't I do it right?" He sat upright.

"Oh, yes, you did everything right. It's my husband. He doesn't want to make love to me anymore, since I found out about him and my sister. I needed tonight so much . . . to feel like a woman again."

"Does that mean you will see me again?"

"Oh, yes. . . . I mean, if you want. Sure."

"I think we could have something special, Norma Jean."

It turned out that we did have something special and developed a wonderful sexual relationship. Whenever I saw Jerry, I told my husband that Sylvia and I were going out. When I was finally ready to leave my husband two months later, Jerry helped me find an apartment.

Not long after I moved into my new apartment and started a new life, sadly for me, Jerry and his wife reconciled. Although we remained good friends, we were never lovers again. He was the first of many lovers, and he will always remain dear to my heart for giving me the strength to leave a bad marriage.

My police training was progressing. The weeks seemed to fly by, and soon it was September. At the end of our six-week course Supervisor Gerny told us we would be assigned to a field officer for six months for further training, and if our field officer passed us, we had a permanent job! The first six months on the job is very crucial to weeding out unwanted employees because after that it takes an act of God to get rid of an established civil servant. Even if one gets fired, it sometimes doesn't stick.

Take the case of Officer Michael Lybarger, a vice cop assigned to arrest bookmakers. He decided to go for a little piece of the action by giving the big guys some notice before the arrests came down. It was reported that the big guys happily provided Michael with some extra spending money—until he got caught. Then he got fired. But six years later, after a successful lawsuit, Michael was reinstated. He received six years of back pay and was eligible to retire within a month of his reinstatement, with a partial pension!

When we got our assignment slips, mine was to Hollywood Division, Sylvia's to Van Nuys. Sylvia and I promised each other we'd stay in touch. We did for a while but then made other friends and lost contact. The last I heard, she had married a captain and was living well.

Sylvia Carter wasn't the only woman I encountered who suggested that I make friends with as many of the higher-ups as possible. By friends she meant bed partners.

Barbara Folsom, blond, blue-eyed, tall, and broad-shouldered, also possessed a noticeably large bosom. Barbie Big Boobs is what everybody called her, but not to her face. She seemed pleasant enough when we were first introduced, but she gave new meaning to the expression "two-faced." Looking into the vast emptiness of her small, pale blue eyes left one feeling one had met a dead soul. I made the mistake of confiding in her once and discovered that whatever she heard, she twisted into unrecognizable and vicious gossip.

When I finished training and began dating, Barbara took me aside. She leaned toward me and whispered in a confidential tone, "I hear you give good head."

My face burned crimson. I was still too soft, or I would have slapped her face. Instead I stammered, "Where'd you hear that?"

"One hears these things, Norma Jean. If you fuck around with the boys, everybody's gonna know it." Her eyes narrowed. "Listen, the only reason I'm taking the trouble to talk to you is that I think you've got what it takes to get ahead. Take a lesson from me. It's tough being a woman in a man's job. Know where a few bodies are buried. You gotta work it right. All you gotta do is accommodate the right guys."

My mouth dropped. I was speechless. Barbara misunderstood the silence and continued. "There's lots of brass who like good head, and they remember a gal who's nice to them. Trust me, I'll steer you right. Cops are lousy lovers, all of them. So if you're going to put out, at least get something in return."

I looked her in the eye. "Thanks but no thanks. I don't put out for favors." I started to walk away.

But Barbara grabbed my arm. "You're a nice kid, Norma Jean. I'd hate to see you waste your talent. The way you're going about it you'll just get a reputation for being easy. Do it my way, and you'll thank me someday. You might need friends in high places."

Barbara may have been way off about many things, but the one thing she did get right, as I sadly learned, was that cops make lousy lovers. Most of the ones I went to bed with thought that making love was like using their gun—that all they had to do was take aim and shoot!

Many years later, Barbara's words returned to haunt me. I did need friends then, and I didn't have any. The ones who were friendly didn't have enough clout to do me any good. Looking back, I still wouldn't have done *that* any differently.

My training officer, Bob Clifton, was a union man all the way, making certain that the city didn't overwork him. He taught me how far one's salary can be stretched with free lunches, dinners, and half-priced clothing. These were some of the many perks offered by local businesses to members of the police department in exchange for leniency toward various owners and employees who just might infract the law. He also showed me how much one can accomplish on a fifteen-minute coffee break.

I was naive. "Gee, Bob, weren't we in the bank an awfully long time? Are you sure the supervisor won't get upset?" I was careful not to do any personal business on city time. I was certain we would get caught as we sat in the back of his friend's family grocery store and he played poker.

It was amazing that I ever passed probation. Traffic Supervisor Fishbeck had a chip on her shoulder bigger than her four-foot ten-inch, ninety-pound body. She drove a canary yellow Harley-Davidson to work, which clashed with her coppery orange hair. She always had a Lucky Strike cigarette dangling from her mouth, and in a voice as rough and gravelly as Popeye's would spew obscenities that would make a truck driver blush. She sometimes even came to work drunk. Our clashes extended beyond her flaming red hair and mine. From the beginning we had conflicting personalities. She had an immediate aversion to my looks, my style, and my youth.

Fortunately, I did pass probation, and not long afterward the police department implemented a new night watch program for traffic officers. Normally assigned to a three-wheeled motorcycle, the night watch traffic officers would be driving a police car, and riding in pairs for safety reasons.

At first they asked for volunteers. When no one volunteered, they drafted from the ranks of the newly hired, like me. And like Frank Maloschitz. He was the one who made rude noises the first day of training. Roll calls just weren't roll calls without a few of his rectal recitals.

It was difficult getting used to the night watch arrangement. Frank and I didn't always get along, and what made it more unpleasant was that we were paired for the entire eight-hour shift. Where I went, he had to go, and vice versa. Everyone called us the Siamese twins—we were joined at the ticket book.

However, night watch did have its benefits. There were more eligible, interesting cops working nights than days. Sergeant Tom Mahony was the most memorable of the many I dated. I met Tom soon after I was assigned in October 1972. He was the night watch commander. Finding another cop to date was the last thing on my mind, but when I walked into the W.C.'s office, I was stopped in my tracks by this gorgeous male animal sitting behind the desk. Wow! I smiled and batted my eyes at him. "Well, hi there!"

"Hi there yourself." He smiled back. His voice was deep and resonant.

"I came in to drop off my Days Off Request. You the new sergeant?"

"No, I just got back from vacation. You're a new charlie unit, aren't you?"

"Well, I've been on the job since August, and I just got assigned to nights."

As I began to mentally ravish this hunk, my partner Frank walked into the office. "Norma Jean, did you turn in our Days Off Requests yet?" As usual he passed wind.

The romantic electricity in the room vanished. I sighed. "Yes, Frank."

"Then let's get out of here. I want to eat dinner."

When I finally got Sergeant Mahony to ask me out, he told me that as attractive as he found me, he had hesitated because he was involved in a long-term relationship. After we had dinner he invited me for a walk in Griffith Park. If it was dark and secluded, I wanted to be there with him. I was determined to make him seduce me. Hours later we were still making small talk.

It took several more dates before he got the hint. He took me back to my apartment. As he hesitantly undressed me and made love to me, I just lay there, a victim of the cop credo that women who enjoy sex are whores. I did not want Tom to think I was a whore. Only inwardly did I yell, moan, groan, shriek, and carry on like a wicked woman. I didn't know how to let him know that he was pushing the right buttons and should keep right on doing what he was doing. He gave up too easily. Just as I was nearing a climax, he retreated. He quietly had his release and then kissed me good night and went home.

I still don't know how we ever managed it, but that one night turned into a year-long relationship, and it was good while it lasted. I thought I was in love with him, but he didn't reciprocate. I learned to express myself better, and after he got over being so nervous with me, he proved to be a wonderful lover, earning a Number One A+ on my scoreboard. Of the many police officers I dated he was one of the very few who cared about my pleasure.

One day I found a card that another woman had sent him. I became jealous and confronted him. He didn't deny it. I thought I could make him give her up by telling him that I thought we should break off our relationship. He agreed we should. I was bluffing; he was not.

It took me years to get over him. I thought of him as my hero and wanted to win him back. Actually my vivid imagination had attributed to him more hero qualities than he actually had, but there is still a soft spot in my heart for him (which is probably moldy by now).

Working nights turned out to be a pleasure. Besides the fascinating cops I met, it was great because I could stay up until the wee hours of the morning and sleep past noon, something I really enjoyed.

Sergeant Peter Leonard, who became a Number One B on my scorecard, came into my life at almost the same time as Sergeant Mahony. A spectacular cross between Clark Gable and Frankie Avalon, Peter wasn't as tall as Tom but was just as ruggedly built. He had just recently divorced and wasn't ready for a full-time relationship. Neither was I. We both decided to engage in a purely sexual relationship. It didn't take nearly as long to seduce Peter as it had Tom, and before long we had a regular weekly ritual.

He got off from work earlier than I did and parked outside my building. When I got home I knocked on the window of his car because he usually fell asleep. But he'd be wide awake and waiting for me in bed by the time I put on my robe. Once I jumped in beside him, feeling his warm hairy chest and accidentally hitting his erection under the covers.

"Oh, excuse me, Peter. I didn't mean to hurt you. Let me give you a kiss and make it better."

He laughed and threw back the covers. "If you're going to kiss anything, kiss that!" He pointed to his erection.

"Oh, Peter, you know that's illegal! Oral copulation is a felony! We'll go to jail!" We giggled. It was true, however. At that time in California oral copulation between consenting adults was still a felony and it was punishable by up to five years in state prison. The penal code number was 288A, not that any cop I knew obeyed this law. In fact, it was quite a joke around the police station. Every cop I knew was a felon. They may not have been very good felons, but that was the law. One cop was so blatant in his scorn, he had a personal license plate that read 288 AHH.

Peter looked at me with his beautiful big brown eyes, a happy grin on his face. "Ah, go on. I won't arrest ya!"

Smiling, I looked him square in the eye and said, "Yeah, well what about the vice cops? Will they arrest me?"

I have to admit that back then I wasn't very good at giving head. I didn't know how to practice deep throat on a cucumber. *That* was a trick I learned later as a call girl! In my years as a call girl I learned that most wives won't participate in oral sex. Pity!

Our relationship continued for several years, until Peter transferred out of Hollywood to the Metro Division. We occasionally got together for old times' sake. Then he got married.

I ran into him years later, after I had left the department and became an infamous call girl. Still working Metro Division, he and other Metro cops were at the Universal Sheraton Hotel guarding Vice President George Bush and California Governor George Deukmejian who were having lunch there. I was running for lieutenant governor at the time and was there to film a segment for "Good Morning America," several floors up.

He saw me and waved. "Norma Jean! What are you doing here?" He still had that magical grin. His full head of wavy brown hair was tinged with silver, but he was still a fox.

"I'm here to do a show."

"Yeah, I've seen you on several. You look great on TV!" He coughed and looked down at his shoes. "Say, listen, Norma Jean, am I going to be in your book?" he asked shyly.

"Of course, Peter. You were an important part of my life. But don't worry, I've changed your name."

"Oh, I wasn't worried about that. I just wanted to be sure you mentioned me. Do I get a whole chapter, a paragraph, or just a short sentence?"

"Heck, I don't know. Those things get changed several times before the final draft."

"Well, how will I know who is me?" He pouted.

"Don't worry. You're the only cop in the book who looks like Clark Gable. Okay?"

He leaned over and kissed me on the cheek.

I laughed. "Won't you get into trouble for kissing a convicted felon on duty?"

"Norma Jean, I don't care what anybody says, you're all right! And a lot of other cops think so, too. We're going to vote for you!"

After Peter and Tom I dated other cops I met during the night shift, mostly married officers. The majority of the relationships were brief, often only sexual. All were unsatisfactory, and some were painful.

Whomever I dated, it was expected that sex would be involved. Prior to my marriage and joining the police department I had little dating experience. I had no female friends to confide in. I had not kept in touch with Sylvia from the academy, and Barbara Folsom's advice was not usable. I learned to be more careful the hard way—through a particularly unpleasant encounter with a psychotic vice cop.

I walked up to the driver of the dark green Chevrolet and knocked at his window. "I am sorry, sir, but you can't park here." The driver reached into his pocket and then rolled down the window.

"Oh my God, he's going to shoot me," I thought, rapidly stepping toward the rear of the car.

He laughed and shoved his wallet at me. "Hey, don't worry. I'm not going to shoot you. I'm a cop, too." He showed me his badge.

He looked at my nametag. "Al–mo–do–var. I like your last name. Mind if I call you Al? I'm Ralph. I work vice, and I'm on a stakeout. My partner is across the street in the hamburger joint. We're trying to move the whores off this street."

He got out of his car. He was not much taller than me. We walked over to the sidewalk, out of the traffic.

"So, Al, what are you doing after work? You free to have a cup of coffee or something?" he asked with a hard, cynical grin on his face.

"I don't drink coffee."

"Yeah, whatever. Ya want to go or what?"

"Okay. I get off at two. Where should I meet you?"

"Don't worry, honey. I know where to find you. I'll pick you up outside the station at two-fifteen. Don't change clothes."

I went into the W.C.'s office to sign out, then grabbed my civilian clothes from my locker. As I came out of the locker room, Ralph was waiting outside the door.

During breakfast he became silent and sullen. He finished his last sip of coffee, stuffed a piece of cold toast in his mouth, and picked up the tab. He walked to the front and presented his badge. Breakfast didn't cost him a penny.

In silence we drove back to the station to pick up my car. He didn't even get out to open the door for me. "Al, I'm going to follow you home," he announced flatly. "I want to make sure you get there okay."

I had a garage underneath my apartment building. When I walked out from the parking space, he was waiting out front. I indicated that my apartment was upstairs.

"Let's go. I want to talk." He nearly shoved me up the stairs.

I offered him a drink from my meager bar. He declined, then plopped on the couch while I went into the bedroom to change. It was four-thirty in the morning.

I stopped in the bathroom to dab on some cologne. After a hard day's work, I needed something to make me smell less like a traffic officer and more like a woman.

He stared at me long and hard as I walked over to the stereo to turn on a little mood music.

"I don't want to listen to anything," he snapped. "Come here and sit down."

Meekly, I obeyed. I shuffled to the couch and sat beside him. He put his chubby arm around me and kissed me on the mouth. His stubbled face tore my skin, and his lips pressed so hard, he hurt my lip. I backed away. "Ouch! Not so rough!"

He opened my gown and leaned toward my breasts. I closed my eyes as his mouth descended on my flesh. Then I shot up like a rocket! The bastard bit my nipple—hard! I yelled and slapped his face. "Shit! What the hell do you think you're doing?"

"Ah, come on, honey. I know you like it that way! All women do! You're all whores, and you love to be treated like shit."

He pulled me into the bedroom and tore off his clothes. It was obvious what he wanted, with his erection sticking out of his Fruit of the Looms, but what kind of fucking did he have in mind?

He grabbed my shoulders and spun me around, then took my head between his hands and again kissed me savagely. He pushed me on the bed, laying his heavy, hairy body on top. I tried not to yell. I figured this guy had a screw loose, and it would be easier if I just went along with the program. The term "date rape" had not yet been coined, and with my reputation it would be difficult to convince a jury I had been unwilling.

He was brutally twisting and pulling on my nipples, and when he kissed me, his stubble continued to tear my flesh. I could feel my lip beginning to swell where he bit me. Finally the pain became unbearable. I began sobbing hysterically. "Oh, stop, please. You're hurting me!"

He jumped off me and stood up beside the bed. "You little whore. You get a man all turned on and tease him, and then when he gives you what's comin' to you, you crawl and scream bloody murder! You cunts are all alike! Women! All goddamn whores!" He threw his clothes on, grabbed his jacket, and walked out the door, slamming it behind him.

I lay there in pain, moaning, for several hours before I at last fell asleep.

Afterward I saw him on Hollywood Boulevard and sometimes in the station, bringing in the street prostitutes he had arrested. Mostly we avoided each other, but once he tried to apologize for his behavior and asked me out again. I declined politely. Whatever his problem was, I wanted nothing to do with him. Ralph worked vice for several more years before joining the F.B.I.

After the encounter with Ralph I needed a breather from dating. I started to hang out with the after-work crowd. When we got off work, it was too late to go to the favorite cop bar hangouts, such as the Stop on Sunset Boulevard and the Police Academy restaurant and bar. We had our own little hangout behind the police station, in the far corner of the parking lot. Out came the ice chest with the cold beer, and the morning watch guys would deliver a fresh, hot, free pizza from our favorite pizza place, Two Guys from Italy on Hollywood Boulevard.

We sat for hours in the early morning fog, eating pizza and telling stories. Sometimes the guys would get drunk and make passes. I wasn't interested in group sex, so I ignored them. But they tried. When the sun came up the guys belched, pulled their T-shirts down over their bloated beer bellies, took a last leak in the corner, and drove home, just missing the morning traffic.

Occasionally other young ladies joined us. And I do mean young! The police department had an Explorer Program, which is a branch of the Scouts of America. These young boys and girls assisted the police with traffic and crowd control at events such as concerts at the Greek Theatre and the Hollywood Bowl. They were supervised by police officers, and all of the officers in charge were men.

The young ladies on the Explorer Program were as young as ten. Most of them were cop groupies. They wanted to hang out with their idols after work and flirt. Some of the events ended at midnight or one o'clock in the morning, and I wondered why the parents of these youngsters didn't worry when they didn't come home. Maybe they unwisely assumed that since their children were with cops, they were all right.

When I realized the young girls who joined our after-work parties were leaving with some of the cops to have sex, I stopped hanging out with the group. Sooner or later these parties would mean trouble.

One might wonder why I didn't tell someone these young girls were having sex with the cops. Hell, it was going on all over the place. Who would I tell? A sergeant? Ha! One of the sergeants was having sex with a fourteen-year-old; he married her when she turned fifteen so he wouldn't get fired for having sex with a minor. A captain? Our captain participated in illegal gambling at the "steak fry" get-togethers and wanted me as a going-away present.

Early on I learned there was no one to tell. One night I was directing traffic at the scene of a bad traffic accident. Frank was up the street writing tickets. The poor victim was already in the hospital and would probably die before morning. Officer Smith was taking the accident report. Rifling through the car, he found some jewelry and slipped it into his pocket. There wasn't much traffic to direct by that time, so I was standing beside him. My mouth dropped. "What are you doing?"

He winked. "Ah, Norma Jean, come on. The guy is going to die anyway. He's never going to miss it. Besides, if I don't take it, the tow truck driver will." He returned to his report.

I stayed awake all night thinking about it. I didn't know what to do. He was a thief, no doubt about it. But to squeal on him? Hell, we have to stick together! There really is a code of silence. It's us against all the assholes out there!

After roll call the next day I pulled aside a sergeant I thought I could trust and took him to the coffee room.

"Sarge, I have a problem." I cleared my throat a dozen times. "I, uh, saw something . . . um . . . and I'm not sure what to do about it."

His eyes widened. For a moment he said nothing, then he frowned and mumbled, "Oh? What did you see, Norma Jean?"

"I saw an officer take something that didn't belong to him."

I thought I saw the sergeant's face twitch. "Well, well. Where did you see this happen?" His voice was low but calm.

"I was directing traffic, sir, and this cop took something from the car that was in an accident."

He looked positively relieved. Then he went on the offensive: "Well, Norma Jean, I think you have a problem. You should have called a supervisor to the scene of the crime when it occurred. By not doing so you are an accomplice. I would suggest you forget what you saw so you don't get yourself into trouble. You wouldn't want to get suspended for failing to make a report on the scene, would you? It's not worth it to you, is it?"

My face paled. I couldn't believe what I was hearing. *I* was going to get into trouble? "No, sir. I guess not. Forget it. It was probably just my imagination."

Was the sergeant trying to save my ass from trouble? I doubt it. Several years later when the Hollywood burglary scandal came to light, I believe he was involved. But I could be mistaken.

3. Captain Quirk, Cops, and Characters

Prithee tell me, my fair lass,
How fares a cop in bed?
Does he sit you on your ass
While he stands upon his head?

Do show and tell us all, my dear,
What cops are all about.
Do tell us what we want to hear
And let it all hang out!

Animals, you say they are,
But don't know how to screw?
Oh, what a pity it is there!
And how sad but true!

"I DON'T CARE what you were promised. I have seniority, and I want to work the night watch!" Barbara Folsom informed me late one afternoon as I changed into my uniform in the ladies' locker room. "My daughter Debbie and I are moving to Santa Monica for the summer, so I need the extra money. There's really nothing you can do about it, Norma Jean."

Astonished by her blunt announcement, I grabbed my briefcase and closed my locker. "We'll see about that, Barbara. I'm not giving up nights without a fight!" I stormed out.

Originally only two traffic officers were authorized to work the night detail, Frank and me. We were getting paid five percent more than the traffic officers working days, and the city had allotted only two at that pay rate.

When Frank and I were first involuntarily assigned to nights, it meant changing my life-style. By now I had learned to like the night watch and I certainly didn't want to return to days. Supervisor Fishbeck promised us that no one could bump us if we wanted to stay on nights.

No one, it seemed, except Barbara. She had more clout than I did. She had seniority and she had friends, the kind of friends I had refused to make. When Supervisor Rose Fishbeck confirmed that I was being bumped for Barbara, I went through the roof. I fought back and finally won, and so did she. Barbara joined us on night watch.

With a third person we had more freedom in choosing our days off. The flexibility in the schedule made the job nice. I liked to collect my days off and take a four- or five-day weekend. For a while we called a truce.

When Barbara and I worked together we went to her house to watch TV or to the movies, where we got free passes, as did all the other members of the police department at that time. This was done on duty, of course. When we weren't at her house, at the movies, or shopping, we spent hours gossiping at the House of Pies on Hollywood Boulevard with Sergeant Pinky McDirth.

I realized we were taking advantage of being unsupervised, and it troubled me that no one seemed to care whether we did anything at all. I'm a workaholic, and I resent time wasted. People who know me know that I have always been this way—when I worked at camp as a teenager, as a clerk in New York at eighteen, and for the phone company before I became a traffic cop. I hate goofing off. After probation, when I worked alone, I always tried to find something to keep me busy. I was chided for working too hard. On night watch Barbara was the senior officer, and I had to be wherever she was since we had to be together at all times. Though my conscience was bothered, I enjoyed the freedom, so I didn't care to challenge the situation. Besides, I was still relishing my active social calendar.

"Say, Norma Jean, what are you doing after work?" Wally Struman came up behind me and tugged on the keys hanging on my belt. I was in the office finishing the paperwork on an impounded car.

"Oh, hi, Wally." I smiled as I reached for the impound board. "I don't know. Do you have any suggestions?"

"Yeah. Want to have breakfast with me?" He looked at me hopefully. Wally had been asking me out for months now, but I never seemed to find the time for him. He wasn't at the top of my list of eligible cops, although he was sort of cute and entertaining.

I had a list, the now infamous Norma Jean list, and I numbered and rated the cops by my own scoring system. Several factors were taken into consideration, such as looks, intelligence, and the effect the cop had on my libido.

Wally Struman never made the list, but he was persistent in his advances; finally I agreed to have breakfast with him. As I said, he was sort of cute, rather average in height, balding, and developing a beer belly. He worked Metro division (police troubleshooters), so he sported a vice-cop-type mustache and undercover attire—jeans, T-shirt, boots, and a baseball cap.

Breakfast at two-thirty in the morning at Copper Penny's on La Brea, a cop hangout because of the free food, was always interesting. The colorful street people—prostitutes, pimps, drug dealers—and tourists also found it a wonderful after-hours meeting place. It was neutral turf, with the cops turning a blind eye to any possible illegal transactions in exchange for being left alone themselves. Sadly, Copper Penny is no longer in business.

For months I let Wally pursue me. I dated him during the time I was dating both Sergeant Mahony and Sergeant Leonard. Wally didn't seem too eager to rush into my pants, and I was content to leave it that way.

Wally was my date for the Hollywood Division Christmas party in 1973. Both Number One A+ and B were going to attend, and both had asked me, but rather than risk either of them finding out about the other, I chose to go with a nonthreatening "unlisted" date.

Wally was an attentive but boring companion. During the evening he drank heavily and began flirting with my downstairs neighbor, Nancy, who was dating another cop.

After one dance number was over, Nancy grabbed my arm and dragged me to the ladies' room. "Your boyfriend is putting the make on me, Norma Jean. He's been telling me what a great lover he is and how the three of us should get together sometime."

We decided to get even. I went out and began flirting outrageously with him. He was falling for it, and then Nancy came over and pretended to flirt with him right in front of me. He blushed furiously. I was behind him, trying desperately not to laugh. She was doing such a good job!

When it was time to leave, I followed Wally out to his car, deciding that I would make the braggart put up or shut up once and for all.

In my apartment I turned on the fireplace and soft music, lit a few candles, and burned some incense, trying to make it as romantic as possible to give Wally every opportunity to prove himself.

Purring, I rubbed his thigh. He coughed and nervously held my hand. "You know, Norma Jean, my ex-wife and I had the best sex life you can imagine."

"So you've told me, Wally. What made it so good?"

"I guess I just know how to use it."

Feigning innocence I asked, "Use what, honey?"

"Uh, you know, my dick. . . . All the women I've ever met admire the way I use my dick."

"Well, honey, stop telling me how you use it and show me! I'm going into the bedroom. Would you care to join me?"

He fixed himself another drink and followed me. I pushed him down onto the bed and unzipped his pants. Like most cops I dated, he was wearing Fruit of the Loom boxer shorts. He turned to me with his manhood—shriveled up to about an inch and a half.

I let out a hoot. "Well, where is it, Wally?" All the anticipation, for this? What a letdown! Maybe he knew how to use it, but now Wally's brutal big tool had retreated.

Wally jumped out of bed, dressed, and left without a word. We never spoke to each other again. Not longer after this incident I heard a rumor that Wally had been caught by the vice squad in Griffith Park, being buggered by another man. He was retired and given a psycho pension. I hope I wasn't to blame for pushing him over the edge because I laughed at him that night.

I decided I needed to move. I wanted to get a place close to the ocean and searched for months for something I could afford, but rents at the beach were way beyond my budget.

Nancy, my downstairs neighbor, also wanted to move. After much hunting we found a three-bedroom house with a swimming pool and a real fireplace on a quiet cul-de-sac in Van Nuys in the San Fernando Valley. Lots of cops lived in the Valley. Unfortunately, it's not near the ocean.

Nancy and I drew straws over who would get the master bedroom with its own bathroom. I won. My bedroom looked out over the huge swimming pool in our spacious backyard.

I had been saving money for months for a waterbed. I found a huge four-poster with overhead mirrors. What a great new playpen! It was put to good use until I moved into an apartment years later and had to sell it.

In the beginning Nancy and I had an ideal relationship. We were both young and horny, and loved the boys. I was twenty-two, she was nineteen, and we both liked to have parties. Now we had the place to entertain. We moved in February 1975, just in time for our first Valentine's bash.

In May 1975 I was accepted as a police reserve officer and started my training at the academy. I was too short to be a regular police officer but tall enough for the reserves where the height requirement was lower for women. For a few brief months life was fantastic. I was dating several cops and a gorgeous fireman. I lived in a beautiful house and had a good job that paid good money. Everything was going along smoothly, too smoothly.

One evening in roll call I noticed a tall, lean, handsome, blond, blue-eyed stranger in a tan uniform sitting in the back row. He had a badge, so I guessed he was from the sheriff's department or something. He smiled at me when I walked into roll call. I smiled back. He sure was cute.

During roll call the sergeant introduced him as Roger Kramer, Air Six, Hollywood's air patrol. After roll call I stopped to talk to him. "Are you the wise guy who shines the spotlight on me on Hollywood Boulevard?" I asked.

"Yeah. Are you Charlie-Seventy-five?" He attempted to mimic my high, squeaky voice but ended up sounding like one of our Hollywood drag queens. " 'This is Six Charlie-Seventy-five. Requesting a tow truck at Hollywood and Vine!' You are always towing somebody away. And you sure got a cute ass when you bend over to put the tickets on those cars!" He grinned.

I turned red. "You can see my butt from your helicopter?"

"Oh, heck, that's nothing! In the summertime, me and my partner fly over the houses in the hills and see all those lovely naked ladies by their pools all alone, playing with themselves! With the powerful telescopes our birds carry, we can see each pubic hair on their fine tan beavers. Hey, why'd you think I became a pilot on the P.D.? It's got some great perks!"

"Do you ever land your helicopter long enough to go out on a date, Mr. Air Six?'" The days of women's lib had finally arrived for me, and I felt no guilt about making the first move.

Roger took me to dinner at a quaint little Italian restaurant in the Valley. When dinner was over, he flashed his badge and got us two free meals. As we were leaving he smiled and waved at the owner. "Freebies sure help extend a policeman's paycheck!" he confided.

Nancy wasn't home, so we got comfortable on pillows in front of the fireplace. I had taken to wearing soft, lacy nightgowns instead of the dowdy flowered cotton nighties. They weren't as sexy as the ones I would come to wear as a call girl—nor as expensive. Roger had stripped down to his skivvies, the standard F.o.L. boxer shorts. He pulled them down. His magnificent dick hung out in all its glory—hard, long, and thick, just as I had imagined it would be. With a sigh and an "Oh, God!" he achieved deep penetration. Thrust one . . . I felt my aching desire grow. I arched my neck, closed my eyes, and waited for the second thrust. And waited.

I opened my eyes. He was wiping his brow and breathing deeply. "Oh, that was good, baby! I really needed that!" Oh, yeah? Needed what?

"Um, what about me?" I asked timidly.

He smiled and looked down at his inert organ. "Sorry, babe, we got a limp lizard now!" He looked at his watch. "Ooo, honey! I gotta go! My girlfriend's gonna wonder where I am."

The evening had turned out to be a disaster. I didn't even bother to walk him to the door. He had the nerve to blow me a kiss. "Thanks, babe. You were great. Let's do it again sometime!"

"Oh, pleeease!" I thought. "Should I throw up now or wait until the next time I see your helicopter overhead?"

Feeling he wasn't worth any more of my time, I gave him the finger as the front door closed. I wished I had the courage to do it to his face.

Fortunately, I did not let guys like Roger or Ralph the vice cop depress me for long. I had the good sense not to blame all men for the flaws of a few. It is sad but true that most of my sexual experiences with cops were negative. There were a few good fucks in the lot, but most saw me as an easy lay and didn't want to know me well enough to find out that there was a real person inside the body.

When I later became a whore, many people asked about feeling degraded when I "sold my body." I felt degraded when cops used my body without even trying to give me sexual satisfaction, and didn't have the decency to pay me for playing the role of a prostitute.

Because I was a sucker for a tall man with a handsome face, a well-built body, and a deep voice, there were many affairs. People have said the cops on the L.A.P.D. look as if they came from Central Casting. I agree—all hero types, macho men. Unfortunately, I think the image gets in the way of their performance.

Sergeant Dixon was almost too handsome, big and beefy. The first time we had sex was in the backseat of his police car. I was driving around with him after work, and he pulled into the parking lot of the Great Western Bank on Sunset Boulevard. He got out of the car and pulled down his pants. "I want you to eat it, honey."

I looked around. "Out here, in public?"

He grinned. "You're right. We'll get in the backseat." We had a real quickie without even taking off our clothes.

I finally got him to come home with me one night so we could do it properly. The backseat of a police car may be fun for a guy, but it is no place for a lady to get her rocks off. He was a wimp in bed, complaining that sex made him break out in large strawberrylike marks. He ran into the bathroom, whining like a baby. "My wife is going to kill me! It takes hours for these to go away!" I heard that after he was transferred to Internal Affairs he was named in a paternity suit. He claimed it was impossible because he was impotent.

Officer Garcia was in training with me when I joined the police reserves and then "went regular," becoming a full-fledged police officer so he could get away with doing drugs, as he once told me. He was romantic and charming when we met, seeming to want to cater to my every whim. Two dates later, when we were sitting at dinner with some friends, he ignored me completely and wound up going home with another girl he met at the restaurant. He apologized later, and we wound up in bed once or twice.

He ultimately left the L.A.P.D. to join the Drug Enforcement Agency because they had a better grade of drugs. On April 16, 1991, he was convicted in a federal court of drug trafficking and corruption.

In late June 1975 I received a job offer from the San Diego sheriff's department, which had to comply with a Supreme Court decision and hire more women. In order to make it easier to qualify, the height requirement for women was lowered. I was scheduled to take an exam on July 9.

On July 5, 1975, I had my first major on-duty traffic accident. Despite guarantees to the contrary, I had just been reassigned to day watch. Cruising along Sunset Boulevard just past Gower, checking the meters, I was driving one of the department's old Harley-Davidson three-wheeled motorcycles. At night I had been driving a patrol car, and I wasn't used to the motorcycles anymore. I kept one eye on traffic ahead of me and one eye on expired meters. I saw the traffic light in the next block change and was slowing to stop.

There is a double light at that intersection, and a Cadillac up ahead was apparently going to run them both. Then he checked in his rearview mirror and saw me. He screeched to a halt and backed up. The Volkswagen behind him, which was directly in front of me, stopped abruptly to avoid a crash with the Cadillac. Unfortunately, I didn't avoid him. My old Harley rammed into the back of his car and twisted around, turning my upper torso sharply. My lower torso was still turned to the front. There was no damage to the Volkswagen and not much to the bike, but my back and neck have never been the same.

I was beginning to become aware of the shortcomings of my employer and my peers, and the accident was definitely the beginning of the end of my law enforcement career. Even though I returned to my job after an absence of a year and a half, never again would the same old Norma Jean roam the halls of the Hollywood police station. The new disillusioned one would hang on for a few more years, trying to effect change within the system, but the one who looked the other way so long and so often, was gone.

4. UNDER THE GUN

How will I last?
I got ten years to go!
Will it ever get past?
Darn, it's going so slow!

I want to escape.
I ain't having no fun!
I'm just marking my time
While I'm under the gun.

BY CHRISTMAS 1975 I was still off duty from the accident and in a lot of pain. I had been hospitalized five times, endured a myelogram, and for a short time was even in a wheelchair. I was on pain pills and muscle relaxers. Periodically I was able to work light duty in the office, which was an eye opener. I was introduced to some of the inner workings of the power structure. Working outside at night, I had been sheltered from this damaging information.

One alarming, unofficial, illegal but routinely practiced policy was "creative report writing." Through the use of ambiguous and vague language an officer could justify the arrest of someone who shouldn't have been arrested. When the police wanted to arrest someone but had no probable cause, the officer or officers would attack the person. If the person tried to defend himself or herself, the police could claim the person had assaulted an officer. (Years later the "policy" would come to worldwide attention through the notorious Rodney King case.)

I observed how the police "misplaced" files and "lost" valuable information, especially on weekends, so a suspect had to remain in jail until arraignment the following Monday or Tuesday. Even if the poor guy or gal had the money for bail, this was not possible because the paper-work was lost or the computer was down or the jailer had gone home and nobody else could do it. "So sorry, fellow. You know how these things go. It's not our fault. Hey, believe me, I'd like to let you go—you're taking up valuable space!"

During this period one of the prisoners had a fatal accident. He hung himself in his cell—right after he choked to death in a chokehold. One of the more honest officers decided he couldn't take the deceit anymore and threatened to expose the death for what it was. I understand he was subsequently fired.

A black traffic officer was canned after being arrested one weekend for driving drunk off duty. He gave the arresting officers some trouble, and the supervisor told me the captain wanted him fired. He hadn't done anything more than thousands of other cops do all the time, but he was black and a troublemaker.

I watched in puzzled bewilderment as my supervisor deliberately changed his rating report, a legal document that gave the captain the ammunition he needed to fire the guy. As I saw it, what my supervisor did was a felony. When I suggested it was wrong, it was recommended that I keep my mouth shut.

I returned to disability. In addition to my aching back, I now had problems with my stomach. The place made me sick.

Just before my accident I had begun dating George, a gorgeous married fireman. He was tall, dark, and handsome, nearly all the requirements I had for a lover. We had a very special relationship. I was happy he was married because I didn't want to be. He told me his wife didn't understand him. It was an old line, but I didn't care. I was hot for his beautiful body. While our sex life wasn't that great—he seldom brought me to a climax—he was a terrific guy and I loved him. I might still be dating him if it hadn't been for fate.

My roommate Nancy and I had several misunderstandings during the first few months of my disability. She decided to move out. I gave her back her share of the deposit. Before she left, she made long-distance calls all over the world and left me with a $500 phone bill. When I couldn't pay it, my phone was shut off. I was in despair. Dear sweet George lent me the money, and I finally had a phone again. I placed an ad in the paper for a new roommate, certain it would not be difficult.

Meanwhile, because of my horrible back pain, my doctor admitted me to the Panorama Memorial Hospital for a myelogram. I didn't follow the doctor's advice not to raise my head for twenty-four hours and was stricken with the worst headache of my life. For two weeks I lay in excruciating pain. Powerful medication put me totally out of it, and I didn't remember anything. After my recovery, my hospital mate, Rita, told me what had happened.

My hospital room was on the ground floor. One night, well after visiting hours, there was a knock at the sliding glass door. Rita opened it to find my young friend Tina Wright with a pal of hers, Patty, whom I had never met before. Tina and I had become good friends while she was in the Explorer program and worked out of Hollywood.

The medication I was on was so effective, I don't remember her being there, much less what was said. Apparently Tina and Patty had come all the way out to the hospital on a bus, and arrived long after visiting hours. They had also failed to tell their parents where they were. When they realized how late it was, they were concerned that their parents would be upset. Tina asked to use the phone, but unfortunately the switchboard was closed. Tina had a brilliant idea: They would borrow my keys, go to my house, which was right up the street, and call their mothers from there.

In my medicated state it sounded like a fine idea. They would be safe while they waited for Tina's mother to pick them up. I told her the keys were in my purse under the bed. Tina said her mother would return the keys in the morning. I fell asleep shortly after they left and the next morning didn't even remember they had been there. Rita had to remind me.

Tina and her mom walked in late that afternoon. Tina wasn't smiling. I vaguely remembered her visit the night before.

"Here's your keys, Norma Jean," Tina mumbled.

"Go on. Tell her what you did," her mom prompted her.

"Um, well, Patty and I saw your car in the parking lot . . . and . . . well, we decided to drive it to your house so we wouldn't have to walk."

"Do either of you know how to drive or have a driver's license?" Of course not; they were both only thirteen.

"Patty knows a little bit, so she drove."

Okay, so they drove the car to my house without a license.

Tina's mother poked her. "Tell her all of it, Tina."

Tina began crying. "We didn't call my mom last night. We stayed overnight at your house. I was going to call my mom this morning, but Patty wanted to go shopping, so we took your car. Patty knows how to drive forward, but she doesn't know how to drive in reverse. She hit this other car. The lady is really mad that you let someone without a driver's license use your car. She's going to sue you."

I was ready to strangle Tina. How could she do this to me? I was trying to recover and certainly didn't need this aggravation. "Here I am in the hospital on strong pain medication and don't even remember you were here last night, and I'm going to be sued because you took my car and drove it without a license?"

Tina just kept crying and saying she was sorry. Ultimately everything was settled by my insurance company, but unfortunately it was just the beginning of my problems with Tina and her friend.

Patty was a runaway. When her parents found out that the girls had come to see me and that I worked for the police department, they threatened to charge me with harboring a runaway (because she stayed overnight at my house) if Tina did not tell them where their daughter was hiding. I told them that I had never met their daughter before, that I had not given her permission to stay overnight at my house, that I was under medication when she and Tina came to visit me—and the hell with them!

They called my supervisor, Rose Fishbeck, who was more than happy to make certain that charges would be brought against me if I didn't put pressure on Tina to tell Patty's parents where she was. Internal Affairs investigators visited me in the hospital. After they were convinced I had been heavily medicated the night the girls paid me a visit (the nurses showed them my chart), they went away.

This whole affair resulted in an increase in my insurance premium, and Tina and I didn't speak to each other for quite some time. I forgave her when she reimbursed me for the expenses associated with the car accident, and I attended her wedding two years later. Incidentally, Tina was one of the girls who was having sex with the cops and was the one who at fifteen married the sergeant so he would not get fired for having sex with a minor.

Arriving home from the hospital just after Christmas, I was very depressed. I hadn't yet found a new roommate, and the rent was now overdue. But by the middle of January I had found two new roommates: One was a waitress at a local Italian restaurant, and the other was a female California Highway Patrol officer. They lasted until the summer when they both found boyfriends and moved in with them, leaving me alone again.

What I desperately needed in my life was a little magic. It came just in time for Valentine's Day.

5. ROMEO AND PIGALETTE

The glimpses that you show me
Of the you I've grown to know
Do not tell me all you are, but even so
In the few I chance to see, I realize
The person that you are, and in my eyes
I cannot know enough of you . . .
Not now or ever find
I'll ever tire of learning from the wisdom of your mind.

THURSDAY, FEBRUARY 12, 1976. My back did not seem to be getting any better, and I was tired of taking pain medication. All it seemed to do was make me groggy and depressed. I decided I needed to do a little shopping to cheer myself up.

Driving to Panorama City to Robinson's Department Store, I noticed movie industry trucks parked all around. A catering truck parked in Robinson's parking lot was serving lunch to the actors and crew of the show. Ignoring the throng hoping to see a movie star, I parked the car as close to the store as possible. Walking was still very painful. I decided to look for a shirt for George.

"That's a beautiful shirt! Whoever it's for is a lucky guy," a deep, rich voice said behind me. I turned around to see a very tall, silver-haired man with a Vandyke beard, blue eyes, and very handsome. It was difficult to tell how old he was—maybe forty-five, maybe fifty. I thought he resembled Edward Mulhare, the actor who played the captain in "The Ghost and Mrs. Muir." He was wearing a wonderful after-shave.

He grinned. "I'm Victor, pretty lady. Who are you?" Oh, so suave!

"I, um, oh, I'm Norma Jean."

"Norma Jean. Are you an actress?"

"No. I work for the Los Angeles Police Department. I'm a traffic officer."

"A cop, huh? Well, I'm an actor, and my buddies at the lunch truck bet me you were an actress. They will certainly be surprised to learn you're a lady cop. You are too pretty to be a cop. I don't see a ring on your finger. That mean you aren't married?''

''I'm not married anymore!'' I made a face. ''And I'll get married again when pigs fly!''

He laughed. ''Well, now that we've established you're not interested in marrying me, would you at least consider going out for a drink?''

I had never been picked up this way before. I smiled my consent.

''So, beautiful lady, where do I find you?'' He took my hands. His hands were so soft! I gave him my address.

February 13, 1976; Valentine's eve. He arrived at seven sharp wearing a suit and a shirt with no tie. Around his neck was a silver chain. I put it all together: An actor who wears cologne, his hands as soft as a baby's bottom, and wears a silver necklace has to be gay. Comparing him to all the men I had ever dated and to what the cops had told me about fags, he just had to be!

We went to Monte's in Westwood and had a wonderful evening. I amused him with anecdotes of my sexual escapades with the cops, figuring it wouldn't hurt to share my private sexual secrets since he was gay. It was like talking to another woman.

When he took me home, we stood outside the door. He picked up my hand tenderly and kissed it. ''Good night, beautiful lady. I had a delightful time. I hope we can do it again.'' Then he left. He didn't make a pass at me, definitely confirming that he was gay.

For six months we dated almost every weekend. He took me to the theater, to musical concerts, and to museums, places I had never been. And he never tried to make it with me. He was my older, sophisticated, well-educated cultured gay friend, and I loved him.

Then I invited him over to dinner one night. When he arrived, he kissed my hand, as he usually did. He had brought a bottle of wine. ''Even though you don't drink, I thought I'd like some with my dinner. Okay, Norma Jean?''

I don't remember what I cooked that night. I do remember it turned out awful, and I felt bad. He assured me it made no difference to him; he still thought I was terrific.

After the disastrous dinner we went into the living room. He sat on the couch, and I sat in front of the fireplace. He had more wine. Before long it began to affect him.

''I've just got to tell you, Norma Jean. I love going out with you, but I don't know how much longer I can take this platonic relationship."

My mouth dropped. "What do you mean, Victor?"

"I mean it is absolute torture to see you and want you so badly, and you don't even seem to be aware I want you!"

"You want me? You mean you want to go to bed with me? But, Victor," I protested, "you're gay!"

He looked at me indignantly. "Who's gay? Where did you get that idea?"

"Well, I thought . . . Well, you never made a pass at me . . . and your hands are so soft . . . and you wear cologne and . . ."

He laughed. "I never made a pass at you because I didn't want to frighten you away. I didn't want you to think I was like all those macho cops you used to date who got into your pants and were gone five minutes later. I wanted you to get to know me first so it wouldn't be just another one-night stand for you."

Victor moved from the couch to the pillow where I was sitting and put his hand on my thigh. "Could you be interested in me in a sexual way, Norma Jean?"

I didn't answer.

He grabbed my hair and began kissing my face all over. He planted his lips on mine. I didn't resist. He picked me up and carried me to the bedroom.

He lay me tenderly on my waterbed. He stroked my hair as he unbuttoned my blouse, reached in under my bra, and caressed my breast. Then he slowly undid my bra and began gently sucking my very erect nipple. I moaned.

With one hand he pulled off my skirt and then lifted me up and pulled off my panties. One of his soft fingers found its way between my legs. I was so embarrassed, being so wet. I thought he would think I was a whore.

My hands were buried in his thick silver hair as he caressed me with his mouth. I twitched and moaned and didn't know which way to turn first. Oh my God, he was good. Suddenly my body was convulsed with orgasm. It burst from me with a powerful rush. I screamed with pleasure. It was my first oral orgasm.

I was sure once I had my release Victor would enter me and have an orgasm of his own. Instead he remained buried between my legs, relentlessly continuing, sending shivers of pleasure throughout my body. I tried to pull him away. Didn't he know I had already had an orgasm?

Then my body was convulsed again with the intense spasm of a climax. Still he didn't stop. I felt the delicious sensation of another powerful orgasm building up, aching for release. His tongue dove deeper into me, sending every little nerve ending the message of exhilarating delight. I screamed again as I rode the beautiful wave.

As I came down from the pleasure, he stroked the inside of my thighs with his tongue. It was pure heaven. I couldn't stop moaning and groaning, forgetting my embarrassment. This man was incredible. If he thought I was a whore, that was too bad. If whores enjoyed things like that, well then maybe I was a whore after all.

Now for certain I expected Victor to have his orgasm. I tried to lure him up beside me, but he stubbornly remained where he was. In a minute he began licking me again. Slowly, deliberately, he worked me back up to the peak, and as my desire rose, his intensity grew. Once more my body reacted to his insistent tongue. I exploded a fourth time into his wonderful mouth, shuddering all over. As I opened my eyes and came back to reality, he came up beside me.

I began stroking him. His penis was strong and hard like a powerful tool. He knelt over me and stroked my breasts with his cock. No man had ever done that before. It felt good. Deliberately he lowered his body and plunged, surprising me again. In and out, slowly, sweetly, he plunged deeper and deeper. With each powerful, unhurried thrust he rekindled my desire. I couldn't believe it! He was so sure of himself. He wasn't after his orgasm but after another one from me. And he got it! It was followed by another, equally intense climax. When I couldn't move anymore and it tickled to have him inside my body, he withdrew. I wondered why he pulled out. We had been making love for almost two hours now, and he hadn't come yet!

"Did I do something wrong?"

"No, my darling, you didn't do anything wrong. Just stay still." He kissed my forehead and was still caressing my body.

After a while he got up and got dressed.

"Where are you going?" Panicked, I grabbed for his hand.

He sat on the bed beside me as he pulled on his pants. He ran his hand through my hair. "I am going home and let you get some sleep."

"But, you haven't . . . you haven't come yet!" I protested.

"And I'm not going to come, not tonight."

"Did I make you mad or something?"

"No, sweet lady. Of course you didn't make me mad. In fact, you made me very happy."

"But I don't understand. Don't you want to come inside me?"

"More than anything in the world. But I am not going to until you really want me to."

I quickly protested: "But I do want you to—"

"No, you just expect me to because every other man you've ever fucked has. I am not like every other man."

I didn't know what to say. He was right. I expected it more than wanted it because it was the thing men did with women.

I lay in bed thinking about him all night. I was very confused. The next day I called him. I wanted to have lunch. He made me feel some powerful emotions, and I needed to sort them out.

He agreed to meet me for lunch at Musso and Frank's in Hollywood during a break from his production.

"So, pretty lady, how do you feel today?" He kissed me on the cheek.

"I don't know. I'm confused. I feel awful." I looked down at the table.

"I made you feel awful last night?" His voice was low and gentle.

"Oh, no, no! You made me feel wonderful. That's the problem. I never had a man make love to me for my pleasure before. What are you trying to do to my head?"

He smiled. "I just want you to know that I know what a woman you are, and I appreciate it. Nobody has ever tried to tap your sexual potential, have they?"

I stared at my drink. "Um, what do you mean, my 'sexual potential'?"

"Women are very lucky. They are multiorgasmic. Nobody ever let you know that before, did they?"

I was embarrassed. "No."

"I thought not. Well, you said you're confused. If I confuse you, do you want to see me again?"

Sighing heavily I said, "I don't know. I mean, I do, but I don't know what to think about you. First I thought you were gay, and you're old enough to be my father. And, well, after last night I—"

"You either want me or you don't. If you don't, well, I can't see you again just as a friend." He kissed my hand. I thought I would faint from sheer pleasure.

"So when, Victor?" I barely contained my eagerness.

He laughed. "Don't be so impatient! I waited six months for you, remember?"

I am very grateful that he is a patient man. He did wait for me. The relationship we have developed over the years we have been together is special and wonderful. The man I grew to know and share my life with is the most interesting, colorful, loyal human being I have ever known. But it took a while to get to know him.

Victor is a very private man. As we spent more time together, he gradually shared his background with me. I was thrilled with each new part of his life he revealed to me.

His father, who had been a bootlegger in the hills of Tennessee, was killed in a shoot-out when Victor was very young. Victor worked in the coal mines as a child and learned about sex from his young female cousin. When he was nine, he ran away from home. He rode the rails around the country, worked on shrimp boats, and educated himself along the way. At fifteen he ended up in New Orleans, at the Oak Knoll, one of the famous whorehouses. First he worked as a towel boy, then graduated to bouncer when he reached his full growth a year later. The prostitutes taught him how to please a woman, and believe me, they taught him well. He developed a positive attitude toward working women and viewed them as human beings, which is probably why he was able to deal with my career change.

Somewhere along the way he fell into acting, doing summer stock at resort theaters on the East Coast and working at odd jobs between gigs.

His other love was architecture, and he studied at Taliesin with the master, Frank Lloyd Wright. He had two careers simultaneously.

In his late thirties he married an actress, with whom he had three daughters, and they moved to California to be near the studios. He and his wife became politically active in the civil rights movement. When his second wife, namely me, became a political activist, I guess he was not surprised.

Victor is a man who loves booze and the ladies, so his first marriage didn't work out. He has mellowed in the years I have known him, and for health reasons doesn't drink as much anymore. He still loves the ladies . . . but so do I.

This is not a book about my relationship with Victor, but because he is very much a part of me, I cannot leave him out. Because of him I was able to free myself from the sexual hangups I grew up with. He was patient while I overcame them, and he never stifled my sexual needs. He always encouraged me to find pleasure within my own body. I discovered it was all right for women to have sexual desire and to experience sexual gratification.

I fell deeply in love with Victor for many, many reasons. He is the tenderest, most thoughtful man I have ever met. He is every inch a man and yet has gentle qualities. He is sentimental, romantic, passionate. He is well read and knows about many subjects. He is a fabulous cook, and it doesn't kill him to wash the dishes, do the laundry, or vacuum. *He is definitely not gay.*

In October 1976, more than a year after my auto accident, I had a tubal pregnancy although I had been using an I.U.D. for birth control. The night the tube ruptured, with severe hemorrhaging, I almost died. My new roommate informed Victor, and he rushed to the hospital in the pouring rain and sat holding my hand all night. After surgery, as I lay unconscious in the intensive care unit, Victor talked to me, telling me I couldn't die because he had just found me.

My memory of the next few days is vague, but I remember that Victor moved in. He took care of me for the next six weeks when I was as helpless as a baby. He fed me and my cats, took me to the doctor's, did the laundry—in short, he was there when I needed him, a first in any relationship I had ever had.

While I recovered he brought me books to read, including several by Ayn Rand. Reading Ms. Rand's most famous book, *Atlas Shrugged*, influenced the remainder of my career with the L.A.P.D. as well as my decision to enter politics.

In the six weeks Victor and I were together day and night, I got to know him and love him like no other human being I had ever met. We talked for hours about philosophy, self-esteem, and many other subjects I had never heard of. He exposed me to a world beyond my own small, shallow life. He taught me to know my own worth and challenged me to change my life accordingly.

He has faults, admittedly, but very few. Sometimes he drinks too much champagne and becomes slightly obnoxious. Sometimes he becomes impatient when I take too long to get dressed. He complains that I spend too much money, which I do when there is money to spend. But he is the man I always wanted, and I know I wouldn't have made it through all the rough times without his love and support.

He was the miracle I needed, wished for, and got. He was my Valentine's present.

6. Catch Me, Catch Me
if You Can

I am a cop, I have a gun.
My gun and dick both work as one.
I rape and pillage, rob and steal.
I do about damn what I feel.

Don't mess with me . . . I'll mow you down.
No one is safe when I'm around.
Don't you be walkin' on my street.
I am a member—L.A.'s elite.

L.A.P.D. . . . we're number one.
"Protect and serve!" but that's no fun!
From sun up and down again
We will always get our man!

Oh, he is innocent, you say!
That's all right . . . more fun that way!
What's that you say? How can that be?
'Cause I commit more crimes than he!

So catch me, catch me if you can!
When in L.A., I am the man.
And hey, my man, I'm no one's fool!
I'm L.A.P.D., and I am cool!

WHILE STILL OFF DUTY, recovering from my back problems, the newspapers began printing some startling stories of police involvement in sexual activity with underage girls.

In October 1976 the *Valley News* headlines read: 5 SEX CASE LAWMEN CHARGED. Four Hollywood officers and one Rampart officer were charged with having sex with underage female Explorer scouts.

The outcome of the investigation was the dismissal of those officers and the suspension of several others, including Michael Casados, an officer I knew well in Hollywood. He did not lose his job, but ten years later, in 1986, he was accused of having sex over a five-year period with a fifteen-year-old girl—ten years old when they started. This time he resigned, but under the terms of a plea bargain he received no jail or prison time.

Remembering the late evenings I had spent with the cops after work prior to my accident and the young ladies who joined them, I was surprised that so few cops were charged, considering how many were involved. Several stories were floating around about other forms of police misconduct and brutality. The things I heard when assigned to work in the office I found troubling, but I needed the job and wasn't ready to let the misconduct of others stop me from returning to work.

I passed my health exam and was allowed to go back to work full time on January 17, 1977. I remember the date so very clearly because it was the day Gary Gilmore was executed in Utah.

I was reassigned to Central Traffic. The area included downtown L.A. and the Rampart Division, made famous in Joseph Wambaugh's *The Choir Boys*. Central Traffic did not yet have a night watch so I had to work days.

I returned to work with great enthusiasm, but it wasn't easy for the first few months. My back still caused problems, and I could hardly walk. Sometimes I shuffled like an old lady, but I still worked an eight-hour day for eight hours' pay and did not join the others on their two-hour coffee breaks.

I soon gained a reputation for working too hard. I was driven to prove that I could do the job, bad back and all. My peers nicknamed me "the bionic arm." They meant it as an insult, but I liked it, really. My bionic arm came in handy when I changed careers.

While my coworkers wrote ten or fifteen tickets a day and towed away one or two cars, I sometimes came in with three hundred tickets at the end of the day. The senior supervisor asked me, "Do you get your rocks off writing tickets?" It hurt to think a supervisor, of all people, would insult me for doing the job I was paid to do. Unfortunately, he was not alone.

One Saturday afternoon while I was completing the paperwork on an impounded car, Supervisor Carl Farley called me into his office and closed the door. He signaled the traffic officer at the desk to take a break and assured him we would answer the phone.

"So how do you like it downtown? Is it better than Hollywood?" He smiled as he looked directly at my chest.

"Well, it's okay, but it's farther to drive from home."

"You live in the Valley, don't you?" He leered at me.

"Yes. So what?"

"Well, I live in the Valley, too. Not too far from you." He scratched his head. "Um, maybe we could work out a deal so you get out of here a little bit early so you could miss the rush-hour traffic . . . if you're interested."

I wanted to slap his face. I knew what the deal was. Another female traffic officer had warned me that Supervisor Farley might try to make such an offer. I wanted to hear it for myself. "What kind of deal, Supervisor Farley?"

"Call me Carl." He smiled, warming up to me. "I was thinking perhaps some night after work we could . . . that is, I could . . . um . . . stop by your house for a little drink or something . . . you know. Then maybe you could leave every night just a little earlier than the rest, so they wouldn't know you were leaving or anything. And if you need to take a few hours off for anything, well, I'll just mark you present, and nobody will know."

Keeping a straight face I said, "I heard you offered somebody else a deal where they could turn in extra overtime slips working the Dodgers' games and get some extra cash."

He almost fell out of his chair. From the expression on his face it was clear he wasn't certain whether I was accepting his offer and simply asking for a better deal. He decided to play out his hand. "Uh . . . well, I could work out the same thing for you if you want. Of course I'd expect to see you a little more often . . . at your house."

I stood up, smiling. "Let me get this straight. What you are asking me to do is go to bed with you, and in exchange you will falsify legal documents, lie, cheat, and steal in order for me to get some kind of remuneration for going to bed with you. In other words, you want me to be your whore. Well, Carl, if I ever take up hooking, I'm going to get a hell of a lot more out of it than that!" I picked up my paperwork and started to open the door. "Oh, was there anything else you wanted to ask me?"

Finally an opportunity to work nights came along. I transferred to the night watch in Rampart Division.

There were four of us: two on the 3 P.M. to 11 P.M. shift and two on the 6 P.M. to 2 A.M. shift. I chose the latter. We reported directly to the sergeants in Rampart, and except for picking up my paycheck every other Wednesday, I never had to see the downtown supervisors.

Being a workaholic, the sergeants in Rampart loved me. I thrived on hard work and felt I was making a positive contribution to taxpayers' lives. When someone called the police on a traffic matter, it often took others up to four hours to respond. The callers were very grateful when I showed up in under an hour. I had my pet peeves, and cars that blocked fire hydrants and driveways or were parked on private property—for which numerous radio calls were received—topped the list.

The night watch traffic officers were required to attend the roll call held for the regular police officers. As the only female in roll call every night, I got teased a lot by the guys. With eight brothers in my family, I was used to it, so nothing the cops did could embarrass me. One sergeant thought he was very funny when he told me I would have to participate in a "short arms" inspection. He thought I wouldn't know it was an old military term for lining up and sticking out one's penis for disease inspection.

One night, suspecting this sergeant was going to order an inspection, I attached a latex male organ sculpture, made by a friend of mine, underneath my heavy winter jacket and stood ready for inspection. It was flesh-colored, fourteen inches long and eight inches in circumference. It even had hair on the balls—very realistic.

When the sergeant announced a short arms inspection, the cops all laughed as usual. I smiled politely, unzipped my jacket, and out popped my fourteen-inch peter. His jaw dropped. I remarked casually, "Will this do, Sergeant?" He never picked on me again.

I consistently wrote more tickets, impounded more cars, and handled more radio calls than my peers—who were, rumor had it, at their girlfriends' houses smoking pot on duty. Eventually the three other night watch traffic officers began complaining to the day watch traffic supervisors that I was making them look bad by writing too many tickets. The Rampart police sergeants who supervised the regular beat officers wanted to know why my peers couldn't keep up with me. As a method of handling their complaints, the day watch traffic supervisors decided to make all of us report at the same time to the downtown Central Traffic office. Then all four of us would drive in one car back to Rampart where we each got our own patrol car. At the end of watch we had to wait for one another and drive back downtown to sign out.

This ridiculous, time-wasting idea cut our productivity and usefulness in half, and I said as much to the traffic supervisors. Even the Rampart sergeants complained. The night watch program was jeopardized because we were not out there when we were needed most.

Being torn between two sets of authority was difficult: the police sergeants who wanted me to continue to work as hard as I did, and the civilian traffic supervisors who wanted me to do as little as everyone else.

Night watch was a seven-day-a-week operation, and on weekends it was necessary to have at least three officers on duty. However, when we were back under the control of the day watch supervisors, they decided that only one officer was needed on weekends. It was crazy, I said. Why were we out there if we were of no use to the people who paid our salaries?

Finally, one weekend when I was working alone, I became fed up with the insanity. At the end of the shift when I went downtown to sign out, I left the day watch supervisor a little note: "You are the epitome of the Peter Principle," I wrote, "and it is disgraceful that the taxpayers have to shell out their hard-earned money to pay you to go to your girlfriend's house while you are supposed to be working. I don't see how you can live with yourself." I didn't sign it, but my handwriting was distinctive; I knew he would know who wrote it.

On my next work shift I was summoned to his office. He was not amused. I was given an ultimatum: Either I returned to day watch where I could be supervised more closely, or I could transfer out of Central Traffic immediately. I was being punished for having a big mouth. I requested a transfer to Hollywood.

When the transfer came through, I was assigned to night watch. I was back on Hollywood Boulevard again, citing and impounding cars. Because Hollywood was experiencing a problem with cruising by cholo gangs, as the Mexican gangs are known, the NO PARKING signs had reappeared, and it had become a tow-away zone.

In a city block twelve cars long, only one sign was posted to notify the hundreds of tourists that they couldn't park on the street at night. And the signs that existed were blocked by the decorative trees used in the annual Santa Claus Lane Parade. It took an act of God to get those trees pruned before the Christmas season. It was clearly unfair to motorists, and during the first three months I made nightly requests for more signs and for the trees to be pruned. I was so disgusted that at one point I was ready to buy gardening shears and prune the damn trees myself.

I was harassed nightly by tourists who had not seen the signs and whose cars had been towed away; they were fined $26 for illegal parking and had to pay $57 for the towing. They usually reported to us that their cars had been stolen, and when they learned the truth, they cursed the police, vowing never to return as tourists again.

Not only was it an unfair policy for the tourists but it cost the shop owners thousands of dollars in lost customers, and they were understandably upset with us for destroying their business. One of the shop owners parked his car on the street one night rather than in his lot around the corner. As I was standing in front of his Volkswagen van, preparing to tow it, he came storming out of his bookstore, yelling, "Oh no you don't!" Twice my size, he tackled me, knocked me into the back of a tow truck, and then got into his van and tried to run me over when I attempted to prevent him from leaving.

I pursued him around the corner. As he was easing into his own parking space, several more heated words were exchanged. When the backup officers arrived, the shop owner tried to convince them that he hadn't seen me standing there. Fortunately for me the tow truck driver had witnessed the whole thing. He explained to the officers that this "gentleman" had not only seen me but had deliberately tried to run me over with his van.

The man changed his excuse, saying he had been so angry with me for towing away his car that he didn't know what he was doing. He had lost so much business because of me, it had made him crazy.

In spite of his sob story, he was arrested and taken to the Hollywood station for booking. The paperwork took an hour. By the time the officers were finished, the shop owner had been released on his own recognizance. Although he had been charged with assault with a deadly weapon and assault on an officer, both felonies, the watch commander didn't feel it was necessary to take him downtown to the central jail facility. Meanwhile, I was taken for treatment to Cedar Sinai Hospital.

My natural resentment turned to indignation when the shop owner went to court and was acquitted. The city attorney's office didn't put much effort into his prosecution.

When I began to act sullen and rude, I sought professional help to combat my overwhelming anger. My supervisors knew I was seeing a therapist, but they still wrote me up for being insubordinate. Granted, I *was* a bit intractable. I was very angry and didn't know how else to express it. In addition, the scandals concerning the Hollywood Division were becoming public knowledge, and I was embarrassed to work for the L.A.P.D. All my illusions had been shattered.

The only positive result of this experience was that it gave me incentive to start writing again. I had occasionally used writing, of both poetry and short stories, as a catharsis for my frustration. When handling a radio call, I sometimes had to wait hours for the towing service to arrive. While sitting in the patrol car I jotted down observations and anecdotes for possible use in a book I might write someday. After my encounter with the shop owner, and in response to my growing disgust with the disgraceful behavior of certain Hollywood police officers, the book took a more concrete shape in my mind.

By this time Barbara Folsom had been promoted to supervisor, and she made her position quite clear. She often stayed in the office late to discuss issues with me, which were merely petty personal attacks. When I called her on it, I was admonished. Once she informed me that I *had* to take my lunch break and two fifteen-minute coffee breaks. At the time I didn't take any at all, and instead, when I finished my work, I went "end of watch" a half hour early.

Another evening Barbara stopped me in the office. "Norma Jean, dear, I just wanted to tell you that there is a new policy for writing up personalized license plates. From now on I want you to fill the ticket out like this." She pointed to the bottom of the ticket where she had written "Personalized Plates."

I followed her directions, but several days later I found correction slips in my mail slot. I was puzzled. I went to work early the next day so I could ask the other supervisor about the problem. He told me there had been no change in policy.

When I arrived at work the next day he told me Barbara said I had lied. I was shocked. Things just kept getting worse.

I was finally called down to West Traffic to see the captain. In his pompous, condescending way he kept harping on the fact that I didn't take my lunch break as I had been told. I tried to explain, but he refused to listen. Then I got mad, and rashly aimed a few barbs his way.

He wasn't amused. "Almodovar, we don't need your editorial remarks around here. Either you take your lunch breaks as you were told and fix those tickets, or I'm pulling you off night watch. Captain Spierol was right: You are a troublemaking bitch."

I shook with anger. At a time when several cops were being investigated for their part in a burglary ring, a drug ring, and a murder-for-hire ring, I was being dressed down for not taking a lunch break!

Not long after my meeting with the captain another incident occurred that pushed me even closer to the end.

As I was towing away a car parked in front of a fire hydrant, a woman came running out of her house waving a baseball bat and yelling obscenities at me: "You stupid bitch. Why are you towing away my car? All the fucking cars park there all the time!"

With unusual calm I replied, "Well, ma'am, when all the 'fucking' cars park here, they all get 'fucking' towed away."

I gave her a break and released her car without impounding it, but she called the station and reported that I had been rude to her.

The sergeant who made the investigation came to interview me in the field. I told him exactly what had happened and what I had said. "Yes, I told her it was a fucking car. That's what she called it. I was just repeating her language."

The sergeant looked at me strangely and said, "I wish you hadn't told me that. You should have said no. It's her word against yours, and the tow truck driver would have backed you up. Now I'm afraid you're in big trouble. The captain has been looking for something like this to punish you. He won't go easy on you."

The sergeant's lecture on the virtue of lying only irritated me more, especially when the captain meted out the punishment for my "crime": a ten-day suspension without pay.

Several weeks earlier two police officers had driven their police car beside the car of a known prostitute, threw a lit flare into it, and drove off. Her leg was badly burned, so she went to the station to file a report and press charges against the officers. She was laughed out of the station and told that if she didn't want things like that to happen, she should get the hell out of Hollywood. After an investigation the officers were suspended for two days.

My much-needed vacation was scheduled to begin April 19. My mom was visiting from New York, and we were planning to drive to northern California to visit my brothers, Dave and Doug. I was looking forward to getting away for a while with my mom. It was the first time in four years that I could afford to bring her out to California.

My bags were packed, and I was scheduled to get off work an hour early so I could get a good night's sleep before we left in the morning. With a couple of hours left on my shift, I decided to check Hollywood Boulevard one more time. Driving north on La Brea Avenue, I noticed a car weaving slowly and unsteadily in the next lane. It pulled over to the curb and stopped. Figuring the driver must be having car trouble, I shrugged and continued up the street. The light was red at Hollywood and La Brea. I glanced at my watch before I made the right-hand turn. It was 11:08 P.M.

As I pulled onto Hollywood, I glanced across the street and noticed a car blocking traffic. I honked the horn, but no one responded. "Guess I'll just have to give it a ticket," I thought.

The light turned red before I could make the turn. I heard car brakes squealing loudly as the old clunker I had seen weaving on La Brea a few minutes earlier rounded the corner. Just as I glanced in my rearview mirror, the car rear-ended mine. My head jerked forward. I turned to look at the driver. His mouth dropped when he realized he had hit a police car. His lips formed the words "Oh, shit."

All I could do was smile. I didn't know who he was, but the minute I had been hit I knew my life would never be the same. Before I could inform the dispatcher of my accident, the man drove off. I called for help, and soon there were patrol cars all over the place. It developed into a Keystone Cops chase scene with the fleeing car circling the same block several times, pursued by a string of patrol cars and a helicopter overhead. Fearing for his life, the passenger finally leaned over his drunk friend and switched off the ignition.

When the driver was taken to the station, blood was flowing from his mouth, soaking his ripe T-shirt. He was missing all his bottom teeth—the result, I believe, of a police beating.

After having X-rays, I returned to the station. It was 3:30 in the morning. The doctors at Cedar Sinai Hospital told me I would have to stay in bed for at least a week and undergo daily physical therapy. So much for my vacation!

The drunk driver turned out to be an illegal alien. The car he had been driving was stolen and filled with stolen property, but by the time I got back from the hospital, he had already been released.

I drove home in pain. It was the last time I worked for the Los Angeles Police Department. My mother was worried when I told her about the accident, but she was relieved that I had made the decision not to return to my job.

At 4:30 A.M. on April 19, 1982, I changed clothes and put on pajamas. I fixed Mom a cup of coffee and made myself some tea. Then I took a pair of scissors from the desk in my workroom and in a symbolic gesture, reflecting my basic middle-finger approach to life, I shredded my uniform and cut my black heavy-duty men's shoes into a hundred pieces. Realizing how much it would cost to replace them, I knew my decision was firm.

My ten-year career was over. I didn't know what I was going to do, but I did know that anything would be better than working for the Blue Mafia. I was no longer under the gun.

7. THIS LITTLE PIGGY WENT TO MARKET

This little pig went to market
After spending ten years in the sty.
Her old "black and white" she did park it,
And went off, her sweet ass to ply.

◇

As I STUFFED the money in my purse and pulled out my coral lipstick, I adjusted the rearview mirror toward me. The face in the mirror resembled mine, but the last time I had looked in the car mirror, not even an hour earlier, I was a "virgin." Now I was not.

I was thirty-one years old and had just committed my first *honest* act of prostitution. I touched the bills, my fingers lingering over the features of Benjamin Franklin. Two hundred and twenty dollars wasn't an enormous sum, but it was more than I had ever held at one time. More important, it represented a major change in my life.

It wasn't that my paychecks were so small at the Los Angeles Police Department. As a traffic officer I made more than I could have earned in private enterprise, at least with the business skills I had at the time. My paychecks were deposited directly into the bank so I never got to see any of the money. I had never held a one-hundred-dollar bill before.

What sinful act did I commit to earn that kind of money? Nothing I hadn't already done with many men before—except then I hadn't charged for it and, come to think of it, I had received nothing from them at all, not even sexual pleasure.

It wasn't an easy transition from traffic officer to call girl. Deciding not to return to work for the police department was one thing. Deciding to become a prostitute was quite another. It was one of the most difficult decisions of my life.

*   *   *

Since the car accident involving the drunk driver was duty related, the City of Los Angeles was obliged to pay me disability. In addition to the physical therapy I was receiving for my back and neck, I was being counseled for suicidal depression. I was not emotionally able to deal with the new pain that added to the discomfort I still suffered from my original accident in 1975.

On top of that, my disillusionment with my former heroes had turned into outrage. I was angry at myself for having been deceived by them. At one point I became so overwhelmed with despair that I made a half-hearted suicide attempt. I deliberately took an overdose of the medication I was taking for pain, but then I vomited and slept for what seemed like days. After this incident my psychiatrist prescribed an antidepressant and instructed me to call him whenever I had the urge to overdose again.

The doctors who reviewed my workers' compensation case said I was not ready to return to work, but the city's doctors insisted I was. So the city stopped paying me and tried to force me back to work. (When I became a call girl, I was in legal no-man's-land, still technically employed by the police department but not being paid. I knew I would never voluntarily return to that job. Ultimately I had to sue to be reinstated on disability, and eventually I won a small settlement.) It was time to think about my career options.

I had permanently injured my back as a result of the three duty-related accidents. I felt vulnerable from the emotional stress, and the last thing I wanted to do was find another job where I might have to put up with someone's nonsense. By now I had decided to get serious about the book I was writing; maybe that would help me get over my anger toward the police. Meanwhile, with no more disability payments from the city, I needed an income.

Legally I was already a prostitute because I had participated in "a lewd act for money or other consideration" more than once. Even in my early years in the department I went into the sergeant's office, sat on his lap, and blew into his ear. Not only did I get off from work early, but I also committed "a lewd act"—and it was definitely for other consideration! I was just a very cheap prostitute!

Still, it was one thing to brazenly give away sexual favors and quite another to sell them! I once turned down an "opportunity" when a couple of cops offered me $200 to be a "going-away present" for a retiring captain. At the time I was highly offended by the offer because I didn't consider myself "that kind" of woman.

All I knew was that I preferred to have a job rather than starve or ask for charity. I also preferred a job doing something I enjoyed, was good at, and that would pay well. Prostitution offered all the things I wanted in a career: I could choose my own hours, see only men I liked, and go to the finest restaurants with my clients. And I loved sex. What more could I ask for?

Getting into the business as a call girl is not easy unless you know someone. Nearly six months prior to my final on-duty auto accident, I was driving my old "black and white" patrol car late one night when I noticed a car behind me flashing its lights, trying to get my attention. I was in the residential area of Hollywood Boulevard. As I pulled over, a red Porsche drove alongside me. A stunning young blonde rolled down her window.

"Officer, can you help me? I'm being followed." She pointed behind her, and my eyes focused on her long, polished fingernails. I thought of my own stubby nails, chewed down to the quick. It was not within the realm of my experience to have hands that looked like hers.

She indicated a black and green Chevy. "That man has been following me all night. I don't dare go home, or he'll know where I live. Could you follow me home and see that he doesn't?"

This was out of my line of duty as a traffic officer, but all the regular cops were changing shifts at that time of the night, and it would be an hour before one would arrive.

I nodded. "Okay, ma'am. Where do you live?"

She let out a sigh of relief. "Back there, up on Nickolas Canyon."

She started up the Porsche and whipped a U-turn. I tried to get my tank to turn like that. Skreech . . . draggg . . . the wheel turned as if it was drugged and ten months pregnant. Goddamn city car. It would be nice if they'd fix them, I thought. I don't know how many times I had turned in a repair request for this heap of junk.

I followed her up the narrow canyon road to her home. She stopped in front of a large house, then waited for the electric garage opener to let her enter. She parked, then walked back to my car. I couldn't help but notice her expensive-looking purple suede outfit.

I tried to sound authoritative. "Well, I think we got you home okay. You shouldn't be out at this time of night by yourself in this town. I guess your husband will be happy to see you get home safely."

"Oh, thanks, officer. By the way, my name's Karin. I'm not married. I live here alone. I do get worried sometimes, but I can usually find a cop to escort me home!'' She laughed as though she were telling me an inside joke. I didn't get it at the time.

Suddenly it dawned on me: This lady's a prost . . . a prost . . . a hooker! I got up the nerve to ask her. She told me she was indeed a call girl.

For a moment I felt self-righteous, superior, and smug. Then I took a second look. She was young, had a Porsche and a house. Her hands were beautifully manicured, her makeup was impeccable, and her clothes were expensive. She did not seem to be suffering from stress. Then I looked at myself: stressed out all of the time, angry with the world, angry with my peers, nails bitten to the quick, cheap mascara flecked under my eyes, tattered uniform and ugly men's shoes for work, and my personal wardrobe consisting of jeans and T-shirts, period. My purse was designer K mart, done in regulation black vinyl. No house and certainly no Porsche. In a society that views material goods as evidence of success, where did that leave me?

In my ten-year career with the police department I had met many street prostitutes and a few call girls, but I was never interested in their job. It appeared to be a miserable, degrading occupation, but I had never bothered to ask a prostitute what it was like.

As we talked it became clear that Karin had made a better career choice than I had. Even with my moral career and her so-called immoral one, morality and ethics, as I understand them, were on her side. I believed it was ethical (right) to give value for value but unethical to violate someone's rights or intentionally defraud him or her. It was moral (good) to make life better for others, to be honest, and not to hurt anyone. By that standard how could I continue to justify working for an organization that tolerated—and sometimes even encouraged—brutality, racism, violations of civil rights, and corruption?

When I decided to try being a call girl, I sought Karin out, hoping she'd introduce me to her madam. I drove past her house several times, but it took me a while to find the courage to knock at her door. When I finally did, it was as if she had been expecting me.

She casually mentioned she had heard from some of the officers that I had been in another accident. I told her I did not intend to go back to work for the police department.

She smiled and crossed her legs. "What do you plan to do?"

I took a sip of water. "I was kind of hoping to go into your profession. I mean, if you could introduce me to your madam or something. I'd at least like to try it."

She tipped back her head and laughed. "If I hadn't heard so much about your sexual escapades, I'd think you were setting me up, Norma Jean. But I don't think you are a moral hypocrite. Sure, I'll call Liz. She'll like you." She cleared her throat and then continued tactfully, "Of course, you do need some fixing up—just a little. I want you to promise me you'll stop biting your nails!"

I looked at my fingers and smiled. "I'd be happy to stop biting them. I'd love to have nails as beautiful as yours!"

Karin went into the other room and made the call. When she returned from the kitchen she announced that Liz would like to meet me immediately.

"Right now? What about my nails and my clothes?"

"Just keep your hands in your pockets! You look fine, but you are going to have to improve your wardrobe."

We took Karin's Porsche since I was driving my beat-up old blue Honda. It was just not the thing to drive into Liz's neighborhood, the plush Wilshire Corridor, a community of expensive high-rise apartments and condominiums just outside Beverly Hills. As we drove past them I noticed that the smartly uniformed parking attendants were maneuvering mostly Rolls-Royces, Jaguars, Mercedes, and Ferraris. I laughed to myself when I imagined handing them the keys to my old blue heap, then nonchalantly sauntering past them to enter the multimillion-dollar lobbies of the high-rise palaces of the rich and mighty!

Liz's apartment was on beautiful Beverly Glen, a favorite street of several madams and call girls. The very efficient staff parked Karin's car and opened the large glass and brass doors to the pink marble lobby. A well-groomed, effeminate desk clerk announced us to our hostess. He languidly lifted his manicured hand and pointed toward the elevator. "Darlings, fifteenth floor, apartment C. Liz is expecting you," he sang in a high, sweet, lilting voice.

Several prominent people rode in the mirrored elevator with us. One elegantly coiffeured but overweight dowager with at least a two-carat diamond weighing down every finger was trying to keep her bad-mannered pedigree pooch from peeing all over the neatly pressed trousers of a very famous comedian. He wasn't laughing. Seems he never gets any respect.

I don't know what I expected Liz to be like, but I was delightfully surprised when she greeted us. Liz looked like a blond, female Howdy

Doody, minus the freckles. With an incredibly proportioned body and a smile that was at once sweet and lewdly suggestive, she was a combination of badwy seductiveness and sincerity.

Her long Gucci gown was cut to her navel, and two immense rubies sparkled in her earlobes. Her wide smile revealed a pair of braces, and at first it was difficult to make out what she was saying. Her voice was high and soft, and she seemed to be as shy as I felt.

She invited us into her living room, which could have been the centerfold of *Better Homes and Gardens*. Trendy magazines were strategically placed on the smoked glass and bronze coffee table. The open curtains revealed a small, intimate tropical balcony that overlooked the pool fifteen floors below. In the distance, the towering buildings of West Los Angeles made geometric patterns across a pink-streaked sky.

She offered us a drink, and I asked for my usual glass of water, which she served in a beautiful cut-crystal goblet.

Devilishly, Karin told Liz of my very recent employment with their natural enemies. "What a great gimmick for some of my clients to know they are fucking a lady cop!" Liz's eyes twinkled as she thought of the possibilities.

I was fortunate to have Liz as my first madam. If my first call girl experience had not been as pleasant as it was, I don't think I would ever have pursued it. What surprised me was that Liz told me up front that she truly did not care for the business. She said she had no respect for men who couldn't control their sexual appetites: "When their little peckers sprout, they have to find a hole to put it in!" It seemed to me, however, that if men didn't have that powerful sex drive, an awful lot of women would have starved to death over the centuries, not to mention all the housewives who would be without mink coats, diamonds, and Mercedes. Porsche-titution, we call it.

Liz was very excited to launch my new career, so excited that she put me to work that very afternoon. I hadn't quite expected to be inducted so soon. Since I had worked so long for a bureaucracy, I forgot that in a private enterprise things are not bogged down by red tape.

But there were still things I had to know before I committed myself. Naively, I asked about medical coverage, dental plans, group insurance, and practical things like that.

Liz laughed. "Honey, you are on your own with those things! I'm afraid they don't give call girls special group rates even though we go to the doctor often enough! Got to keep the merchandise in top condition! But don't worry about it. We have a few doctors who will take care of your equipment on a regular basis in exchange for an 'office visit'! They see just about all the girls who work in this town.''

I decided that there was no time like the present to get started. If I left without trying it, I might not have the courage to return. Liz called her client. Within an hour of arriving at Liz's I was preparing to break the law. I bathed, nervously fussed with my makeup, and combed my short hair a thousand times. I slipped on the lacy pink silk negligee Liz lent me. I was as ready as I would ever be.

Returning to the living room, I waited with Liz and Karin until he arrived. When the knock came, Liz just smiled and held my hand. "It's going to be all right, Norma Jean. You'll see. He's such a dear!'' She opened the door, and a very tall, stout gentleman entered.

Heinrich kissed Liz and Karin on the cheek and held a friendly hand out to me. "Vell, hello, Norma Jean,'' he said in his warmly accented voice. "I am so very pleased to meet you. Liz told me vat a vonderful surprise she has for me, and here you are!'' He kissed me on the cheek. "Let me have a goot look at you!'' The way he said it, I did not feel like a piece of meat but like a woman who was appreciated by a man.

Taking me by the hand he maneuvered me toward the bedroom, waving a thank-you to Liz.

Liz's bedroom had a magnificent four-poster brass bed, covered with stuffed animals and antique dolls. The bedspread had matching draperies, and the overstuffed chair was done in colors that complemented the wallpaper. There were mounds of lacy pillows on the bed, and the room smelled of lilac. It might have been a bit too feminine for some men, but it was the perfect place for the seduction of an ''innocent''!

Heinrich removed the stuffed animals, dolls, and pillows, and disappeared into the bathroom while I removed my negligee. I was as shy as a bride on her honeymoon and felt sorry for this poor fellow. Little did I realize the desirability of my ''virgin'' status to some clients, who pay highly for the privilege of breaking in a new whore.

When Heinrich returned to the bedroom, I was under the covers. Walking over to my side of the bed, he cupped my chin in his hand. "There, there, *Liebchen*. This will not be as bad as you think. I am not a mean old man. I will not hurt you!''

It wasn't the first time I had been with an older man, but it was the first time I had ever been paid for it and I didn't know how to react. In this one quick encounter I was knowingly, willingly violating ten years of blind obedience to the law. Yet it didn't feel wrong. I was only nervous because I was at a beginning. Perhaps I should have been there all along.

With a tenderness I never knew one could feel for a complete stranger, I kissed him. He put his arms around me and began to stroke my hair. I took his hand and nibbled lightly on his fingers, then reached to play with his semi-hard organ, which no amount of stroking made firmer. He told me not to worry, that despite his lack of rigidity, he could still have an orgasm.

He ran his hand down my body. It felt good to have him touch the body I had worked so hard to keep fit. "You are a lovely woman, Norma Jean. You shut have no twouble at all in dis business."

I smiled and ran my tongue along his body. The goosebumps he sprouted told me I was doing something right, and he quietly moaned with pleasure.

When Heinrich reached the peak of arousal, he slipped on a condom and inserted his half-hard penis into me. With a sigh he achieved orgasm, pulled himself off my body, and lay beside me, breathing heavily.

Reaching for his face, I began to stroke it tenderly, as though he were my dearest lover. I thanked him for being so easy with me my first time. He laughed heartily and said that if he weren't, Liz would never let him have the cherries of her new girls. He asked if I would be interested in seeing him again. Gratefully, I told him I would love to have him as a steady client.

He handed me two $100 bills from a wad of bills and a business card that had his phone number on it. I thanked him solemnly. He smiled with a twinkle and pulled out another $100 from the stack.

"Dis is for you, my dear, because you have been such an angel to dis old fart. You don't have to share this with Liz. And believe me, the pleasure was all mine!" As I had learned from Liz earlier, forty percent of the fee belonged to the madam, but the tip was all mine.

He got dressed, went into the living room, and gave Liz a glowing report of her newest girl.

"Well, honey, how did you like Heinrich?" she asked after he'd left. "He seemed to be quite pleased with you. I think you will work out just fine in this business if you want to give it a try."

I burst out crying, I was so relieved. It had been easy and very, very pleasant. I sat there looking at the money Heinrich had given me and thought of how ridiculously simple it had been. I asked myself why I hadn't done this years before.

Liz misunderstood my tears and tried to comfort me. She thought perhaps Heinrich had said something to hurt me or maybe I was full of self-reproach. I shook my head and assured her my tears were tears of joy, and Heinrich had been a real gentleman. I handed her the $200, and she gave me back my share. I told her he had tipped me, and she was very pleased to hear that. It was a sure sign he liked me and would probably become a steady client.

"Let me know when you are ready to start working full time. I know I can keep you busy." She smiled and patted my hand.

As Karin and I rode downstairs in the elevator, I was certain everyone in the elevator knew what I had just done. What was worse, I wanted them to know. In fact, it was all I could do not to announce it to everyone I met.

Contemplating my earnings, I was overcome with new emotions. I had just made in a half hour's time what it would have taken me two whole days of hard work to equal. That alone impressed me, to say the least. But it also seemed wonderful that I could actually make a career out of bringing people pleasure.

Although this kind of work is not for every woman, if prostitution was "acceptable," a lot of underpaid secretaries, file clerks, waitresses, telephone operators, and even traffic officers would leave their jobs. The hours are great because you make your own. As a call girl you pick and choose your clientele, and by practicing safe sex there is little worry about AIDS or other diseases. What horny woman wouldn't opt for such a life-style?

After my first experience as a call girl, I had a talk with Victor. He had always encouraged me to be independent, so I did not feel the need to get his approval to become a prostitute. I did want to make him aware of my new profession for several reasons. I hadn't done any research yet to know that the image of the "beaten, victimized prostitute" was mostly a myth, particularly for call girls, so I harbored concerns about my physical safety. Also, even though the possibility of being arrested seemed remote (because of the cavalier attitude the police had toward call girl operations), I wanted Victor to know what I was doing in case anything happened to me.

Victor's response was what I expected. Since jealousy was not part of our relationship, he was mainly concerned that I not become "hard and jaded.'' I pointed out that I had endured ten years dealing with the darkest side of the public and was not yet hard and jaded, so it was doubtful that bringing pleasure to people would make me that way.

His next concern was that I not burn myself out trying to make all the money I could. I assured him that I intended to work only enough to pay my bills, buy a few new clothes, and occasionally treat us to dinner. The rest of my time would be spent writing my book, sculpting, and being with him.

In my entire career as a call girl I never had any problems dealing with the many men who came into my life. Instead, we grew closer because I was always able to share the excitement of my expanding sexual horizons with him.

In the first few months of my new career Liz kept me busy, and I went through her entire list of clients. She loved to send me to her "fantasy clients"—the ones most of the other girls didn't want to see. The fantasies required a vivid imagination, some acting skills, and the ability to keep a straight face. I enjoyed the challenge of being sexually inventive. People have asked me what else I got out of my work besides money; well, it certainly made my own love life interesting.

Miles Falconne deserved the grand prize for imaginative use of raw chicken. Miles, a very wealthy stockbroker from New York, single and reasonably attractive, had a fantasy that was without a doubt one of the most puzzling I have encountered. It wasn't dangerous, and as was true of many of the fantasies, it didn't involve intercourse.

The fantasy centered more around Julia Child than chicken, but the chicken had a definite role. I enjoyed the challenge of figuring out what turned my clients on and why.

When Liz called to tell me about Miles, I was intrigued. She often had trouble finding anyone to see him. "I haven't heard from Miles in quite a while because I usually don't have anyone for him. He needs a real actress, someone who won't start laughing in the middle of his fantasy. If you make him happy, he can be a good bread-and-butter client. He pays well." (A bread-and-butter client is a good, steady client who can be called upon when business is slow and who will always see you if you call, even if he hadn't planned on it. B and B clients paid the bills and were a working girl's dream.)

I told her I was interested.

"Do you know who Julia Child is?"

"Yes, of course."

"Well, he has this hang-up about her, and he wants you to pretend to be her."

"That doesn't sound so bad."

"And he wants you to pretend to cook a chicken for him."

"Just pretend to cook a chicken? What's so difficult about that?"

"I can't get anybody to impersonate Julia Child and keep a straight face. The last girl I sent was still laughing when he told her to leave. He threw the chicken at her car, and she laughed all the way down the street. He was really upset. He pays five hundred dollars an hour, and he reimburses you for the groceries."

"What groceries? You mean I have to go grocery shopping for him, too?"

"You have to get the chicken at the Farmer's Market. He wants to hear about how you shopped for just the right chicken. You have to tell him the name of the butcher you bought it from. He will call the butcher after you leave and find out if you bought it there. If he finds out you lied, he'll never call you again."

"Oh, wow, Liz, he sounds like a real piece of work!"

"He's harmless, really, and I think he'd like you. You are really into this job. Try it once. He still pays even if he kicks you out."

It was just too interesting a fantasy to pass up. "Okay, I'll try it."

"He wants to see you tomorrow night. By the way, when he calls he'll ask for Julia. He will always call you that."

Miles called about an hour later. "Julia? This is Miles. How's my favorite chef?" The role-playing had started already.

"Oh, Miles, how lovely to hear from you." I raised my voice and faked her accent.

"Can you come over tomorrow night for a private cooking lesson?"

"How about eight o'clock?"

"I can't wait!" His voice actually trembled at the thought. He gave me directions to his huge home in Trousdale Estates, one of the most exclusive areas in Los Angeles.

Early the next morning I was off to do the shopping. Sometimes I had to buy special sexy articles of clothing or some whips and chains before a date, but never food. At the Farmer's Market I went from butcher shop to butcher shop looking at the poultry. Did he want a whole chicken or just the breasts? Or maybe wings and thighs?

I caught the eye of one of the butchers. "Hello, young lady. Do you need some help?"

I smiled. "I'm looking for a nice, plump, juicy chicken." I was already starting to sound like Julia. How could I explain to this friendly butcher what I wanted it for?

He gave me a knowing look. "Are you shopping for Miles Falconne by any chance?"

He wiped his hands on the bloody apron and reached in the meat case for a healthy-looking whole chicken. "You want a whole one. This one is nice. I'm sure he'll like it." He patted it tenderly. "That will be eleven dollars and seventy-eight cents, and tell him you bought it from Sandy." He gave me a wink.

I handed him a twenty and grabbed my chicken. "Thanks. I will," I mumbled and hurried away.

"Hey, Julia, you forgot your change!"

I needed some time to work myself into the role. I also needed some coaching from Julia, so I rented a videotape. If I was going to play this game, I wanted to do it right.

At 7:15 I finished putting on my makeup. Then I kissed my darling and said in my most Julia Childish voice, "Good-bye. This is Julia Child. Bon appetit!"

Driving to work was such a pleasure now, in contrast to my former occupation. The lush landscaped lawns of Beverly Hills were far more pleasant to look at than the seedy neglected streets of Hollywood.

Miles Falconne was awaiting my arrival. The door flew open as I walked up the steps. He was wearing nothing but a pair of green socks and an apron. His toupee had slipped slightly, and his face reflected the glow of those wholly engrossed in a fantasy world. He grabbed my hand and pulled me inside.

"Oh, Julia, Julia," he panted, his voice raspy with lust. He took the bag with the chicken, potatoes, onions, butter, and cream. He unwrapped the chicken and sighed appreciatively as he squeezed it tenderly. "Oh, it's lovely, just lovely! Come on upstairs and let's get ready."

His house was enormous and well appointed. Aloud, I admired his collection of artwork—in Julia Child's voice, of course. An important thing I learned early was that with a client who had a particular fetish or a repetitive fantasy, it was best to stay in character from the beginning. It was important to reassure the client that for the time he is paying you, his fantasy is real.

Upstairs in his bedroom Miles had a closet full of aprons. I chose a utilitarian blue number, similar to the one Julia wears in her videos. I slipped out of my clothes and donned the apron. He paced the room while

I undressed. As soon as I put on the apron, he grabbed my hand and rushed me downstairs. I almost tripped in my five-inch heels.

His kitchen was the center of his home. It was twice the size of my living room and was equipped with every imaginable convenience for those who love to cook. Done in chrome and black and white tile, it was spectacular—high tech but warm, inviting the guest to stay.

He opened the cupboard and pulled out several bowls. Then he reached up over the stove for a small skillet and into the other side of the oven for a roasting pan. He quickly gathered other cooking instruments for me—a whisk, measuring spoons, a measuring cup, a sharp knife, and then salt, pepper, some herbs, cream, and a stick of butter.

With a flourish he wiped his hands on his apron and said, "Okay, Julia. Let's begin!"

I smiled nervously. Could I pull this off without laughing? I cleared my throat and gave it my best shot. (Note: The following is not a recipe for stuffing a chicken. It was my improvisation for a man's sexual fantasy. I do not recommend that anyone use my directions for cooking *anything*.)

"This is Julia Child, and today we are going to prepare stuffed chicken. There are many, many wonderful things you can do with your bird. Stuffing it is just one delicious way to prepare it. I went to the Farmer's Market today and found this lovely, succulent, juicy bird. Notice its pale pink flesh, tender but firm to the touch."

Miles was perched attentively on top of a high stool in the corner. His hand was underneath his apron. He was oohing and ahhing my performance.

I picked up the chicken by its legs. "It has two beautiful, firm, meaty breasts." That really turned him on. I think he was a breast man. Not interested in *my* breasts but . . .

"We are going to start by washing this baby." I stuck the chicken in the sink and rinsed it off.

"Then we need to gently dry our bird with a paper towel. . . . That's enough. There now, he's ready to go. We'll just lay him down for a minute while we prepare the stuffing."

I reached for the small skillet and the butter. "But first I'm going to melt some butter to baste our bird."

While the butter was melting I kept a constant monologue going, to keep Miles basting himself.

"Oh, look at that butter! Doesn't that look good! Let's stick our impeccably clean finger in there and get a taste of that sweet butter.

Mmm, isn't that yummy! I just love to lick the juices off my fingers, don't you?''

When the butter was ready, I removed it from the stove. I took the onion and chopped it carefully, trying to avoid making my eyes tear so I wouldn't ruin my mascara. When that was done, I set it aside to work with the cream. There is no recipe I know of for a stuffed chicken that involves heavy cream, but I knew enough about fantasies of this sort to know it wasn't the recipe that was important. It is the words that are used, the way they are said and then repeated over and over, and the voice inflections that make the fantasy work. Words such as ''rich, heavy cream'' rolled on the tongue.

Miles was breathing hard, groaning loudly. He jumped up and sat on the counter, closer to the chicken and me. I went back to the bird, to our make-believe stuffing, and began to talk rapidly.

''I'm going to baste our bird before I stuff it. I'm going to take some herbs and rub them into the meat. And I'm going to take this rich, heavy cream and rub it over the breasts like this.'' Magic words. I massaged the chicken.

''And then I'm going to stuff it. Miles, I'm going to stuff the bird.''

Miles almost fell off the counter.

My voice was husky, and I spoke faster and faster. ''And then I'm going to put this lovely, succulent bird in the pan, and I'm going to baste it some more. Then I'm going to put these two round, firm potatoes down here by the breasts, and I'm going to cook the bird slowly. The juices will drip down in the pan, mixing with the rich, heavy cream, making the stuffing moist. Our bird will be so tender and juicy. . . .'' I stressed the words ''tender'' and ''juicy.''

''Oh, yes!'' A loud sigh came from Miles as he reached orgasm. He remained ecstatic for several minutes, then he snapped back to reality. He stood up and took off his apron. He was now as naked as a jaybird except for his green socks.

''Don't worry about the kitchen, honey. I'll clean up. You were terrific!'' He kissed me on the cheek.

Back upstairs I got dressed and noticed an envelope on top of my clothes. Inside were six crisp one-hundred-dollar bills.

Miles walked me to the door. He kissed me on the cheek again.

''Norma Jean, you were very good.'' So he knew my real name! ''Can we do this again?''

''Of course, Miles. Anytime.'' I was using my real voice now; I could be myself. But the next time, if there was a next time, I would have to start out again as Julia.

Miles became a semi-regular, and each time the fantasy was exactly the same. As we got to know each other better, I learned which words were effective for his fantasy and which weren't. I was better able to regulate the sessions for his maximum enjoyment. I wanted to make sure he got his money's worth.

I always wondered what he did with the chickens after each session. I never did ask him, though. As for me, well, I definitely look at chickens in a whole new light.

8. My Daily Bread

Off I go to fight the war
To earn my daily bread.
Wouldn't I earn a little more
If I gave some daily head?

ON EVERY TALK SHOW I have done, the same questions arise: Why do men see prostitutes? Why do married men pay for sex when they can get it for free at home? Why do single men pay when they can get it for nothing in a bar? Why did my famous clients, some of whom were actors and movie producers, come to me and pay the kind of money they did? Surely they could find all kinds of women willing to sleep with them for nothing!

Call girls and other prostitutes offer something all of these men just can't get at home or from a free encounter: a nonjudgmental relationship with no strings attached.

Every job has built-in stress, as do personal relationships. A married man has stress at work *and* at home. He may love his wife very much, but she is part of the twenty-four-hour-a-day stress. When he needs to get away from it all, he needs to escape from everything that causes stress. Some men play golf, while others play tennis, work out with weights, or jog to relieve stress. And some men see prostitutes.

It's true that seeing a therapist helps some people, but a therapist must sit across the room, far away, while a man sits in his chair, fidgeting. What he really needs and wants is some tender loving care. A prostitute can hold him while he shares his troubles with her. She will listen, pass no judgment, and make no demands. In the end he will usually have a climax, which is very relaxing, and then he leaves. He is happy to pay her for the service—it simplifies his life enormously.

For single men who are busy moving and shaking the world we offer the ideal relationship. I had several unmarried clients who were so busy with their careers, it just wasn't possible for them to cultivate relationships with one woman.

My clients in show business were willing to pay a call girl for their sexual entertainment because women who offered it to them for free were usually after something, and at least we were up front about it. The producers, writers, and directors preferred our "honesty"; they didn't have to promise us movie parts as they did some bimbos who pretended to be in love with them.

Some clients had gone through messy divorces and weren't ready to jump into new commitments, which many "straight" women demand after the second date.

Some clients come to us because they have fantasies in which their wives or girlfriends do not want to participate. Sometimes the client won't tell his wife or girlfriend about the fantasy for fear of ridicule. A woman who is being paid usually won't laugh, no matter how unusual the request.

One of my favorite clients had an irresistible and charming fantasy. He would call from New York and book an appointment whenever he was coming to Los Angeles. Martin Sarranti, a wealthy real estate developer, and his wife were always being mentioned in the *New York Post* society columns.

In our secret little world, far from his fancy friends and his elegant, aggressive wife, he was a pirate who landed on my island, where I was the queen of a society of beautiful women. He and his men tried to capture us, but my women outwitted and captured them instead. I took him as my special prisoner and tied him to my big brass bed.

I had most of the equipment for bondage, but he wanted his own special fur handcuffs. He brought me a lovely pair from New York, which I used only on him. I tortured him for hours (in reality, just a few minutes) by standing naked in front of him, playing with myself. I taunted and teased him, and told him what I was going to make him do to me.

"You little worm!" I yelled as I cracked my latex whip across his stomach (lightly, of course). "I am going to make you my slave. You will service me and my beautiful women."

I used my vibrator on myself, standing so close to his face he could barely breathe. I put a gag in his mouth so he couldn't talk. Sometimes I removed the gag and forced him to suck my breasts.

"You'd like it if I made you my slave, wouldn't you, you little bastard!" Again I used the whip. "Just what can I do to punish you? I know. I'll bring in my beautiful girlfriend Simone and make you watch us make love to each other. Simone will eat my pussy, and I will suck on her big beautiful breasts. And you can't touch us! That's what I'll do! How would you like that?"

I would reach down and rub his very hard penis between my breasts. He'd wiggle his tightly bound body frantically as he had an orgasm all over my breasts.

The whole episode sometimes took less than fifteen minutes because he would come to me so excited. We tried to make it last longer by doing an elaborate tying-up scene, but since I talked to him in character while I tied him up, he still climaxed very rapidly, which is the whole point anyway. Since all fantasies take place inside the mind, it is an art to get inside a man's head and enliven his fantasy even for just a little while.

Martin often brought me little presents, things like sexy underwear and sex toys for my briefcase. Whenever I saw one of my clients who was into this kind of fantasy, whether in his home, office, or a hotel, I usually brought my briefcase of "toys" with me. It looked like any other business woman's attaché case, but inside it had a whole arsenal of goodies: handcuffs (metal and cloth), several cock rings, vibrators, adult magazines, and, of course, some lacy underwear in extra-large sizes for the man who wanted to dress up a little. And condoms in an assortment of colors and sizes.

In the event I was ever stopped by hotel security, I was prepared to explain that I was simply a sales representative for an adult store! Most of the hotels my clients stayed at never interfered with their guests' private activity. After all, for the kind of money my clients dished out to stay there, I should have been supplied by the hotel! I never did have an opportunity to shock a hotel detective, though, which was fine with me.

Herman Feinberg was one of the sweetest, gentlest clients I had. He was short and plump, in his late fifties, and could have been a stand-in for Santa Claus except that he was completely bald. His wife had died many years earlier, his only daughter was grown, and he was not interested in remarrying. He had sacrificed his whole life for his wife and daughter, and now that he was financially successful and retired, he wanted to enjoy himself.

He bought himself a Ferrari and a Jeep. He toyed with photography, spending thousands on cameras and accessories. His favorite hobby, outside of S&M, was flying a remote-controlled helicopter out in the desert.

Herman had a problem with women. They knew he was an easy target and often took terrible advantage of him. It hurt him every time it happened, but he still fancied himself a ladies' man and never stopped pursuing them. He was often lonely, though, and had frequented prostitutes for quite some time.

When we were first introduced, he wanted to make me his mistress. Actually, he wanted to become my sex slave. He was serious.

"That's a lovely thought, Herman, but I don't need a slave, and I have a boyfriend." I tried to be as diplomatic as I could.

He pouted. "Well, you could use me when you come to my house! I'll do anything you want me to . . . anything!" I could see how some women would try to take advantage of him.

Herman had one room in his house entirely devoted to his playthings. The walls were covered with hundreds of devices of torture: neat, orderly rows of whips, chains, nipple clamps, ropes, cuffs, and every other instrument of bondage and discipline a sadist or masochist could ever dream of. He had many boxes, all indexed and labeled, of leather and latex clothing, props, costume jewelry, and makeup, and two large closets, one filled with wigs in every color and size, and the other with high-heeled boots and shoes, in small and large sizes.

Although he liked the way I looked, for his fantasy I needed to exaggerate every feature and become the wild tigress dominatrix of his dreams. This meant an hour of preparation, going through the boxes, finding the right clothes and jewelry, the right wig, and an elaborate makeup job. While I prepared myself, he was busy donning his own getup.

I often used an orange wig, studded black leather body harness, fishnet stockings, and a pair of six-inch heeled boots that came nearly to my crotch. I completed the outfit with black opera gloves, studded leather arm bands, and a collar. I wore tons of makeup, huge false eyelashes, and blood-red lipstick. After my transformation into this exotic mistress of dominance, not even my own mother would have recognized me.

When I emerged from the dressing room, he was ready and waiting. He had on black lace panties, a garter belt, black stockings, six-inch-heeled shoes, a padded bra, and a face mask. He had already tied himself and was hanging by his arms from an overhead hook specially constructed for this kind of activity.

The room was softly lit, and appropriate background music was playing. I didn't know where to start. I removed the ball gag from his mouth. "What do you want me to do, Herman?"

I didn't think I would be very good at being a dominatrix since I was not an aggressive person. But I found that while in makeup and costume I did very well, especially after a little practice. The first session was difficult for me, though, and I had one hell of a time with his first request. I really don't like to see anyone in pain if I can help it.

From inside the tight face mask he gave me explicit instructions: "I want you to take a pair of nipple clamps and put them on my nipples."

Walking over to the wall, I tried to find a comfortable set. All I could find were some heavy, long-handled clamps with sharp teeth that looked as though they would tear his entire breast off. My hand passed over them briefly. Surely most of these props were for show, not actual use!

"Yes, those. They'll be fine! And get that brick down. I want you to tie it around my cock."

"I beg your pardon?"

With great trepidation I took the brick off the wall and gently tied it around his inert organ. I winced as I let go of it and let it hang down between his legs. Then I tenderly fastened the nipple clamps to his nipples. They looked painful!

He was so sweet, patiently leading me through my introduction to real S&M. "Please, Norma Jean. You won't hurt me. Believe me, it's what I want! Now twist the nipple clamps."

"Oh, I can't, I just can't." I dropped them and then realized that must have hurt, too. "I'm sorry, Herman."

It took him a while, but he finally convinced me it really excited him to experience the type of pain his requests gave him.

"Now, pick up the brick and drop it."

Was he serious? I gingerly lifted the brick and dropped it slowly, still holding it as it came down between his legs. I couldn't bring myself to just drop it.

"Norma Jean, trust me. It doesn't hurt the way you think it does. Drop it, please."

Who am I to judge what brings another pleasure? I picked it up and tried again. This time I succeeded in letting it go. It wasn't so bad. I did it again. Before long I managed to do it expertly. I was twisting those nipple clamps and dropping that brick as though I had been born to the world of S&M. When the brick fell, I kicked the back of his legs, bringing the chain down from the overhead rack, knocking him to his knees.

I flogged him with the latex cat-o'-nine-tails, cursing him incessantly (at his request): "You filthy swine! I'm going to have to punish you, you bad slave!"

Through his leather muzzle he moaned and twitched.

"You like that, do you, slave? Well, maybe I'll have to whip you harder, something to make you scream!'' I applied the whip with more force. (I think it sounded much worse than it felt.)

"You dildo breath bastard!'' In order to be most effective, I pretended he was the vain captain from West Traffic. It became very easy then to call him every vile and disgusting name I could think of.

When it was time for him to have an orgasm, I commanded him to come while I flogged his ass with the whip. Being an obedient slave, he did.

After my little slave climaxed, I gently untied him and made him get down on his knees again to give me proper thanks.

Herman became a steady client. One of my bread-and-butter guys. He often called me between visits just to talk. Sometimes he called me late at night and asked me to tuck him into bed over the phone.

He was really heartbroken when the judge sent me to prison. When I got home, I found a package from him—a lovely letter and a musical teddy bear. Although I couldn't see him anymore, he frequently called and tried to cheer me up. When people ask me how I felt about my clients, I often think of him. I had a great bunch of guys.

Not all of the madams I worked for were as nice and as ethical as Liz. When I had gone through all of Liz's clients, I had to expand and work for other madams. Donna was, unfortunately, one of the most disreputable. She had a poor reputation with her girls and her clients. She rarely took the time to meet the girls, so she didn't know who she was sending to her clients. And she seldom cared.

One night she called and wanted me to see one of her clients at the posh Westwood Marquis. It was late, and I wasn't eager to go.

"Norma Jean, I've told him all about you, and you're the only one who will do for him. He won't see anyone else!''

I walked through the small but exquisite lobby of the hotel to the front desk, gave the receptionist my name, and asked her to ring Mr. Jones.

Suite 1401 was the first door by the elevator. I knocked quietly. The door flew open, and a very surprised Mr. Jones stood there in his bathrobe, just staring at me.

"You're not a blonde!''

"Well, that's true. Did Donna tell you I was?''

"That bitch! She always does this to me!''

"Could we talk about it inside?''

"Oh, sure. I'm sorry! Here, come in.''

"May I sit down?"

"Of course! Oh, look. I'm sorry. It's not you. It's just that every time I come into town and ask Donna for a blonde, she sends me everything but!" He sighed. "I usually see the girl she sends me anyway, but . . ."

"But you told her not to do it again, and she did anyway. Yes, that sounds like Donna."

"I think you're real pretty and all, and you sure have a body on you, but darn it, it's a real special occasion for me and I wanted to see a blonde. I hope you don't take it personally."

"Of course not, Mr. Jones. We should call Donna and straighten this out, then I'll leave." I picked up the phone and dialed Donna's number.

Her phone machine came on. "We're sorry no one is in right now to answer your call, but please leave a message. . . ."

"Donna, I know you're there. Are you listening? It's Norma Jean! You remember Mr. Jones who I was just perfect for, who didn't want anybody but me? Well, he wanted a blonde! I'm *not* a blonde, Donna."

She picked up the phone. "I know, Norma Jean, but he doesn't really care. Now you're there, he'll see you anyway!"

"No, Donna. I'm not going to stay. I'm not what he asked for, and I don't think it's fair to him or me!"

"Calm down, calm down! Okay, so you aren't his type. I have another call for you to go on. It's right up the street. Here, I'll give you the address. Then let me talk to Mr. Jones."

"It's getting awfully late, Donna. I want to go home."

"Aw, come on. You're already out, and it's so close by. And he's real easy! He just flew back from Europe an hour ago. He'll be too tired to do much!"

"Okay, Donna. But if he wants a blonde, too, well, I just won't work for you anymore!"

I jotted down the address and handed the phone to Mr. Jones. I waited, hoping he would at least give me a few dollars to pay for the parking.

When he finished yelling at Donna, he turned to me and smiled. "Well, I may not get a blonde tonight, but Donna's gonna think twice before she pulls this again!"

"Why don't you find another madam? I'm sure there are some out there who have blondes available this time of night."

"Oh, Donna and I go way back. She used to be a real beauty when she was young, and I wouldn't feel right going to someone else. Donna was the first hooker, er, call girl I ever saw."

"Well, I had better be going. She has another guy she wants me to see. I hope he likes redheads." We both laughed.

"You're nice, Norma Jean. I'm sorry it didn't work out. Here, let me give you a little something for coming all the way over here." He shoved a fifty into my hand.

"Thanks, Mr. Jones. I'm sorry, too. Maybe next time you'll want a redhead." I kissed him on the cheek and left.

The valet took my ticket and smiled. "That was a quick visit!"

As I drove out of the parking garage, I thought I really didn't want to see this other guy. I was tired and grouchy and mad at Donna. But as she said, I was already out, and it was right up the street.

Steve Kirschbaum, my next date, owned a penthouse in this magnificent building. Another client of mine lived in the building and had a beautiful apartment, but it was nothing like Steve's!

I knocked at the double door, and knocked and knocked. I was ready to give up when Steve finally answered. He was tall and absolutely gorgeous, a tanned athletic body dressed in black silk pajamas. Mmm. He was rubbing his eyes.

"Oh, hi. I'm sorry I didn't hear the door. I feel asleep. Come on in." He had a deep voice, too.

He took my coat and led me into a huge living room with windows on three sides. What a spectacular sight! The view inside wasn't bad, either: a rich, single, gorgeous hunk of a guy with a fabulous penthouse. Boy, this would be an evening to remember! I licked my lips. I knew there was a reason I liked this job!

We went right into his bedroom, definitely a man's bedroom, a real bachelor's paradise. It had a neat yet slightly rumpled appearance. The obviously expensive matching sheets and bedspread on his king-sized bed were macho gray-and-black striped. Even the paintings on the wall reflected masculinity. There was nothing feminine or soft about this room, and yet as a woman I was not uncomfortable in it. There was a large TV and a VCR next to the bed and dozens of adult videos on the floor. The TV was on, and an old Gable movie I had been watching at home was still playing.

"Okay, Norma Jean. How much do I owe you? I want you to stay two hours." He slipped off the top of his pajamas. He had a beautiful chest, muscular and hairy! This was getting better every minute!

"Well, uh, I guess five hundred dollars. I don't usually negotiate the money, Donna does. What does she usually charge you?"

"Five hundred is fine. I just want you to stay with me for two hours. I want you to give me some head. Do you give good head?"

"I don't want to brag, but some people think I do."

"Great. Well, let's go!" He took off his pajama bottoms. A large, firm erection greeted me.

He propped himself on several pillows while I undressed. I was wearing my favorite black garter belt, bra, and panties. He whistled.

"Not bad, Norma Jean." He was holding his erect penis for me.

"You're not too bad yourself, Steve!" I jumped in bed beside him. "Mmm, wow," I managed to mumble.

Steve kissed me on the mouth and rammed his tongue down my throat, then he gently nudged my mouth down. I began licking and sucking him.

He moaned. "Oh, that's good, baby. I like that!"

He moaned, and moaned, and I thought I must be doing a super job. Suddenly I noticed his erection was fading rapidly. He hadn't had an orgasm. I looked up to ask him what was wrong. He was snoring! He had fallen asleep!

I gently shook him. No response. I watched TV for a few minutes, hoping he would wake up soon so we could resume our activity. He didn't wake up. I sighed. What was I going to do?

"Okay, Norma Jean," I said to myself. "This guy paid you for two hours, and he's going to get two hours. He wants head, he'll get head."

I turned back to his inert organ and shook my head. *"C'est la vie, girl!"* I picked it up gingerly. It wasn't so big when it was asleep. I pulled on it, stretching it as far as it would go. I let go of it. Boing! I pulled it again. Stretch, boing, stretch, boing! I stretched it again and pretended it was a fiddle. I plucked at it—boing, boing, boing! I amused myself quite well while I waited for him to wake up or until it was time to leave.

I talked aloud to him, knowing he couldn't hear a word I said. "So you want a blow job, do you, huh? Well, I'll give you a blow job like you've never had before!"

I took his penis and began to blow it like it was a flute. I hummed the "Star-Spangled Banner." Every now and then I checked to see if I had awakened him, but he was dead to the world.

"Do you think it's very nice of you to fall asleep on me, you cad? I have a reputation to maintain, an image to uphold. Think of the scandal, the loss of income. I can see the headlines of the *National Enquirer* now:

BEVERLY HILLS CALL GIRL LOSES TOUCH. CLIENT FALLS ASLEEP! I'll be ruined!''

Finally I looked at the clock. It was nearly time to go home! I got out of bed and got dressed very slowly.

"Ah, you dirty rat. You don't know what you missed! We coulda had a wonnerful, wonnerful time, yessir! But no, you have to insult me and fall asleep. We could have had a night of wild, hot sex!'' I sighed. "But now you'll never know!''

I left him the following note:

"Dear Steve—You were incredible tonight! I've never had a lover quite like you! We made beautiful music together! Thanks for the memories!''

I stopped working for Donna right after that, and I never saw Steve again.

"Hi, Norma Jean, this is Sarah.'' Sarah was my best friend in the business. We often did doubles together. She and I both loved our job, and our clients certainly appreciated our close relationship.

"Oh, hi, sweetheart. What's up?'' It was 7:30 on a Saturday night. I had spent several days and nights hard at work on my manuscript, and I certainly needed to get out and work a little. The book that had started out to be a police exposé had grown to include anecdotes about my new profession, and it was taking up quite a bit of my time.

"Honey, I've got an emergency. I have a date tonight with Mark Hillsinger, and my friend Pete Rosen and his wife just called. Are you busy tonight?''

"No. I was just going to do some writing. Is that *the* Pete Rosen, the actor?''

"Yes, it is. I told you about him, didn't I? I met him and his wife through Rosanne [another madam we worked for] several months ago. He's a doll! He's a little different, but he's not dangerous. And he pays real well. I mean real well. He's so rich, money doesn't mean a thing to him. His wife Barbara is a little strange. She may or may not like you. She wants to pretend it's her very first time with a woman, and she gets real spaced out on coke. If she likes you, she'll join the two of you. If not, she'll go to sleep.''

"Isn't his wife an actress, too? I think I've seen her in a commercial lately.''

"Yeah, that's her. I know for a fact she's been into the 'bi' scene for

years, but she'll say she's never done it before. You'll have to call and
tell him I gave you his number.''

I dialed Pete's number and a woman answered. I panicked for a
moment, thinking I should hang up. ''Hi, I'm Norma Jean, a friend of
Sarah's. She is busy tonight and—''

''Oh, hi. Just a minute. I'll let you talk to Pete. Peeete, telephone!''

''Hello, this is Pete.''

''Hi, Pete. My name is Norma Jean. I'm a friend of Sarah's. She's
busy tonight so she asked me to give you a call.'' I coughed. ''I understand you're in the mood to play—''

''Yeah.'' He sounded stoned. ''Me and Barbara want you to come
over and suck her pussy. Oh, and park your car in the alley and knock at
the gate by the pool.''

It took me exactly twenty-five minutes to drive through traffic to their
beautiful two-story house in the flatlands of Beverly Hills. I passed their
house three times before I found the entrance to the alley. It was dark in
the back and very difficult to see the house numbers.

I knocked at the gate marked 864 and stood there for almost fifteen
minutes before Pete let me in. I almost gave up. ''Shush,'' he whispered.
''Here, follow me. The kids are going to their grandparents', but they
haven't left yet, so I'm going to put you in the guest bedroom for a few
minutes.''

He grabbed my arm and pulled me behind him. We tiptoed past the
swimming pool and into the back part of their enormous house. The guest
wing had three huge bedrooms behind the kitchen. He stashed me in the
last one, turning the lights off as we entered.

''Hey, it's dark in here,'' I complained.

''It's just for a few minutes. They'll be leaving soon. Don't worry.
I'll pay you for the time that you're sitting here.'' With that he left.

I took off my coat and sat in a big overstuffed chair by the window.
The bright lights by the pool filtered into the room and cast a large
shadow on the wall. I could hear laughter in the distance.

Ten, fifteen, twenty minutes went by. No Pete or Barbara. I twiddled
my thumbs. Another twenty minutes passed, and the sound of voices in
the front of the house continued to drift back to my room. I was getting
bored and restless. To relieve the monotony of the situation, I began to
make shadow figures on the wall with my hands. ''The life of a high-class
call girl!'' I sighed. ''Oh, the glamour, the glitz, the glory of it all! Ha!
If the world could only see me now!'' My animated fingers came to life

on the wall. Dogs, dragons, butterflies, and other strange creatures ran amuck. What a waste of my talents!

About an hour after I arrived, Pete finally returned, only to tell me his parents hadn't left yet. "Just be patient, Norma Jean. Oooh, I can't wait to watch you eat my wife's pussy. She'll like you. You're beautiful. What are you wearing under that dress?" He kissed me on the lips and pulled up my dress with one hand to feel my garter belt and stockings.

Still another hour passed, and at last I heard farewells and the closing of a door. In a few minutes Pete entered the room and turned on the light. He was clearly under the effects of drugs. "Hi, sweetie. I'm so horny." He grabbed my bottom. "Oooh, are we going to have fun tonight. I like your eyes, baby."

"Pete, before we get started, don't you think we should straighten out business? I have been here for two hours already, and I don't know how long you want me to stay. Sarah didn't tell me."

"Oooh, baby. You and me and Barbara are going to have a great time. I'll pay you whatever you want. How much do you want to stay all night?"

Because the madam always took care of the financial arrangements, I had never had to negotiate the money. And I had never stayed overnight with a client before. I didn't know what to charge him. "Well, that's a long time," I said slowly. "How about two thousand dollars?" I didn't think he would go for this sum. I expected him to argue it down to a thousand.

Instead he agreed to pay it. He pulled out a wad of hundred-dollar bills and peeled off twenty. I took it and gratefully tucked it away in my purse.

Pete walked to the closet and brought out a large shopping bag. He dumped the contents on the bed: a wild assortment of lingerie in every color imaginable. Pete picked up a pair of high-heeled shoes.

"Where's your wife, Pete?" I was anxious to meet the famous Barbara Rosen. I wondered if she was as pretty in person as she was on TV.

"She'll be here in a minute. I'm going to get dressed first." He took off his crisp blue silk shirt and unzipped his pants. He was wearing ladies' black lace panties, a tad too small and pulling tightly across his coke belly. (Men who are habitual cocaine users frequently will party for days, when they usually don't eat. After they come down from their high, they eat enormous quantities of food. Their bodies will remain thin and reedlike, but they get a large belly, which I called a coke belly.)

"Oh, Norma Jean, take off your dress. I want to see your body."

I complied quickly. He began fondling my breasts. Then he resumed donning his costume. He pulled the black panties off and picked a red pair from the tangled pile of dainty undergarments. I held on to his arm as he pulled them up around his fleshy stomach.

Out of the pile he pulled a bright orange teddy and a white lacy bra. The bra was very tight and bunched up badly across his chest. He pulled the orange teddy over his head, and that, too, didn't quite fit over his tummy, so he left it all bunched up on his chest. He found a black garter belt to complete his outfit, and we tugged and pulled at it for several minutes until we got it fastened. He wanted to wear my stockings. I refused. They were brand new and very expensive.

Going back to the pile, he found one green fishnet stocking and one seamed black one. He pulled them on, and I hooked them to his garter belt. Who was I to argue with his sense of fashion?

The final touch to his charming ensemble was a pair of heels. The only ones that fit were a pair of silver open-toed sandals. He put them on and strutted his stuff before me. "Well, what do you think? Am I beautiful or what?"

"Or what" was more like it, but if he wanted me to think he was beautiful, then he certainly was. I admired his outfit. "Oh, Pete, you look really hot. Now when do I get to meet Barbara?"

"Let's get her right now." He took me by the hand and led me through the house. On the way through the kitchen he lost one heel, and the single green fishnet stocking broke loose from the hook, falling down around his ankle.

Up the back stairway we went in the dark to the huge master bedroom. He opened the door slowly. Barbara was already in their enormous four-poster bed with the covers drawn over her head.

"Barbara, look who's here to play with us! She's going to suck your pussy."

Barbara groaned. "I've got a headache. I don't want to play tonight. You two go play downstairs in the guest wing. Leave me alone!"

Pete wasn't about to let his creative wardrobe go unnoticed. "Honnnney, look at me. I got all dressed up to play. Come on. The kids are gone and everything! Here . . . Norma Jean stopped at the store and bought us some cigarettes." He tossed a pack on the bed.

"Pete, go away! I don't feel good. Take that hooker and get out of here." She threw the cigarettes back to Pete.

I looked at Pete. "Maybe we should go downstairs until she feels more like joining our party."

He sniffed. "Okay. But first I'm going to do a little more coke. Do you want some?"

"No, thanks. I don't do any drugs." (I saw Pete and Barbara several times over the next two years, and between the two of them they went through a mountain of that horrible white powder.)

Opening the beautiful satin robe I borrowed from the closet, I posed sexily on the bed, expecting Pete to get romantic with me. Instead he paced the floor for at least an hour, chain-smoking and cursing Barbara. He finally calmed down.

"I'm going to get another hit, and then I want you to put some makeup on me. Okay, Norma Jean?"

He returned in a better mood. "Barbara says she'll come down and join us in a little while. She just wants to take a nap. Let's get ready by talking hot. I want you to tell me what you're going to do to her when she comes down here."

I had pulled out my makeup case and was already applying eye shadow to his puffy, famous eyes. I could just imagine a picture of him like this on the cover of the *National Enquirer*. If Joan Rivers ever got hold of information like this, he'd never live it down. And if the millions of viewers who watched him every week saw him like this, they would think he was gay, which he was not.

Pete got out a mirror to inspect his face. "Oh, I like it. Don't I look beautiful? Aren't I as pretty as Farrah Fawcett?"

"Much prettier, Pete."

"Rub my tits, Norma Jean."

I began to stroke his hairy chest. He moaned and groaned. "Oh, Pete, your breasts are as sensitive as any woman's!"

Pete reached under the bed and pulled out a stack of movie magazines. He thumbed through the well-worn pages.

"Do you and my wife fuck these women?"

"What do you mean, Pete? I just met your wife tonight."

"No, no. Just say that you do. It's my fantasy."

"Okay, then, we fuck them all the time."

"I wish I was there to watch! Do the two of you ever fuck Jackie O.?"

Playing along with his fantasy, I said, "Yes, sure. She's really hot!"

"Does she pay you lots of money?"

For a minute I was puzzled. "Who? Barbara?"

"No, Jackie and all the famous women the two of you fuck!"

I suddenly saw where the fantasy was going. It would be much easier to play now that I knew what he wanted. "She pays me and Barbara so much money, it's unbelievable! Just for sucking her delicious cunt!"

"Barbara works with you, doesn't she? She's the best hooker in the world!"

"Yes, Pete. How did you know? She wasn't supposed to tell you."

He smiled, his crooked, coked-out smile. The telltale white powder was all over his famous mustache. "I just knew you two must work together. She's the best and you're the best, so you have to work together. Where do the two of you work? Do you use this house when I'm on location?"

"No. She has an apartment in the valley, a big, beautiful place where we bring all our famous women to fuck."

"Oooh, tell me what she does with them when you get them home."

"First she fixes them a drink, then she sits down on the couch next to them and rubs their leg."

"What do you do?"

"I unbutton their blouse and play with their breasts, like this." I fondled his nipples.

"Then what?"

"Then Barbara kisses them on the mouth and neck, and by that time the woman is so hot, we take her into the bedroom."

"Oooh, I wish I could watch."

"What would you do, Pete?"

"You could dress me up like a beautiful woman and I could come out of the other room and you would let me suck their pussy and they would think I was a lesbian hooker like the two of you and they would pay me big money to suck their pussies."

"How much would they pay us, Pete?"

"Oh, thousands of dollars! We'd be the best lesbian hookers in the world, and every rich woman would come to us and pay us so much money!"

While Pete talked, I removed his bra and sucked on his nipples.

"What are you going to do to Barbara when she joins us?" Pete wanted to know.

"I'm going to throw her on the bed, pull off her nightgown, and bury my face in her hot little cunt, stick my tongue up there and suck out all her sweet juices!''

''Oooh, that sounds so good. Then what?''

''I'm going to get out my vibrator and make her come until she screams.''

Pete's penis was finally visibly erect through the lace panties. The panties ripped ungraciously. I tried for several hours using manual and verbal stimulation to get him ''off.'' Even though we worked our way through every famous actress in the business, I never succeeded. He supplied an endless list of names of women I had never heard of, but he assured me his wife and I fucked them. Every time I thought we were even close, he would excuse himself to do one more hit of coke.

I was beginning to feel exhausted. He seemed to have endless energy. Barbara never emerged from her bedroom. Pete knew it was hopeless. He had used too much coke.

Pete went upstairs one last time. It was 5:30 in the morning. When he returned I was half asleep under the covers. He shoved a chair in front of the door so it couldn't be opened. ''What's that for, Pete?''

He crawled in beside me. ''My kids will be home in the morning. I don't want them to walk in here. I took a Quaalude to go to sleep. D'ya want one?''

''No, thanks. I won't have any trouble getting to sleep, believe me!''

Within minutes Pete was fast asleep. I looked at him lying there, the famous Pete Rosen, snoring. I shook my head, rolled over toward the window, and fell asleep.

Drifting off in a dream, I was somewhere between a late-night talk show, where I was entertaining the world with amusing anecdotes of my glamorous profession, and the television station where I had become Pete's full-time makeup person. I heard a doorbell ring far away. Then there were loud voices, children's voices. I drifted back pleasantly to my dream. The Reverend Jerry Falwell was now patiently waiting for me to fasten the back of his . . . dress? He had on a long blond wig, and his false eyelashes were covered with silver glitter. I reached over to straighten his padded bra. ''You look beautiful, Mr. Falwell,'' I mumbled in my sleep.

There was a knock at the door and then it was pushed. It would not open, thank goodness! ''Daddy, are you in there?''

Pete snored. I shook him. ''Pete, wake up. Your kids are trying to get in.'' He grumbled and rolled over.

I slapped his face. "Pete, you have to wake up!" He finally opened his eyes. "Your kids are trying to get in here. What'll I do?"

The kids ran down the hallway. A minute later, heavy pounding on the door. Barbara managed to push the chair out of the way. She was waving a butcher knife wildly in the air.

"Get that hooker out of here! How dare you keep that woman here all night! Get her out of here, *now,* Pete, or I'll call the police! I mean it! Get her out of here!" She lunged toward me with the knife.

I grabbed my clothes and briefcase and threw my raincoat around my naked body. I wasn't going to wait to see if that night's TV headlines would feature a "famous actor's dick cut off and stuffed in the mouth of a lady of the night as his horrified children restrain their famous actress mother."

Barbara had already made it to the telephone as I raced through the cold morning grass of the backyard in my bare feet. I reached my car and tried to get it started. My heart was pounding. I had to get out of there quickly. I could almost hear sirens in the distance.

As I drove up Sunset Boulevard, I looked at the clock. It was 7:30. Two hours of sleep. Were my eyes red!

When I arrived home, I immediately fell into bed without even undressing. Victor was awake but didn't ask me to explain my disheveled appearance.

A good night's sleep (or in this case a good day's sleep) can put things in perspective. When I awakened, the preceding night's adventure and that morning's near disaster were almost funny as I recounted the events for Victor.

Later that afternoon Pete called to apologize and to invite me back that night. I laughed. "Yeah, right! Are you crazy? Your wife was going to kill me this morning!"

"Oh, that. She's sorry. She'd really like you to come over!"

"Yeah, I'm sure!"

"Here, she'll tell you herself." He put her on the phone. She apologized and assured me she meant me no harm. And yes, she did want me to join them that evening. She promised not to chase me with a butcher knife.

She seemed sincere enough, but to make sure it was okay, I called the madam who had originally given them to Sarah. After all, I owed her a cut of the money, since it was her client. Rosanne assured me it would be perfectly safe to see them again but urged me to charge them more money to make up for my inconvenience.

Hesitantly I called them back and promised to join them that evening. I explained what Rosanne had said about the money, and Pete said it wasn't a problem.

When I got to their house, Barbara met me at the door. She was cordial and invited me in. We had a wonderful time. Barbara joined us, and for the one and only time in our two-year relationship, the three of us made love together. I didn't stay over that night, but I was well remunerated for the time we spent together.

Pete, Barbara, and I maintained a very strange but financially agreeable relationship. When Pete invited me over and Barbara didn't want to play, she gave me $500 and asked me to leave. When she wasn't home, I saw Pete alone. With the exception of the second night when we all made love together, never again did Pete and I have sex. He didn't want sex, just sex talk! Most of the time I never even took off my clothes. When Barbara was home and wanted to play, Pete would only watch, or the three of us would sit and talk about the fantasy. I never saw Barbara alone.

Pete always took good care of me because he figured if I was the best whore in town, I was naturally the most expensive. He wanted only the most expensive (that is the best) whores. If I charged him less, he wouldn't have called me again.

One time Barbara was out of town filming a commercial. Pete called, and I ended up spending the night. I made $10,000.

He told me he wanted me to stay for only a little while. He was lonely without Barbara, and the kids were at their grandparents'. I arrived with his two packs of cigarettes. (He and Barbara smoked only when they were doing coke and playing. There was no way I would or could supply the coke, but I always stopped to buy him cigarettes.) He paid me $500 to stay for one hour.

As usual we started discussing his fantasy. The hour went by quickly. Pete did not want me to leave. He offered me $1,000 to stay for two more hours. I agreed.

Whenever it was time to leave, Pete renegotiated the deal. At six o'clock in the morning I could stay no longer. My eyes would not stay open, and my voice was gone. Although I could have made another $10,000 if I stayed all day, I figured $10,000 for one night without even taking off my clothes was enough of a record.

Even though I had to pay forty percent of the night's wages to the madam and a percentage went for taxes, I still made enough money to live on for quite a while, leaving me plenty of free time to work on my book.

*   *   *

Certainly not all of my clients were as generous as Pete. Nor as nice. A few were downright offensive. A man was once so rude when I got to his hotel room that I gave him his money back and left. I told him I didn't want to waste my time or his money. His attitude toward women was just awful, and he treated me as though we were engaging in something dirty and shameful.

I really grew to love the ones I saw on a regular basis—not in a romantic way, although that certainly could have happened with several if I weren't already in love.

Lars was a handsome man, rich, smart, and sweet, a real catch for any woman. His was a tragic story but one that illustrates the service and support that prostitutes can provide for men in his situation.

The head of a multinational company, with the wealth and power that accompanied his position, he was happily married and in love with his beautiful wife. They had an idyllic life, traveling the world, spending lots of time with each other. Then the doctors discovered she had cancer, and shortly after, she died.

Unable to cope with a permanent relationship and weary of the many women who threw themselves at him, Lars still needed the warmth and companionship of a woman while he healed. On the advice of his doctor and good friend, the solution was to see call girls. We bridged the gap until he was ready to find a steady relationship.

Whenever he was on the West Coast, he stayed at the Bel Air Hotel. He called me each time he came to L.A., and we became good friends. He knew about Victor, which made him feel secure in his relationship with me. He was always charming and witty, and gave me some great business advice. Then I didn't hear from him for a while. I was worried and sad. I really liked him and missed seeing him. Not for the money because he never knew my fee was higher than what he was paying. He paid what he had been charged by the madam in the past, and I didn't have the heart to tell him it was more. He could have afforded it, certainly, but I thought he had more important problems.

I heard from Lars a year later. He was dating a woman he had decided to marry. He was ready to start living his life again.

Bobby Frank was a terminal colon cancer patient in a well-known hospital on the west side of town. He had a colostomy bag and was emaciated. Rather than let his misery and pain get the best of him, he decided to live life to the fullest.

He had plenty of money, so he treated himself to a pretty girl every week until he died. His wife didn't want to entertain him on his deathbed, so she discreetly called the madam I worked for and arranged for him to be entertained at least once a week.

It was painful for all of us who saw him because we knew he was going to die, but we were professionals and tried hard not to become too attached to him. I saw him quite often, and although he couldn't have intercourse or an orgasm, he liked to be given oral or manual stimulation. Mostly, though, he just liked talking with a pretty girl who would sit in his luxurious private room in her garter belt, panties, and high-heeled shoes. Whenever he had company the nurses put a DO NOT DISTURB sign on the door and let him enjoy himself. They used to wink at me when I came to see him, and some of his male neighbors smiled knowingly when I walked by their rooms.

It was painful for me when he died because I had grown quite fond of him. I admired the way he handled his approaching death. He lived his life with gusto, something many healthy people don't do. I will always be glad I could brighten his last days.

Jim and Paul, whom I affectionately referred to as the boys, were divorced men who had decided never to marry again. They were best friends and business partners in a very successful ad agency. With pooled resources they bought a magnificent house on Sunset Plaza Drive overlooking Hollywood.

Once or twice a week they played and invited their favorite call girls. I was on their list of favorites and saw them as often as time permitted. When I arrived they were always wearing their playtime outfits—a black turtleneck sweater and black slacks. While I entertained one in his bedroom, the other sat in the living room watching TV until it was his turn. They were both quick and easy; I was out of there in less than half an hour. Whenever they traveled, they always sent postcards, and frequently they called from Europe just to say they missed me.

Although I never saw them again after prison, I kept in touch with them through the years. In 1991, Jim called to tell me Paul had passed away and that he was moving to Europe for good. I cried. They both meant a great deal to me.

*   *   *

While I was still working for Donna, I had the pleasure of seeing a man who later became a close personal friend. The first night I met him, however, I was certain Donna was setting me up. Larry Asher looked like a cop.

Donna had called Sarah and me to ask if we wanted to double-date two "swell" guys who owned a yacht in the marina. I always liked working with Sarah; in fact, if I'd had my druthers, I would have worked exclusively with her. Donna gave us directions to the yacht. We were to meet them at 10 P.M. in the parking lot. We found the place without any trouble, but no one was there. We sat talking in Sarah's car for twenty minutes, trying to decide whether we should split.

Just as we were about to leave there was a knock at the window. Two guys dressed in typical vice cop undercover attire stood outside the car, grinning like Cheshire cats. "Oh, shit!" I thought. "We've been set up!"

Sarah rolled down her window. We made small talk long enough to make sure they were okay and figured it couldn't hurt to have dinner with them.

My date was Larry Asher, a good-looking, slightly chubby guy who claimed to own a meat-packing plant that supplied hamburger patties to all the major fast-food restaurants. He seemed to know enough about the meat-packing industry to be legitimate, but I wasn't sure. He said he was single, and if what he said about the meat-packing plant was true, he was also very wealthy.

Sarah's date was a cute little guy who was getting married in a few weeks. This was his last wild fling before he settled down.

After dinner we went on board their yacht. If these guys were cops, the city had certainly gone to a great deal of trouble and expense to rent this well-appointed luxury vessel. Larry and I went below and had a good long talk. I explained that I thought he might be a cop and proceeded to tell him just what I thought of him if he was. He laughed! In the future, whenever he introduced me to his friends, he always told them about the lecture I gave him that night.

He finally convinced me that he was not a cop, and we had sex. When Sarah and I left that evening, Larry tried to get my phone number. I explained that since he was Donna's client, he would have to call Donna if he wanted to see me again.

Larry lost Donna's phone number but fate intervened. I was attending a New Year's Eve party with another client at the exclusive El Caballero Country Club in Encino. My date for the evening was Mark, a nice Jewish boy from the East Coast. It was strictly an escort assignment from Liz. I was seated at a table with Mark and his friends, who didn't have the slightest idea I was a working girl. Mark had asked if I would pretend to be an old friend of his younger sister and go along with the story that he had looked me up and asked me out. It was awkward, pretending to be a friend of someone I didn't know, but it kept me on my toes! I made up amusing anecdotes of wild escapades his sister and I had pulled when we were in high school.

Dinner was unrelenting boredom. His friends were nice, but the conversation mostly revolved around people and events they all knew. I decided to make a trip to the ladies' room. Just as I rounded the corner, a man nearly knocked me over. When I recovered my balance, I looked up and realized it was Larry! He explained he had lost Donna's phone number and had been desperate to get in touch with me. Since I had run into him on my own, without Donna's help, I decided it would be okay to give him my number, so I did.

At first Larry and I dated in a client–call girl relationship, but after a while we became friends. I grew to love and respect him for his gentleness and consideration. He was one of the few clients I've ever had who did not drink or use drugs.

We could have developed a much deeper relationship. Larry hinted several times at getting married, and I must say it was tempting. I probably could have fallen in love with him, and since he was rich, I probably could have lived happily ever after. But Victor had my heart, and with Victor I would stay.

Larry proved to be a very good and loyal friend. He lent me money to help pay the bills when I went to prison the first time, and he supplied a ton of hamburger patties to my defense fund-raiser. He now has a lovely wife and two little girls.

Almost all the men who became regular clients gave their real names and occupations. Of course it would be difficult for a famous movie star, singer, musician, or comedian to hide his identity. And most of the hookers I met were exceptionally bright and talented. Many were on their way up the corporate ladder or breaking into show business. There are women in the business whose I.Q.s match their shoe size, but luckily I never worked with them.

Robert Bloomfeld was a well-known State Supreme Court justice from the East Coast. Whenever he was in L.A., which was quite often, he called Liz to have a young lady sent to his suite at the Beverly Hills Hotel. He requested that the young lady wear a very short skirt or, if it was raining, nothing but a raincoat. Once I started seeing him, I became his favorite, and I went so far as to get a short skirt wardrobe just for him.

He would parade me through the lobby of the hotel, making me bend over in front of the bellmen as though I had dropped something. Why? To arouse them! Robert would be right behind me, excitedly watching their reactions. We would leave the hotel and go shopping for the same reason. When wearing a raincoat, I was to "accidentally" let the coat fall open, exposing my nakedness to unwary male salesclerks. Afterward, in the darkness of his hotel room, I would manually stimulate him while reminding him of the various men I had turned on that day.

Robert was also a transvestite, and he enjoyed wearing lacy, frilly ladies' things under his judicial robes. We shopped for the things he wore on the bench at places like Trashy's and Victoria's Secret. We always pretended the oversized garments were for his mother, to prevent saleswomen from asking embarrassing questions. I wondered what the East Coast district attorneys, defense attorneys, and convicted criminals would think if they knew what went on under the good judge's robe!

Late one night I received a call from Barry, one of my favorite clients, who lived in a high-rise condo on Wilshire Boulevard. Barry had a business associate coming to visit and asked if I would entertain him. He asked me to wear nothing but a raincoat and a pair of very high heeled shoes.

When I arrived, I noticed a big black limousine pulling away. Knowing many famous and important people lived in the building, I wondered if I would get to the elevator in time to see who had been in the limo. The doorman called Barry's apartment, then unlocked the elevator door. When the elevator door opened, there stood the passenger of the limo. He had returned to the lobby because he had forgotten something. It was Cary Grant!

He asked the doorman to hold the elevator for him while he wrote a note to the limo driver. Then he stepped inside the elevator and grinned at me. ''Expecting rain, are you? I didn't see any clouds tonight.''

I smiled. ''Me, either!''

''You, uh, wearing anything under that coat?'' he continued.

''No.''

''I thought not. Mmm. Lucky man.'' The elevator stopped on the eleventh floor. As Mr. Grant was leaving, he turned and blew me a kiss.

That's what I liked about this profession. I got to meet so many interesting people. Whether I met them in elevators or as clients, rubbing elbows (or other body parts) with the rich and famous was a lot more fun than fighting with Barbara Folsom. I liked what I had to do to earn my daily bread.

9. HUNG OUT TO DRY

They'll never give up till you're dead.
Even then they won't stop, I'm afraid.
If it's your ass that they're after,
You will hang from the rafter—
Either that or it's off with your head!

AUGUST 11, 1982, was one of the most godawful nights of my life. The handcuffs that bound my wrists tightly were a grim reminder that I was no longer a friend of these burly vice officers. All of those naughty jokes we used to exchange didn't seem funny anymore. I was on the other side of the law, and to them it was not amusing.

If I had been a little more prepared for my trip downtown, I might have found the whole situation entertaining. It was ironic, after all, that I should be caught in this massive sting operation of high-class call girls and be taken down and booked in a place that had once been so much a part of my life. Fortunately for me, on the night of my first arrest the cops were no more competent than when I had worked with them. Their complete foul-up of the whole operation was cause for dismissal of the charges against me—at least for now.

As I sat on the hard wooden chair in the vice squad office waiting for the interrogation to start, I remembered one night two years before when their ineptitude and stupidity, coupled with my somewhat overzealous work attitude, prevented them from arresting a call girl whom they had been investigating for three years. (Why it took them three years to determine she was a prostitute and gather enough evidence to arrest her, I'll never know.)

My assignment was to impound the illegally parked cars on the streets behind the Sunset Strip. The clientele from Roxy's and Gazarri's and the Rainbow (nightclubs for the young and rowdy) was a chronic nuisance to the neighborhood, and in self-defense the residents had the city ban all-night parking. Everyone in the station knew I was there every night until two in the morning religiously enforcing the signs.

On this particular occasion, a very windy Friday night in late October, I took exceptional delight in towing away a decrepit old pickup truck parked directly under a well-lit NO PARKING—TOW AWAY sign. It was unlocked, and the windows were rolled down. The front seat was covered with a mass of papers. There appeared to be nothing of value in the vehicle, so when it was hooked up, I left it unlocked.

I completed the impound report and sent the truck on its way. As it screeched and grinded down the hill toward Sunset, two men and a woman exited the Rainbow club. They were engaged in animated conversation as they headed up the hill toward me. Suddenly one of the men noticed the pickup truck hooked to the tow truck as it rounded the corner at the light. He began running and waving his arms in that direction. "We are on police business!" he screamed, flashing his badge. He stopped short and turned back to his partner, just as the young lady who had been walking with them faded into the gathering crowd. "Oh, shit!"

The tow truck driver was unable to look back at his angry pursuers; traffic is rough on Friday nights. After he had turned the corner onto Sunset, he hit a crater-sized pothole in the road. The passenger door of the dilapidated pickup truck swung open, barely missing a parked car and an anxious pedestrian before slamming itself shut. Caught by the heavy breezes, papers flew out of the truck and sailed everywhere. The driver was completely unaware of the disaster that would soon follow. Under strict orders from me concerning the fate of any vehicle already hooked up, he continued to the impound garage. A trail of emancipated papers followed.

Cursing loudly, the two officers were in hot pursuit of the airborne pages. Within minutes word had passed among the denizens of the strip, the punkers and the addicts, the pimps and the whores, that the Man had gotten themselves towed away and their quarry had escaped. A huge cheer rose from the crowd. The punkers jumped on top of parked cars and hooted and jeered at the two cops, who were frantically darting in and out of traffic, desperately trying to retrieve the mounds of evidence from under the tires of cars.

Meanwhile I was a distance up the street. I heard the commotion and went to investigate. Traffic was backed up and horns were honking loudly. The mood of the crowd was rather jubilant, though, and they were applauding. Some idiots were running dangerously through the traffic chasing papers. Probably some crazies, I thought. On Friday night Hollywood is full of them!

Since I saw no accidents or other major disasters and the Strip belongs to the county, not the city, I radioed for the sheriff's department to clean up the traffic. I took the shortcut down Doheny and headed back to the station to finish my report and have dinner. By the time I finished the paperwork and had a bite to eat, I was anxious to get back into the field.

When I got into my patrol car, the R.T.O.—radio telephone operator—sent an urgent message to report to the watch commander's office. I "rogered" the call.

"What's up, Sarge?" I said, sauntering into Sergeant Mahony's glass cage. Unlike the old Hollywood station where the small private offices had been the scene of a few interesting sexual escapades, the new building sported all-glass partitions, eliminating any opportunity for hanky-panky.

Two dour-looking vice cops were sitting against the wall. Their faces looked familiar, although I didn't know them. I flashed my famous flirtatious smile, but they seemed downright hostile toward me.

"Norma Jean, what's the idea of towing away vice's truck up on the Strip?" My old lover looked rather put out. He frequently had to soothe ruffled feathers whenever I was out in the field hard at work.

I suddenly remembered seeing those guys. They were the idiots out in the street. I swallowed hard. "What truck was that?" I asked innocently. Sometimes my big-eyed dumb-little-girl act worked. This wasn't one of those times.

Sergeant Mahony shuffled his papers and continued. "These guys tell me they had their files spread out on the front seat so you would know they were vice and leave their truck alone."

"But Sarge," I said, pouting, "I'm not supposed to look through the property in people's cars. How was I to know?"

"Well, Norma Jean, all those papers are now all over the street, thanks to you!" one of the vice cops growled.

The other cop parroted his partner: "Yeah, thanks to you. Our three-year-investigation of a two-hundred-dollar-a-night hooker is shot to hell. Now she knows we're on to her."

"Hey, you guys parked under a tow-away sign, and I had no way of knowing it was your truck. Besides, I couldn't very well leave your truck on an empty street, now, could I? Your hooker would have known something was wrong."

Sergeant Mahony sided with me. "She's right, fellas. She was justified in towing you away. She's supposed to tow everything."

The vice cops left in a huff. Sergeant Mahony chided me for failing to lock the door. He dismissed me with a perfunctory admonishment to take more care in securing impounded vehicles.

I passed the two disgruntled vice cops in the hall; they were still sputtering their complaints to the record clerk. I smiled to myself. I was actually glad I had been able to help a working girl get away from those two bozos.

On the night of my arrest I was glad for a change that these cops were an incompetent lot. If they had been efficient at their job, I would have had to spend time in court and used some of my hard-earned money to defend my activities that evening. Eventually I had to anyway, but that came later.

The Internal Affairs investigation report given to me as a ''souvenir'' of the evening described how the sting operation had allegedly been set up. I later learned the politics behind it that weren't in the report. The operation had nothing to do with ridding the city of prostitution.

According to the report, two years earlier administrative vice had begun to investigate the two top madams in Los Angeles, Anna Fischer and Jill O'Conner. They had operated successfully in the city for many years and, according to Anna, with the full knowledge and cooperation of the police department. They had established great reputations for having some of the world's most beautiful women in their stables; their young ladies have graced the centerfolds of many men's magazines, and rumor had it that if the price was right, they could procure practically any actress or model for their exclusive clients. In recent years the Arabs composed a large percentage of their clientele.

According to Anna, the police went after her because she failed to continue providing valuable information, such as which politicians used the services of her girls and which actors used drugs, as she had agreed to do in exchange for their blindness toward her operation. By arresting her, the police provided her with incentive to ''get back into the fold,'' as she put it.

The report said a vice cop using the name Roger Ryder and posing as a rich playboy jetsetting around the globe gradually gained the trust of the two madams by sending them postcards and detailed accounts of his travels. Then, one week in early August, he gave them both a call. He announced his planned visit to the City of Angels and requested dozens of gorgeous women to attend the large party he was throwing for many of his equally rich friends. He made them an offer they couldn't refuse. Greed overcame common sense. They jumped at the opportunity of taking care of this wild, extravagant playboy and his rich friends.

The party was in a rented house in Malibu, and most of the girls were to go there. However, as Roger explained to Anna and Jill, there would also be some special friends who did not like parties, and they would be accommodated privately elsewhere.

One gentleman in particular, Mike, was very shy, Roger said, and had a special fantasy. He had never been with two girls before and especially wanted two girls who would "do it to each other." Did Jill know any really beautiful "bi" girls who could entertain Mike?

That's where I came in. I was in the process of expanding my work base, hoping to be introduced to the more important madams in town. Every ambitious call girl hopes to meet someone who can introduce her to the madam with the most exclusive, highest-paying clients. A good madam will not employ a young lady who has not been introduced by a trusted mutual friend.

Unlike street trade, a client at this level of entertainment must wait until the madam calls the girl before he is given her phone number. Men are also usually screened by the madam before they are referred to anyone. I expected this to be the case when I was introduced by phone to Jill. Normally the madam will not give the first assignment until she meets the girl in person. Jill didn't have time to meet me before the party, but on the recommendation of our mutual friend, she decided to use me.

A young woman named Julia was to be my partner. We had worked together several times with a mutual client of ours, and although she was not at all sexually attractive to me, she was easy to work with.

When Roger called to confirm the date for his friend Mike, he suggested we all meet at my place.

"How come we can't meet Mike at his hotel?" I asked Roger, hoping not to have to clean my apartment that afternoon. "If his hotel is downtown, it wouldn't be any trouble for me to get there."

Roger stammered, "Uh, well, uh, Mike's too shy to have you gorgeous ladies coming in and out of the room. He's afraid he'll get teased by the other guys."

"Well, I don't care to have men come to my apartment, either. But I suppose we can have a drink there and then find another place close by."

I gave Roger the directions to my apartment.

"Mike should be there by eight-thirty then, Norma Jean. That's a pretty name. Is it your real name?"

I never felt I had anything to hide, so I always used my real name. "Yes, it is. Why do you ask?"

Roger ignored my question, asking instead, "What's this evening going to cost me?"

Why did little red lights start flashing in my head? I quickly responded, "Whatever Jill told you, I'm sure it will cover everything." I wasn't about to talk money over the phone. I had never done it before, and I wasn't going to start now. Either the client knew what he was supposed to pay, or he wasn't well trained.

It was fortunate I refused to mention money to him.

Julia arrived at eight o'clock. I greeted her at the door, and she kissed me on the cheek. "Hi, Norma Jean," she said breathlessly. "I just saw a real weird client, and he ruined my stockings. Do you have a pair I can borrow?"

I found an extra pair in my lingerie drawer and handed them to Julia.

"Have you ever seen a client with a foot fetish, Norma Jean?" She shook her head as she removed her soiled stockings. "I mean, he didn't want to kiss me or anything, he just slobbered over my feet and then asked me to call him names. He got all hot and ejaculated all over my shoes and stockings!"

"I've had a few like that. At least you don't have to worry about catching any diseases."

At 8:15 there was a knock at the door. I hoped it wasn't Mike. Didn't he know it was impolite for a client to arrive early?

I opened the door. A very tall, badly dressed, average-looking young man stood there.

"Hi. I'm Mike," he said timidly. "Am I too early?" He stuck out a huge, rough paw for me to shake. I should have recognized from his ill-fitting cheap suit that he was a cop, but I only thought he was a bad dresser. (I later realized his inappropriately heavy jacket in mid-August was concealing his gun.)

"No, that's okay. I'm Norma Jean. Julia is in the other room getting dressed. Come on in. Can I take your jacket?"

He flushed and said no, he was fine.

I seated him on the couch and asked him if he wanted a drink.

"Yeah, sure. That sounds great. A vodka tonic. And would you make it strong? I'm kind of nervous and all."

Smiling faintly, I excused myself while I went to the bar for a bottle of Stoli I kept for my drinking friends. I put an extra jigger of vodka into the glass.

For a man who supposedly owned his own business, he seemed terribly boring and not very bright. I hoped Julia would hurry up and join us. Perhaps she could stir up a lively conversation.

"So, Mike, what business are you in?"

"Well, I own a salvage company in Victorville."

"Oh, that's nice. What are you doing in L.A.—I mean, besides fulfilling your fantasy?"

"Well, my buddies and I are going to spend a few days fooling around, and then we have some business to discuss."

What was taking Julia so long? Mike had already finished the stiff drink I had fixed him and was sitting uncomfortably on the edge of the couch, looking at his watch.

"Can I fix you another drink, Mike?"

"Uh, that would be fine." He was sweating heavily and tugging at his tie. "Can you make it a little stronger?"

"Sure thing, Mike. Are you certain I can't take your jacket? It's awfully warm in here. Sorry, I don't have air-conditioning."

"Uh, um, no thanks. Really, I'm fine. So tell me about yourself. What do you like to do?"

Making small talk with this guy was not going to be easy. I did my best. Then I did a really dumb thing. I told him I was writing a book. Of course he asked me what it was about, and of course I told him. "Well I was with the L.A.P.D. for ten years, and I'm writing about my experiences."

"Really?" His eyes grew wide, and he suddenly came alive with interest. "Tell me more! That's something I'd like to hear about."

I should have paid attention to the warning signals, but I didn't.

"What would you like to know?"

Before he could answer, Julia made her grand entrance. "There you are!" I was relieved to have some help with Mike. "Can I fix you a drink? We're going to have to hurry, though, so we can leave for the hotel."

"Sure. I'll just have some juice if you have any." Julia sat down beside Mike.

"Yeah, and I'll have another one of these, Norma Jean." Mike handed me his glass.

I stayed in the kitchen as long as I could, giving Julia a chance to charm this toad into a prince. When I returned, they were engaged in animated conversation. I put down their drinks and turned up the fan in the window. In my marvelously charming older apartment, which had low rent and no air-conditioning, it got warm and stuffy in the middle of the summer.

The couch was too small for the three of us to be comfortable, so I sat on the coffee table. I glanced at my watch. We were scheduled to be with him an hour, so we had to transact business soon and get out of there.

I nodded to Julia. We had agreed earlier she would be the one to ask for the fee. There really is an art to collecting money. It has to be done with finesse so the client doesn't feel we are all business. We have to leave him with his fantasy.

Julia started to ask Mike for the money, but he beat her to the draw.

"So how much is an evening with you two beautiful ladies going to cost me?"

"I thought your friend had that all arranged with Jill." Julia looked at him quizzically.

Mike pulled out a wad of folded $100 bills. "My friend Roger is treating me to you girls, but he didn't say who should get the money."

"Well, why don't you give each of us half?" Julia asked politely. This guy was sure dumb!

"How much of this do you have to give to Jill?" Mike questioned solicitously as he waved the money around. In spite of the fan, he was perspiring heavily. He wiped his brow, a gesture he had made several times.

Before he could give us the money there was a knock at the door.

Quite surprised because I was expecting no one, I went to answer it. Through the little peephole I saw a short mustached fellow with a plaid shirt. There was something familiar about the way he was dressed. I swallowed hard.

"Yes, what is it?" I demanded. A knot began to form in my stomach.

"Hi," he said. "We're looking for Larry." Sure enough, there were two of them. The other fellow was dressed the same way except that he was wearing a baseball cap.

Only slightly relieved, I said, "You must have the wrong apartment, fellows. There's no Larry here."

"Are you sure?" the short guy piped up. "I think he lives here."

"No, there is no one here by that name. Why don't you try next door?" I tried to remain civil. The evening wasn't going well.

"Look, lady, we're the cops. If you don't open the door right now, we'll have to kick it in." The little one tried to sound menacing.

My knees felt weak. This was a setup! We hadn't said or done anything yet, so perhaps I could still salvage the evening. I played innocent.

"What seems to be the problem, officers?" I opened the door and escorted them into the living room where Mike and Julia sat, transfixed.

It had been prearranged that Mike would stand up and identify himself when the cops came into the room. Since no violation had occurred, he figured he might save the evening by playing it cool. Imagine all of us standing around, trying to be cool!

The two cops quickly invented a story about being from a "noise abatement" program; they said they had received several complaints about my apartment. Nice try. I am about as noisy as a librarian. Usually no one came over but my boyfriend, and the stereo played nothing but classical music. "No way, fellas. You've made a mistake."

The leader got huffy and demanded to see some identification. He also wanted to know who my friends were.

Mike spoke up. "Look, officer, we're just sitting here talking and not bothering anybody. Why don't you just leave us alone. You can see we're not making a lot of noise. Go bother somebody else."

The little one sneered at Mike. "I'm sorry, sir. It's just that we've had several complaints from her neighbors, and we had to check it out. It's probably someone else making all the noise. We're sorry to bother you."

"Yeah, we're sorry to bother you," the other pimply-faced cop chimed in. "Let this be a warning to you, lady. Keep the noise down. Next time we'll have to give you a ticket!"

With a sigh of relief I ushered him out. So far, so good. I returned to the living room and asked Julia to join me in the kitchen. I knew we hadn't done anything yet, and if we got rid of the damn cop now, we'd be okay. I told Julia my plan.

I gave the bad news to Mike. "Look, Mike, it really isn't a very good night for either of us, so Julia and I want to cancel the evening. I'll call Jill and see if she can recommend someone else for your fantasy." I tried to make him believe I wasn't on to him.

He looked crestfallen. "Oh, no! Please don't call it off. I've been looking forward to this for such a long time, and I don't want anybody else. You two are perfect for my fantasy."

I shook my head. "Sorry, Mike. It just won't work. I have a headache now. Those damn cops really upset me."

Mike wondered if he could stay until we were sure the cops had gone. As long as he didn't realize I knew he was a cop, it was okay to play along with him. If he thought I suspected, who knows what he might have done.

Julia decided it was time for her to leave. Mike offered to walk her to her car. I walked them both to the door.

Back in the living room I took off my shoes and was about to throw myself on the couch in relief when I noticed that Julia had left her address book on the coffee table. I picked it up and ran down the stairs after her.

She was standing outside her car talking to Mike. I handed her the book. At that moment the two "noise" cops came running through the courtyard to where we were standing.

"Okay, girls. This time it's for real!"

"What's for real?" I asked. "What on earth do you want?"

"You are both under arrest for prostitution!" he snapped at me.

I shook my head and laughed. "You've got to be kidding! We haven't said or done anything!"

Mike turned to us. "Sorry, girls, but you're involved with some terrible people, and we need all the information we can get."

I looked at him, incredulous. If we hadn't done anything, I didn't see how they could make us go with them. I was mistaken. I discovered they can do anything they want.

I asked if I could go back to my apartment to get some shoes, so we all marched upstairs.

The little one went to the kitchen to poke around, and the pimply-faced one followed me to the bedroom. Mike stayed with Julia. Pimply Face saw my note board and began to read my daily schedule. I told him to leave it alone since he didn't have a search warrant.

He remarked that as long as it was in plain sight, he had a right to look at it.

I quickly grabbed my shoes and a sweater and returned to the others. I pulled Pimply Face behind me. Shorty was still in the kitchen, going through my Rolodex. I had to get these guys out of there before they found my records.

Julia was standing uncomfortably against the wall. She asked Mike if he would let her use the bathroom before we went. I thought it was a good idea, too. I remembered the days in Hollywood when the asshole vice cops would drag in girls off the streets and force them to sit in the hallway of the station while they waited to be booked. Not once were they allowed to use a bathroom, and several times I noticed a stream of yellow liquid flowing down the hall.

Before they would let either of us use the bathroom, Shorty had to check it for drugs. He went through the cabinets and found my pain pills.

"What's these for, lady?" He pulled them out and spilled them all over the counter.

"I have a bad back, if you must know," I retorted. At this point only Mike knew who I was. He hadn't had time to tell his buddies. To them I was just another whore.

"Where did you get a bad back at your age, ha, ha, ha?" Pimply Face butted in. The other two laughed at his little joke.

"If you must know, officer, I got it working for you guys."

"Oh, come on, lady. Quit kidding."

"I was injured on duty in April in my black and white. I was working Hollywood division."

Shorty's mouth fell open. He realized I wasn't kidding. "Oh, shit! What the f— did we get ourselves?"

Mike spoke up. "Yeah, and she's writing a book about it, too."

"Oh, really! Say, are you *the* Norma Jean who worked Hollywood? The 'bionic arm'?"

I smiled dolefully. "The same."

"Well, what the f— you doing working as a whore?" Mike asked bluntly.

"Hey, wait a minute, Mike. I was working as an escort. Nothing happened. Besides, the city stopped paying me disability back in June. What do you expect me to do, starve?"

Pimply Face was enjoying all this. I remembered seeing his ugly face somewhere before—probably one of the many cops I had turned down for a date. Mike and Shorty had a quick conference. Julia and I took turns in the bathroom. When I came out, Shorty told me I should take some money with me for bail.

"What for? I thought you said you were only taking us down for questioning. Why on earth should we need to be bailed out?" I was getting downright hostile with my former compadres.

Shorty looked at Mike and then at me. "Well, yes, but you should take some in case you have any outstanding warrants."

Julia looked at me uneasily. "Oh, Norma Jean, I have a moving violation ticket I haven't paid," she groaned.

Our "friends" overheard her remark and sighed with relief. That would make it easier for them to take us in, in case we decided to give them any more trouble.

I went into the other bedroom where I kept my money locked in a filing cabinet. Mike asked me what else I kept in there. It was none of his business, I told him. He muttered he'd see about that. I ignored him.

The two cops had parked their car behind the apartment building across the street. Mike was driving. When he almost ran a red light and barely missed getting sideswiped by a truck, I suddenly regretted how strong I had made his drinks. "Hey, be careful. I'm already off work on a disability injury. I don't think the city will pay me if I get hurt while I'm in custody!"

Shorty, who was in the backseat with Julia and me, laughed heartily. "Ah, Mike is driving just fine! Besides, we could all use some vacation time! I'll tell the city to pay you if we have an accident. That way you can claim to be the only whores to get paid on this raid!"

Mike got into the Hollywood Freeway and drove toward downtown. He was swerving left and right, changing lanes, and speeding past the slower traffic. I held on to the bar on the door.

"Please, Mike, could you be more careful?" I tried not to sound like a nag, but my back was starting to hurt. I was sure we would never make it to the station.

The garage attendant tried to peer into the back as we passed him. "You're the first ones in," he told Mike. "Did you get a couple of beauties or what?" He finally spotted me. He looked puzzled for a moment, then smiled. "Norma Jean, I didn't know you were working vice!"

I smiled back but said nothing. What was there to say?

We walked down the corridor to the vice room. The record clerks we passed were gawking at all the high-class call girls being brought in. I tried not to notice their surprised stares of recognition. This evening was definitely a disaster. I took a deep breath and walked into the office.

Since we were not technically under arrest, Julia and I were not allowed to make any phone calls to let anyone know where we were. We were told we would be out of there in no time so it wasn't necessary to give us the same rights as the other girls.

Julia and I sat there silently, waiting for Mike to complete his report and begin questioning us. The other girls were brought in, yelling and cursing, in groups of three and four. I began to piece together what had happened. The other girls had been at the party in Malibu, were all intoxicated, and were very upset. The cops who were bringing them in appeared to be just as drunk. It must have been one hell of a party.

According to several of the girls, the cops had sex with them before they were arrested. One of the girls was so upset, she fell down the stairs and broke her leg trying to escape from the cop who had taken liberties with her.

Many of the girls were dressed only in their underwear. The cops had been in such a hurry to get them to the station and book them before they got off work, they didn't even give the girls a chance to collect their belongings. The sober cops lining the halls were ogling the nearly naked girls. One had just been the centerfold in a men's magazine, and her picture was gracing the wall of the vice office. One wise-ass cop asked her to autograph it for him. Surprisingly, she did.

The scene in the room turned into a rowdy screaming match as the intoxicated young ladies angrily accused their equally intoxicated arresting officers of unbecoming behavior. The cops yelled back, and no one seemed to know what was going on.

When Roger, the vice cop in charge, finally returned, he was quickly taken into the inner office to be informed that one of "their own" had been taken into custody. This was an extremely serious matter, and Internal Affairs had to be notified.

Roger went back into conference with the arresting officers and the lieutenant. One of the sergeants was assigned to take a Polaroid of each girl brought in. I protested when it was my turn. Since I wasn't under arrest, they had no right to take the obligatory mug shot. He assured me that these pictures were only for their records and not an official pose. Reluctantly, I let him snap my picture. It didn't look much like me, I thought thankfully. (The next evening, when my picture was shown on the eleven o'clock news, I was grateful the sergeant was not a professional photographer.)

The night dragged on as the conferences continued. I was angry, tired, and in excruciating pain. I had not taken any medication in hours, and the stress of the situation was causing my neck muscles to tighten in terrible knots. I asked the sergeant for some aspirin. He nastily replied that I couldn't have anything until after I had been interviewed by Internal Affairs. I asked when that might be.

Gruffly, he said they had to call in my commanding officer, Captain Dills. He had to be interviewed before they got around to me.

"And when will that be?" I patiently inquired.

"He's at dinner right now. It will be a couple of hours at least."

I groaned. I should have known better than to believe I'd be there for only a little while. We had arrived at 9, and it was now 11:30. They wouldn't even let me call my boyfriend, who would be frantic since he hadn't heard from me all this time.

I tried to relax. I massaged my neck, but it didn't help. The pain deepened. It would take a lot of medication to relieve it, and there was nothing I could do now but wait.

Captain Dills finally arrived around 1 A.M., and he grinned at me as if to say he had expected to see me in this kind of situation. I sneered at him in return. (I may even have stuck out my tongue.) "You sick, evil bastard," I muttered under my breath.

All the horrible stories I had heard about Internal Affairs interrogations could not have prepared me for the Gestapo-like interview ahead. Mercifully, my mind was numb with physical pain, and I scarcely seemed to care about the verbal abuse. The officers assigned to my case were not at all sympathetic to my pain. I limped slowly into the office that had been turned into an interrogation room and stoically sat in a chair. At first I refused to answer their questions, reminding them that I was not under arrest and that I was entitled to counsel before I was questioned.

They smugly informed me that I was not entitled to the same rights as the other young ladies. I was not allowed to have a lawyer present, and I was not going to be released until I had answered all their questions. They were prepared to stay as long as they had to. I could take my sweet time if I wished; it made no difference to them.

They weren't bluffing. If I didn't cooperate and get this over with, I would be too weak from pain and lack of food to protest their inhuman treatment.

I agreed to answer their questions, informing them that since I was suffering from stress and was under psychiatric treatment, I might not remember everything. If they didn't believe me, they could call my doctor who was on call for me twenty-four hours a day ever since I attempted suicide months before, after my last accident.

They told me to answer their questions simply and straightforwardly, and we could easily avoid a hassle.

The introductory questions were standard, the ones they ask everyone who is taken into custody. Showing no emotion, I answered them all. Then they progressed to more specific matters: "Tell us, Norma Jean, how you came to be involved with Miss Jill O'Conner."

Jill had also been brought in that evening. She was dressed only in pajamas; they wouldn't let her change after they knocked at her door and arrested her for pimping and pandering. She was a tall blonde with eyeglasses who looked as if she had been spectacular in her younger days.

She flatly refused to acknowledge her participation in the evening's exercise, declaring she had no idea what the cops were talking about. She

claimed she ran a legitimate modeling agency and had supplied a legitimate client with several of her girls for an ad campaign. Nothing more.
If the girls had engaged in anything underhanded, it was certainly not her
fault. All the girls were over twenty-one and made their own decisions.
She was not their keeper.

Bravo for you, I thought. Don't let them intimidate you, honey. Tell
them all to fuck off. They have no right to judge you or anyone else. They
certainly find it convenient to forget *their* morals when it comes to *their*
personal pleasure. I should know, I thought bitterly.

During my first summer with the department I attended a customary
"steak fry" in Griffith Park. In the back of the men's room, the cops had
an illegal poker game going. Even Captain Titwood, drunk as a skunk,
was there, making his hundred-dollar wager. It amazed me that they
could gamble so casually when just the day before, dozens of little old
ladies and men in the Fairfax area of Los Angeles, involved in a series of
penny-ante poker games, had been rounded up and arrested.

On the eleven o'clock news the night before, Captain Titwood praised
the work of the vice squad. He said they had successfully squelched a
vicious ring of chronic offenders who were tainting the neighborhood's
reputation with illicit activity. Hypocritically, he denounced their vice,
saying such activity caused the moral decay of our society; he vowed the
offenders would be punished despite their ages. Further, he asserted that
these older folks should be ashamed of themselves for the bad example
they set for the younger generation.

That same summer I also learned about the use and treatment of
informants. When I started working nights, I noticed there were quite a
few street prostitutes, some of whom were never arrested and others who
were always being booked. When I wondered aloud about it, the answer
was that many of the girls had "friends" on the vice squad.

They were informants, I was told, who served as the eyes and ears
for the police. As informants these young ladies were totally uncon-
cerned with harassment. In exchange for such privileges they frequently
visited their "protectors." I noticed those fellows went around smiling
a lot. (Years later, when Anna was arrested again and this time nearly
went to trial, she threatened to expose how she had "treated" the officers who protected her. She often paid her girls to have sex with the
cops.)

Most of the other cops envy the life of the vice officer. It is a gravy position if you are inconspicuous enough not to look like a cop. You even get to drink on the job.

Two motorcycle officers I once knew would agree. They used to patrol the Los Feliz area and made a game out of being more intoxicated than the drivers they stopped. Fred and Ed kept a little apartment not far from their beat, where they whiled away the time in between their occasional arrests. It was well stocked with their favorite expensive liquor, which had been donated by Hollywood merchants who felt obligated to make friends with the law enforcement officers in their area. At Christmas time it was a regular ritual to collect booty from the grateful civic-minded merchants on their beat.

These two motor cops played the game well, but one day a smart-mouthed lawyer turned the tables on them. On his way home from a hard day in court he was stopped for driving under the influence. He was in no mood for the two clowns who pulled him over. He may have had a few too many, but he could see they had had a few more than he. When they gave him the sobriety test, he made a bet with them. If they took it with him and passed, he would be happy to accompany them to jail. If they failed it, even if he did also, they would have to let him go. They agreed. Needless to say, they made jackasses out of themselves and were forced to let him go at the risk of his turning them in. Wise man that he was, he reported them anyway. Last I heard, they were both permanently assigned to desk jobs.

My reverie was broken when I realized that one officer was about to throw cold water in my face.

"We asked you a question, Norma Jean. How did you become acquainted with Miss O'Conner?"

"I was told about her by a friend who knew I was in desperate financial trouble. She knew I was interested in trying escort work. It is not illegal to be an escort, is it?"

"As you very well know, that is not why you were brought in here tonight. You are being charged with committing an act of prostitution."

"No, sir, that is not true. I was not arrested. I did not do anything illegal. As far as I knew, the man who came over to my house last night was supposed to take Julia and me to dinner. I had no idea it was supposed to involve anything else."

"Oh, come on. Who do you think you're trying to fool? Jill is one of the most notorious madams in the city, and you're claiming you didn't know?"

"No, sir, I did not. I had been introduced to her over the phone, and all my friend told me was that she ran a very respectable escort service and that I could make some money to keep from starving while I waited for the city to get its act together and pay me my disability compensation.''

"Why have you refused to go back to work? Captain Dills said his division has done everything to get you back on the job, but you refused to return. If things are that bad financially, wouldn't it be easier to return to a nice desk job while you wait for the city to send you to its psychiatrist for your work comp claim? Seems to me it would be better than getting caught up in an illegal operation like this.''

"Well, sir, I can't do that. I have reason to believe if I returned to work, the captain would find some reason to fire me. I was a bit of a troublemaker.''

We were both trying to remain civil. He could see I wasn't going to make his job easier and cop out to my guilt.

"When you worked as an escort, where did you go?''

"I have had only a few dates, sir, and each of the gentlemen took me to a restaurant.''

"What kind of restaurants?''

"The kind that serve food, sir.''

He looked very annoyed. "Where were these restaurants located?''

"I don't remember exactly.''

"Don't be a wise guy. Tell me where they took you. Did you go to Chasen's? Or to Jimmy's?'' He named some of the most expensive restaurants in Beverly Hills.

"I don't remember. But I have heard of those places.''

"What were the names of the men?''

"I honestly don't remember, sir.''

"Did you have sex with any of them?''

"I don't remember.''

"Why don't you remember a thing like that? Do you have sex so often you don't remember?''

"I don't think that is any of your business, sir.''

"Did any of them pay you to have sex with them?''

"Only when I was married, sir.''

"What do you mean? Did you engage in prostitution when you were married?''

"Only in that I was a wife, sir, and my husband made a living so he could take care of me, and I would have sex with him.''

His face turned bright red. Obviously I had hit a raw nerve. He bit his pencil. It took him several minutes to write down my replies and consult with his partner.

He turned back to me, his eyes focusing on the pad of paper in front of him, his fingers tapping impatiently. "Is this information in that book they say you are writing?"

"What book? I don't know what you're talking about."

He looked at his partner, who shook his head. He then cleared his throat and continued: "I understand from Officer McCune [the one I called Shorty] you have a file cabinet at home, that he believes might contain some pertinent information on this case. We would like to get your permission to go through it."

"No, sir, I can't do that. You have no right."

"I believe a judge will feel differently, and if we have to get a search warrant, we will. Why don't you save us some time and let us go through it."

I very hesitantly gave them my permission. I wasn't sure it was the right thing to do or even if they had the right to ask me, but I was too tired to argue.

Mike and Bill (Shorty) accompanied the two investigators and me to my home. We arrived at 4:15 A.M. My brother John, who was in the Marines, was staying with me. He had come home from work and was asleep when we all traipsed into my apartment, but the noise awakened him. He thought we were being robbed.

"What the hell's going on?" he demanded as he threw on a robe.

"Nothing. Go back to sleep." I closed the door to his bedroom.

"Who's that, your boyfriend?" Mike sneered. "A little young for you, isn't he?"

"He's my kid brother. You leave him out of this!"

Shorty led the two investigators directly to the file cabinet. They asked me what else was in there besides money, and I told them just my bills and purchase receipts. I also kept doll business information in there.

The older, more experienced interrogator assumed the task of going through my papers one by one. "We'd like to take a look at your book."

I continued to play dumb. "I have a whole library of books. Any particular subject?"

"We could get a search warrant," he said, his anger rising.

"For what? To see if I'm writing a book about the police? I doubt it!"

He looked at me sharply but kept silent. He could see I was not going to be conned into giving him my manuscript.

I kept an eye on the others, who seemed anxious to go through the rest of my house as well. I warned them I had not given them permission to do so, and if they were going to try without my permission, I would sue them. They wisely gave up.

I was angry that they thought they could trick me into letting them go through the rest of my house simply because they were already there. I was livid when the head investigator demanded to hear the contents of the telephone answering machine tape since it rested on top of the file cabinet. I told him to go to hell. He didn't pursue the matter, and we went back downtown. At least this time I felt fairly certain that the officers weren't driving under the influence.

They resumed their interrogation where they had left off, and for the next five hours I told them repeatedly that I knew nothing of this big prostitution ring they thought they had busted.

I had not yet been placed under arrest, so I figured they couldn't keep me indefinitely while they decided what role I had played in this whole mess. I was wrong.

My arresting officer, Mike, finally told me they were taking me to Sybil Brand Institute, the Los Angeles jail facility for women, to check me for warrants. I asked why they couldn't do it at the station, a process that would have saved everybody time and trouble. I had never even been issued a citation for a moving violation, nor did I have any record or outstanding warrants. It did not serve their purpose to check me out there, however, so handcuffs were placed on my wrists.

I reminded them that since I was not under arrest, it was not necessary for them to restrain me. I have a feeling they were told to handcuff me for retaliatory reasons, so I walked out of my old division in restraints, trying to smile bravely. My former comrades had assembled in the corridors to see me. I threw back my shoulders and in great physical pain walked past them proudly. Fuck 'em all, I thought. Or rather, don't fuck 'em. They don't deserve to feel that good.

The pain in my back and neck was overwhelming. When I had to sit in the car with my hands behind my back, I could no longer contain my discomfort. I begged Mike to cuff my hands in front of me. He refused. He also warned me not to mention that I was in pain or they would have to take me to the hospital, and then none of us would get out of there in a hurry.

The women assigned to work at Sybil Brand Institute were members of the sheriff's department; they had a five-year tour of duty there before being allowed on the streets. It was a constant source of friction between the two departments since none of the women on the L.A.P.D. were assigned to such duty after the academy.

The women who worked the jail became hard, bitter creatures who couldn't feel compassion or demonstrate a civil emotion if it were demanded by law. The power they had over the hapless beings who drifted through their domain went to their head, and they played silly, petty games with those who were unfortunate enough to lose their freedom. They were particularly unfriendly toward those who used to be on their side of the law. By the time I came through, the other ladies who had been in the roundup had already been released or were waiting for a friend to bail them out.

I was fingerprinted and body-searched, a process I could have done without since I still had not been charged with anything. I was then taken to wait in the giant holding tank. It was mercifully empty when I went in, though it stank of stale urine and old vomit. The walls were decorated with unintelligible scribblings, and the floors were covered with soiled, wet toilet paper. The open-air john in the corner overflowed with feces and urine. I wanted to vomit.

There was a pay phone on the wall with instructions for making the famous one free phone call. It had been more than fifteen hours since I had been "kidnapped" by my former employer, and not once had I been permitted to make a call.

I picked up the receiver and put it next to my ear, but I quickly dropped it in disgust. It was covered with slime. I searched and found a very small piece of dry toilet tissue to clean off the phone. I dialed my boyfriend's number, hoping he wasn't too upset I hadn't called. I heard a recording: "We cannot complete the call as dialed. Please hang up and dial again."

I tried the number over and over. No luck. I tried dialing the prison operator. All lines were busy, I was told. I went to the door and rapped hard on the glass window.

A large, fierce-looking matron came to the window to see what I wanted. When I told her that I was having trouble with the phone, she laughed coldly and answered, "Too bad." She guessed that I would just have to wait until I was released. Still laughing, she walked away. No amount of knocking or banging on the glass brought anyone back to the tank.

It was just too much. I could hardly breathe, the stench was so bad. I was in a great deal of pain. And I was hungry and thirsty, and had to go to the bathroom again.

I sat on the cold, hard, wooden bench and contemplated my situation. Since no one knew I was there, no one would come to my rescue.

I could be in there for days, I thought, a victim of ''lost'' paperwork. I had seen it happen before. And there was nothing that could be done about it. I realized sadly that I was truly at the mercy of these sadistic bitches, and I had better behave.

Finally, the big, ugly matron returned with news: ''Okay, I guess you don't have any outstanding warrants.'' She sounded disappointed. ''We're going to issue you a citation, and then you can go.''

I was being charged with keeping a disorderly house, an infraction equivalent to jaywalking. I stifled my indignation and signed the ticket, not acknowledging my guilt but merely complying with their demands so they would let me out of there. It was another hour before they got around to releasing me. I bit hard on my lip to refrain from editorializing on their competence. I was much too close to freedom to lose my temper now. I signed for my belongings, which I had relinquished when I was taken into custody. Another half hour passed before my possessions were found.

At last I was allowed to leave. I went to the lobby to look for a phone. I checked in my purse but found no change. Then Jill came into the lobby. She happily lent me money to call a cab and wished me luck. She said she was genuinely sorry that we had met under such conditions but assured me that when things cooled down, we could do some profitable business together. She said she'd be in touch. I thanked her profusely.

I am sure that the taxi driver realized why I had been in Sybil Brand. He must have heard about the big call girl ring bust since we had made the evening news the night before. I handed him a $50 bill to pay my $30 fare. He told me he didn't have change for such a large sum. I jumped out of his cab and told him to keep it.

Running upstairs past the curious neighbors, I was now feeling angry and humiliated. I gulped down several pain pills. God, I was in pain. Thankfully, my brother John was not around to ask any questions.

I called Victor's answering service and left him an urgent message to call me. I made a quick inventory of my apartment, checking every paper and book, to see if Internal Affairs had dropped by uninvited while I was gone.

Picking up every piece of paper that had a phone number on it—those of my clients and the madams I had worked for—I tore them into shreds and flushed them down the toilet.

I removed my stale makeup, which was streaked down my face, following the lines of my tears. My eyes were bloodshot and swollen, and my nose was red-blotched from anger.

I drew a hot bath and laced the water heavily with perfume and bubble bath. I had to wash the stench of jail from my body.

In the tub I began feeling relief from the pain in my back, but I was still incensed. I sighed and leaned back into the suds. If I could ever get through this day, I would never let something like this happen to me again. I swallowed repeatedly, trying to keep the bile in my stomach from reaching my throat. My hands trembled uncontrollably as I tried to wash my body. I took out my contact lenses. They felt as though they had been glued to my eyeballs.

The phone rang. It was Victor. "Where have you been?" His voice sounded as tortured as my body felt. "Oh, darling, it happened." I didn't need to say any more. He knew exactly what I meant.

He groaned. "Oh, honey, I'm so sorry. I'll be right over. You can tell me all about it then." He hung up.

I sighed. My love was on his way, and I wouldn't have to suffer this pain alone. I got out of the tub and dried myself off. All the pain pills had so drugged me by this time, I could barely stand up.

I tried to put on a robe, but it seemed too difficult to drape it around my body. I dropped it on the floor, and then I dropped to the floor. Somehow I managed to crawl into the bedroom and lift myself up onto the bed. I sprawled naked across the covers and passed out.

Several hours later I woke up. Victor was gently stroking my hair. I sat up and vomited all over him. He told me not to worry about it, that he would clean it up. Several times I tried to talk, but he quieted me and said that we would talk about it later. I fell back into a troubled sleep.

When I awakened again, the evening news was on, featuring further developments in the big sting operation. The station had done an interview with Jill after her release, and, not surprisingly, she was claiming entrapment. She mentioned that the police had engaged in sex acts with several of the young ladies at the party and had been so intoxicated when they began arresting them that there was no way the police could remember if the girls had solicited them or not. It even appeared that several of the officers had forced themselves on a few unwilling participants and then informed those girls that they were under arrest.

At least the media had not reported that one of the young ladies in the roundup was a member of the department. I had been spared the embarrassment of a big scandal—at least for now. It had been only a few months since a fellow Hollywood cop had been caught running a brothel out in the San Fernando Valley, and the news of Ron Venegas's and Jack

Myers's burglary ring was still on page one of the paper. I guess Chief
Daryl Gates wasn't ready to have his entire force portrayed as Peyton
Place. His brother, Captain Steven Gates, had recently been caught dat-
ing a madam who operated a business in the San Fernando Valley. Steven
Gates was transferred to another division, while the madam went to jail.

It wasn't until the next day that I had calmed down enough to be able
to describe in lurid detail the events that led to my incarceration. I called
my attorney and told him about the citation I had been given. He said
what they had done was highly irregular, as I had suspected. He thought
we had a good case for a false arrest suit.

Two weeks later my attorney and I went to court fully prepared to take
on the whole city, if necessary, with volumes of prior cases as my
defense. It was unnecessary: The city attorney had conveniently lost my
paperwork. I wasn't even on the court calendar.

I was curious to find out what happened to the other girls who had
been rounded up that evening, and I wanted to know what the police
had done with Jill and Anna. I began checking around—discreetly, of
course—because someone had started the rumor that I was an informer.
For a while no one wanted anything to do with me. Eventually the other
girls realized what side of the fence I was on, but it took a lot of convincing.

Julia, I knew, was still being prosecuted. I received dozens of sub-
poenas from both her defense attorney and the prosecution. I briefly
talked to her lawyer and asked him how the city could prosecute a case
for which they had absolutely no evidence. He told me that it was an
important case to the city, and they fully intended to pursue it.

A year later her case was still being continued, and my presence was
still demanded. I refused to appear at all. My psychiatrist strongly advised against it; if I entered a courtroom in my state of mind, I would
undoubtedly end up going to jail myself.

Rumors abounded concerning Jill, Anna, and the other working girls.
The story most often bandied about was that for $2,000 their paperwork
could be conveniently lost. It cost a girl much more to be defended in
court. The fee for Jill and Anna was sufficiently higher, of course, since
they allegedly made more money. I understand that Jill paid up and then
went into semi-retirement. Anna made other arrangements; she developed
a profitable relationship with the vice cop who started it all, Roger Ryder
himself. She has admitted that they often have lunch together, and he
calls her frequently.

Despite that, Anna was arrested several more times and in 1988 was charged with pandering and pimping. She threatened to expose the cozy relationship she shared with the cops if she went to trial, so she pled guilty on only one count and the mandatory prison sentence required by law was waived. She was given a short probation with no fine and will never serve a day in prison. And life goes on.

10. You Can't Keep
a Good Woman Down

You can torture and maim—it'll turn out the same.
There's no way in the world you'll ruin my game!
So take your best shot, 'cause you'll get only one.
I will still be here when your nonsense is done.

You can make me unhappy, you can ruin my day,
But when it's all over, you will go away!
And when you are gone, you won't see me frown!
Although you may try, you can't keep me down!

AFTER I FELT SAFE enough to go back to work, I decided to work only through madams I had worked for in the past, with one exception: David, whom I had met at a party hosted by one of my clients. Because I trusted the client, I took David up on his offer to work through him occasionally. David always had the most interesting clients. Maybe he attracted these colorful characters because he was such a character himself.

In her book, *Hustling,* Gail Sheehy describes a character named David who resembles the David I know. I am almost certain her David and mine are the same man. Tall, skinny, dark-haired, with a huge nose, David is very New York Jewish. He could be comedian David Brenner's twin brother. Because he looks emaciated, he brings out the mothering instinct in most women.

David pimped for the sake of control over other men. Since he is a man, he must be called a pimp, but in reality he was a male madam. Women who worked for him did so by choice. Although he had many different women working for him at any given time, just as a female madam does, I don't think he had the ambition to run a stable of women who worked exclusively for him. David did not take a cut from the women who worked for him; his clients paid him to procure women for them, and then David paid his employees.

I wanted to see what it was like to work for a man. In some ways he was easier to work for than some of the female madams because he didn't demand that his girls bring him money in the middle of the night or in the pouring rain. In other ways he was certainly more devious because he paid the women far less than the client had paid him for her services. But considering that we were making more per hour with him than with any other madam, it seemed to even out.

David traveled extensively and lived high, courtesy of his rich and powerful friends who were anxious to keep him happy so he'd continue to provide them with top-quality girls. David knew every human weakness and frailty, and how to apply guilt, lust, and greed in just the right doses to make his clients come up with more money.

David had a lovely two-story condominium in Encino. Part of his little empire included a fleet of limousines, some of which he kept parked on the street in front of his condo. He had them in a variety of colors and kept them serviced and ready to transport his clients to his girls or his girls to his clients at any moment, day or night. Sometimes he entertained clients in his condo.

David's pride and joy, aside from his fleet of limos, was a little white Shih Tzu named Pussy. To say Pussy had the run of the house would be an understatement. Spoiled beyond belief, that little white fur ball was a holy terror to uninformed visitors who might find the little mutt chewing on their expensive clothing while they were busy getting a little pussy of their own.

David called one afternoon: "Norma Jean, I'd like you to stop by my house around five-thirty tonight. I have a very interesting client I'd like you to meet."

Arriving at David's condo at about 5:20, I found a parking place about a block away. I brought along my briefcase just in case this client had any interesting fantasies.

David was frantic when I walked in the door. His client was going to be a little late, but he would take care of the extra time I had to wait. He seemed anxious and in a hurry. "Try to get him out of here before seven, Norma Jean, okay?"

"Sure, David. Is he that fast?" Usually David wanted a girl to stay for as long as he could con her into.

Dan, the client, arrived at 6:15, and David rushed us downstairs to the bedroom. Dan was wearing a large cowboy hat, and I recognized his face from the sports pages. He was a member of an NFL football team and has since retired. Tall, good-looking, and charming with his Texas drawl, it appeared he had already started partying before he arrived. David provided him with even more white powder before we began to play.

Underneath my red silk dress I was wearing red silk French underwear: bra, panties, and garter belt. It had cost me plenty. I was always very careful with it because it was very expensive to replace.

Cowboy Dan was very impressed with my underwear. He wanted to hold them and smell them—he even wanted to try them on. Horrified that he just might try to put my lovely expensive French underwear on his massive frame, I hurriedly convinced him it would turn me on much more if he just let me perform oral sex on him.

Fortunately, that idea took hold in his drug-stupefied mind, and he promptly forgot about trying on my undergarments. Relieved, I put my precious underwear in a tidy little pile at the foot of the bed and began orally manipulating him.

He sat at the head of the bed, propped up with several pillows, his legs spread wide, still wearing his leather boots, which dangled off the side of the bed. His cowboy hat was tipped down over his eyes as he serenaded me with Texas love songs in rhythm to my stroking. Every few minutes we had to break stride so he could do another hit, which upset my concentration considerably.

I looked at my watch. It was ten minutes to seven, and Dan wasn't even close to achieving orgasm. Coke heads are so difficult to work with. I wondered if David would be upset if his client left without getting off.

I thought I heard a door slam in the distance and then the door to the bedroom opened. It must be David coming to see how long it would take us to finish, I thought—but no David. Must have been my imagination.

Suddenly I felt soft fur on my bare buns and heard a growl at the end of the bed. Dan started laughing. Pussy had joined us and was playing tug-of-war with my delicate underwear. "Give me those, you little mutt," I shrieked. I tried to ease them gently out of her mouth to keep them from ripping into shreds. But Pussy jumped off the bed and made for the stairs, my lingerie dangling from her mouth, the stockings still attached to the garter belt trailing behind her. "Come back here, Pussy! Give me my underwear before I strangle you, you perverted little feather duster!" I was in hot pursuit. Dan, being the gentleman he was, had taken off his cowboy hat and tried to cover my private part as he followed me up the stairs. "Here, little darlin'. Let me cover up that purty little beaver of yours!"

"Get away from me, Dan. You're going to make me trip!" I tried to shoo him away before Pussy could devour my belongings. Instead of my tripping, Dan tripped, making a very ungraceful landing at the bottom of the stairs.

"Oh, darn! My leg! I think I twisted it!" He got right back up and hobbled after me.

The dog had made it all the way upstairs, through the kitchen and dining room, and was heading for the living room. I was hollering at the top of my voice; "David! Your Pussy has my underwear, and I swear I'm going to kill her if she ruins them!"

I heard laughter coming from the living room. In fact, I heard several voices laughing. Damn! David had more company. And the damn dog had my underwear!

I was running so fast I couldn't stop, and pell-mell into the living room we went. Dan had been hobbling behind me, still trying unsuccessfully to protect my body parts with his ten-gallon hat, his own body in full view of the appreciative audience sitting on the couch. The dog had disappeared under the couch with my garments, with one of the stockings draped over a guest's foot.

Besides David, who was fixing drinks, and Dan, there were five or six men and three women in the room, dressed to the nines. Their faces looked terribly familiar. Then it dawned on me who they were: One man was a famous senator, two were movie stars, and two of the women were well-known daytime soap opera stars.

Horrified, I stood there naked, speechless, covering my bare breasts with my arms. Poor Dan was still trying to cover me with his hat, and when he remembered he, too, was exposed, he tried putting the hat over that instead. Realizing it was a lost cause, he put the hat back on his head.

"Er, pardon us, folks. We seem to have lost something. I think that dog under the couch knows where it is. Will you all excuse me a minute while I get the little mutt?" He handed me his hat, got down on his knees, and tried to reach under the couch, his ass up, balls dangling absurdly. "Oh, ouch. I think I hurt my knee again! David, do you have an Ace bandage?" He stood up, rubbing his knee. David's guests were laughing hysterically.

By this time David was also trying to retrieve the dog and was yelling at me for coming upstairs. "I told you to get him out of here by seven. How dare you come up here and interrupt my other guests! Here, Pussy, give me that!" The dog growled at everyone. She was *not* going to relinquish her prize without a fight. Finally, David coaxed the dog out from under the couch. Pussy exchanged my garments for a dog biscuit. David handed them to me.

I found my voice. "Oh, look! They're ruined! She's chewed them all to pieces! Damn it, David. I didn't know you had guests up here. Why did you let the darn dog downstairs anyway?"

David turned to his guests to apologize. They just laughed. The senator said, "Hey, that's okay, David. I thought this was the entertainment before we head to the charity function at the Beverly Hilton. Your friend has great tits! Maybe she should join us." His blond female companion hit him playfully in the stomach.

While my attention was focused on retrieving my underwear, I had forgotten Dan and I were naked. My face turned red, and I ran back downstairs, clutching my things tightly. Cowboy Dan was right behind me, giggling to himself, rubbing his sore knee.

"So, you ready to get back to playing my fiddle?" He grinned.

"No, I'm not, Mr. Cowboy. I'm going home. I've been embarrassed enough for one day." I felt like crawling into a hole and staying there forever. Imagine parading stark naked in front of a group like that!

"Ah, come on, honey. You have no reason whatever to be embarrassed. You could hold your own among anybody, dressed or naked. Didn't you see how those men looked at you with lust in their eyes?"

"Don't you know who those men are? One of them is a senator, for goodness' sake!" I assessed the damage to my underthings, which were still damp from Pussy's mouth. The bra had three gaping holes in its lace front, and the garter had been completely chewed through on one side. The panties didn't fare any better, with a wide hole from the seat to the crotch. I threw them into my purse. "Ah, damn! I can't even wear them home. That damn dog!" I slipped my dress over my naked body. Fortunately it was dark out now so no one would see me walking up the street to my car.

I left David a note telling him how much he owed me for the time I was there and the damaged lingerie. Dan was disappointed I was leaving, but I promised I would see him again another time. Quietly, I let myself out and hurried to my car.

By the time I got home the whole thing seemed funny. And that senator! I always suspected he was a lech!

Later that night as Victor and I lay in bed watching the news, a film clip of the charity function held at the Beverly Hilton was shown. There was David and his friends getting out of a limousine. Even Dan the Cowboy was there, with some young blonde climbing all over him. He still looked high. The TV reporter interviewed him briefly: "Big Dan Winnemuka. How are you tonight, Dan? How do things look for the

Superbowl this year? I see you are walking with a limp. Did you injure your bad knee during training? I hope you're not going to be out for the season!''

Good old Dan just grinned into the camera and said, ''Nope. I got it chasing a dog!'' The young blonde pulled on his arm. ''Got to go now. Hope you all are rootin' for our team this year!''

''Thanks, Dan. That's Big Dan Winnemuka, here with me at the Beverly Hilton, where all the stars are out tonight for a good cause. Jim Dandy, for Channel Eleven news, reporting live from Beverly Hills.''

Another night David called very late. He wanted me to see one of his clients who was staying at Bernie Cornfield's house. The name sounded familiar. ''Isn't Mr. Cornfield the man who used to date Victoria Principal?'' David always knew those kinds of things.

''Yeah. He's the man who founded the I.O.S. (Investors Overseas Services) in the sixties and made hundreds of millions of dollars. I have a good friend who's staying with him. Name's Chip Gordon. I don't want you to ask him for any money. I'll pay you tomorrow.'' David was so New York, always trying to hustle me. Sometimes when he said I would get paid tomorrow, it was months before I saw any money. And then he forked it over only because I hounded him, threatening never to see any of his clients again.

I reminded him of the difficulty I had collecting my money from him in the past. ''David, that's what you told me last time. And you still haven't paid me for Cowboy Dan and for your dumb dog ruining my underwear. I'm not going to see any more of your clients on credit. You either pay me before I go or forget it!''

Even though I really liked David, he had taken me once too often to be trusted again. He agreed to meet me in front of Bernie's house in Beverly Hills with cash in hand. When I arrived, he handed me $500. ''I want you to stay with him as long as he likes. If I owe you more, can you trust the rest until tomorrow? Okay? Please? Don't give me so much trouble, Norma Jean. When I say I'm going to pay, I'm going to pay!''

''Okay, fine, David. I'm not going to argue with you.''

I knocked at the door. In a minute it was answered by a short, two-ton man in a white bathing suit. In reality, this five-foot-six man weighed only 385 pounds, or so he said. He was Amerasian, and with his size and costume he looked like a sumo wrestler. ''Come on in. I'm Chip.'' He held a plate filled with food, which he was stuffing in his mouth.

Following him through the heavy wrought-iron doors into the Corn-field mansion, I got a good look at Mr. Cornfield's famous living room. With its high-beamed ceiling, dark wood-paneled walls, and deep red draperies adorning the two-story windows, it looked like a mausoleum. Ancient brass chandeliers filled with fake candles hung from huge wooden beams, and the walls were covered with huge oil paintings. Most of the furniture was antique, too. In fact, the whole house smelled musty and old.

Chip led me through the long living room, past the black grand piano, to a hidden stairway that led to a small guest bedroom over the garage. The stairs were narrow, and Chip just barely made it through.

Chip's main concern that evening seemed to be to have company while he gorged himself on food. While we sat at the end of his bed talking, he wanted me to strip down to my garter belt and panties, but thank goodness he didn't ask to try them on. He was babysitting Mr. Cornfield's favorite red parrot, and we laughed hysterically at the amusing things it said.

He never once tried to get romantic with me, and to be quite honest, I was very happy he didn't. I was certain if he had tried to get on top of me, I would be crushed.

It was well past two in the morning when Chip made his last trip to the kitchen for the night. He had made several trips earlier while I waited for him in his room and talked to the parrot. This time Chip decided I should go with him because he was going to make a late-night breakfast for himself. I was getting chilly, so I borrowed his robe to wear, which was yards too big for me.

We took the parrot with us to put it to bed for the night. I don't think it liked the idea because it kept biting Chip all the way down the stairs and into the den where his fellow feathered friends—a green parrot and a white cockatoo—were squawking loudly: "You bastard. Wanna fuck? Squawk! Wanna fuck? Pretty bird!" He put the parrot in its cage and pulled covers over all the bird cages.

We tiptoed into the kitchen, although I haven't the faintest idea why. His "tiptoe" sounded like that of a baby rhinoceros, so if we were trying to keep quiet, we were not successful.

The kitchen was a marvel in modern conveniences. Huge stainless-steel refrigerators lined the entire back wall. The professional chef's stove would be the envy of any restaurant in Beverly Hills. Huge skillets hung from the ceiling in a neat, orderly fashion. Unlike my own kitchen, it did not lack counter space for preparing meals. A homey breakfast nook completed the room.

Chip offered to fix me breakfast. I declined. Fascinated by the sight of a 385-pound man jiggling his sweaty, naked flesh around the kitchen in pursuit of more food, I sat on a high stool in the corner as he plunked two pounds of bacon into a heavy skillet and cracked a dozen eggs to fry, sunny-side up, on the grill. A half loaf of wheat bread became burnt toast, soaked in butter and dripping with strawberry jam. When the eggs were almost done, he remembered the hash brown potatoes. He reached for another skillet and put a whole bag of Ore-Ida potatoes O'Brien on to cook.

The eggs, bacon, and toast were devoured long before the potatoes were cooked. That was no problem; he just made himself a second helping of everything so he would have something to go with his potatoes, of course!

I was amazed at his capacity, but as he confessed to me while he inhaled his breakfast, he was just a growing boy. It must cost a small fortune to keep that boy fed!

An hour and a half later he was finally finished eating. He threw the dirty dishes in the sink and washed his hands.

He decided he needed some milk to wash everything down. Then he thought perhaps he'd better make himself a sandwich to take to his room just in case he got hungry before morning. Back to the refrigerator he went; he guzzled a quart of milk and got out the mayonnaise and cold ham. One sandwich became two, and then he discovered an open bag of potato chips in the cupboard to go with the sandwiches, just in case. Now we were ready to go back to his room. We turned out the kitchen lights.

When we had entered the kitchen two hours before, the lights in the rest of the house were lit. Now all the lights were off. It was pitch-black.

"Uh oh," said Chip. "I think the alarm is on."

"Great. What does that mean?"

"That means we have to crawl across the dining room and through the den and living room so we don't set off the alarm. I guess Bernie didn't see the lights in the kitchen when he came home."

I groaned. Just what I always wanted to do!

He pointed to a thin beam of white light shooting across the room about knee high. "We gotta stay under that light all the way to my staircase. If we trip the alarm, it'll wake up Bernie and he'll get real mad! I don't want him to find out I've got a girl here."

"How are you going to carry your sandwich and bag of chips?"

"I'll show you. Here, get down on your stomach . . . there now. Since you're smaller than me, I'll put them on your back, and you can carry them until we get to the stairs. Follow me."

He plopped down on the floor in front of me and started to slither across the dining room floor, his great rolls of flesh safely guarding his family jewels from harm. I didn't dare wiggle too much or the food would fall off my back. The chips kept sliding off anyway.

"Stop. Wait a minute, Chip. I can't see you . . . and your potato chips have fallen on the floor."

Chip giggled as he reached back in the dark for the bag of potato chips. "Here, I'll carry them in my mouth," he mumbled.

We started forward through the darkness again, slowly, inches at a time. His robe was so big on me, it kept bunching up under my stomach, making it very hard to continue. "Slow down, Chip . . . Chip? Are you still there?" I couldn't see a thing.

"I'm here, I'm here!" He dropped the chips for a minute so he could speak. "I think we turn right here. Watch the wall. Oh, ouch!" There was a crashing sound in front of me.

"Chip, are you all right? What did you hit?"

"The wall! I must have turned too soon! Hold on, I gotta feel for the opening." I heard him pounding on the wall.

"Oh, here it is. Come on . . . this way. Do you still have my sandwiches on your back?"

"Yes. Hold on a minute. I have to fix the robe. I'm caught here. Hey, which way did you go? I can't see a thing." My hand reached out in the darkness, trying to find his foot.

"Go towards your left, and hurry up. I gotta go to the bathroom!"

At last we reached the den, but we woke up the parrots.

"Halt. Who goes there?"

"Brawwwk! Nasty man, masty man! Give me some pot!"

"Aw, dirty bird, dirty bird. Wanna fuck, little girl?"

The cockatoo just squawked.

"Okay, you guys. Shhh! Go back to sleep," Chip whispered loudly.

"Come back here, thief! Stick 'em up. Hello, little girl."

"Hello yourself! Now shut up and go back to sleep!"

The den had a lot more furniture that we had to maneuver around. There was a giant screen television and lots of overstuffed couches and plush pillows. My arms kept hitting the legs of the tables.

As we rounded the corner into the long living room, Chip let out a muffled shriek. "Oh, shit! The floor is cold!" He had been lucky so far because there had been rugs. My stomach was covered, but he was naked.

In the hallway leading to the main staircase, I could see a faint shaft of light coming through the front door. For a minute the light shined right through the crack of his large ass sticking up in the air, and his fleshy thighs were faintly illuminated, rolling together as he shimmied down the few stairs to the living room. He looked so ridiculous, but then I must have, too.

The living room's wooden floor was well waxed, so it was much easier to slide along than the other floors. We made good time to the back stairway. It must have taken us at least forty-five minutes to crawl there from the kitchen.

"How much longer, Chip? Are we almost there?" The light from the front door had faded. Again we were in utter darkness. I hoped we were not sharing the floor with any creepy crawly creatures—spiders, ants, and roaches don't discriminate against rich people.

"We're almost there, Norma Jean. We just passed the piano."

"Yeah, Chip. We're going to make it!" Suddenly something fuzzy and warm was licking my foot. It startled me, and I jumped up with a yell. It was a little dog! Another darn dog! The alarm went off when I sat upright, and Chip began to yell at me.

"Oh, what did you do that for?"

"I'm sorry. That goddamn dog. Where'd it come from anyway? It scared me half to death, licking my foot!"

The lights came on, and there was Bernie at the top of the stairs, putting on his robe. He shut off the alarm. "What's going on down there? What's all the noise?" I looked around and saw that the dog was busy eating—the ham sandwiches had flown halfway across the room, landing in a heap of bread and mayonnaise, with pieces of ham scattered along the way.

Chip stood up and helped me to my feet. "Oh, hi, Bernie. We were just having a little midnight snack. Sorry we disturbed you!" He grabbed his bag of potato chips and my arm, and we rushed up the back stairs.

"Was that Bernie?"

"Yeah."

"He didn't seem too upset to me, Chip."

"Yeah, well I am! We crawled all that way for nothing! I had to pee so badly!"

"No, it wasn't for nothing. This is one for my book. No one will ever believe it, but it'll be there. My life as a high-class call girl. Yes, sir!''

Nights like that were not what I had imagined when I fantasized about being a glamorous Beverly Hills call girl!

The year between my first and second arrest was probably one of the happiest of my life. I was much more secure with my new image and pleased that I had the opportunity to learn so many new things. The bitter memories of my ten-year career with the cops were fading, and I was meeting many wonderful, fascinating people. I felt I was in heaven.

Madeline, a madam I occasionally worked for, called one Sunday and asked if I wanted to make $1,000 that afternoon. She said she had just received a call from a secretary who told her an attractive woman was needed to attend a dinner party at oil millionaire Wilbur Reese's ranch near Santa Barbara. The President and First Lady would be there.

Madeline told me to wear an elegant cocktail dress and high heels, and to be there by 5:30. Santa Barbara is a two-and-a-half-hour drive, so I had to move quickly. She gave me detailed directions to Mr. Reese's house. I was afraid my black cocktail dress would be wrinkled by the time I arrived. I was looking forward to my entree into society. I hoped I had learned enough about the social graces to pass muster.

As I drove, I mused about how far I had come since the first time I had gone out to a really expensive restaurant with a client.

Bob had taken me to Bernard's, a fancy French restaurant in downtown L.A. at the posh, newly refurbished Biltmore Hotel. Thoughtfully, he ordered for me, and when the waiter brought the lobster on a silver platter for inspection, I wasn't quite sure what to do. I thought he was holding it in front of me so I could put it on my plate. I started reaching for it, and my embarrassed client groaned loudly and grabbed my arm, shaking his head at me.

After dinner the waiter brought a bowl of hot water with a piece of lemon, which I thought was to drink. After all, we never had luxuries like that in the restaurants where I had worked as a waitress in high school. My client just laughed and said, ''Honey, I'm not laughing at you. It's just so refreshing to find a beautiful woman who is not hard and jaded because she knows everything. You are priceless. I hope you never change!''

Well, I had learned some things in the short time I had worked. After that embarrassing experience, Victor gave me a crash course in expensive restaurant etiquette.

When I arrived at the ranch, I observed that no other cars were around except for one old Jeep. The garage must have housed at least ten cars, but it was all locked up. Surely there should be Secret Servicemen scanning the place for bombs or something. And maybe a catering truck or two.

Maybe I was early. I looked at my watch. Nope, right on time.

I walked up the long stairway to the front door. From the top of the steps there was a stunning view of the ocean. I rang the bell, and rang and rang. No one answered. Finally an older man wearing a cowboy hat and a dirty old shirt came walking toward me from the stables.

I waved to him. "Hello. I'm supposed to be here for a dinner party this evening. Can you tell me where it is?"

He smiled as he came closer. "Honey, what dinner party is that?"

I felt my heart drop. "I was told Mr. Wilbur Reese was having a dinner party tonight, and I am here to be Mr. Reese's date. This is the right place, isn't it?"

"Oh, this is Mr. Reese's house, all right. I'm Mr. Reese." He stuck out his hand. "Pleased to meet ya. I don't know nothing about any dinner party, though. Guess I could round up something for you to eat if you're hungry. Come on into the house. What'd you say your name was?"

"I didn't. I'm Norma Jean." I followed him inside the rambling mansion. "I feel so embarrassed! I drove all the way from Los Angeles because the lady I work for told me there was to be a very formal dinner party here, with the President and First Lady coming and everything!"

"Ol' Ronnie and Nancy? Yeah, they usually come to my parties when they're out here. They're my neighbors, you know. What kind of work do you do?" We walked into the massive living room that had a huge fireplace on one wall. It was a western-style home. A beautiful buffalo-skin rug covered most of the floor. Stuffed animal heads were mounted everywhere, and numerous hunting trophies lined the shelves.

Since he was a friend of the President's and it was clear he had no knowledge of my invitation to his home, I thought it best to hedge a bit about my profession. "Well, I work for an escort service."

He slapped his knee and laughed. "Oh, you're a call girl! Why didn't you say so? Well, that explains it, honey!"

I shook my head. I must have missed something somewhere. "Pardon me, but I don't understand. That explains what?"

"Honey, my old girlfriend Patty was a hooker, and she's always calling me up wanting money. I won't give her any more so she calls me a cheap bastard and hangs up. When she gets mad at me, she'll call up the madam she used to work for and has the lady send someone out here to see me. She knows I can't turn down a poor little thing that drives all the way out here for nothing, so I always pay the girl. Patty figures if she can't get money out of me, somebody should get some, preferably one of her working sisters. This is the first time she's used a dinner party ruse to get someone out here. What did the madam tell you I'd pay?''

"One thousand dollars.''

"Well, that's more than I usually give the girl. What will you do for me if I give you all that?''

"What do you want me to do, Mr. Reese?''

"Please call me Wil. All my friends do. And honey, if I'm going to give you a thousand bucks, you'd better become my friend! What I'd like is a little head. I'm afraid my old bronco is busted, and it can't do any more mounting. An old war wound, you know. But it sure likes to get a lickin' now and then!'' He laughed uproariously. "You good at giving head, honey?''

I had a delightful time with Wil. He paid me the thousand and gave me a little something extra to pay for my gas. He asked if he could see me again when he went into town. I was very happy to take him on as a regular client. He came frequently and sometimes took me out to lunch and dinner. And he introduced me to several of his friends. What started out as a mean prank by his ex-girlfriend ended with several thousand dollars in my pocket.

11. Tales of the Arabian Nights

Dazzling stories came out of the East
Of harems and other wondrous delights.
The stories were filled with wild, sumptuous feasts,
Those exotic tales of Arabian nights.

My childhood was filled with wonderful stories,
All better, more dazzling than each one before;
But none can compare, there are no greater glories,
Than those that I found for myself as a whore.

"DAMN! Why does everybody call at the same time? I'm doing my nails, and I just ruined them—again!" Rosanne yelled into the phone in her deep, raspy Lauren Bacall-like voice. "Where the hell have you been? I've been trying to reach you all day. Don't you ever check your messages?"

"Sure, but not every ten minutes," I replied. "I've been out all day. Just calm down. What's the plan?"

"Well, the flight to New York leaves at eleven-thirty and arrives at seven-fifteen, and the limousine driver will meet all of you in the baggage claim area. And Norma Jean, Don't you dare tell him how old you really are!"

I said nothing, patiently waiting for her to finish her tirade.

"Are you listening to me?" she shrieked. "I'm telling you, you'll never work again if you blow this for me!"

"Yes, Rosanne, I know. I'm supposed to be twenty-five, and the Pope is Jewish! Are you sure this is going to work?" I couldn't believe she was going to try to pass me off on the richest Arab sheik in the world as a twenty-five-year-old nymphet. I was thirty-two, and I really didn't like trying to fool my clients. If they didn't want me the way I was, they were free to find somebody else.

"Yes, it will work. He'll look at your tits and ass, and he won't even notice your face. Look, girl, you are going to get paid a small fortune to be twenty-five for a few days, and damn it, that's what you're going to be!"

My ears rang as she slammed down the phone. I remembered her saying a thousand times, "If men wanted honesty, they'd be going to a nun, not a whore!"

Just a few days earlier I was sitting at home working on my book when Rosanne called and asked if I wanted to fly to Las Vegas to meet an Arab sheik. He wanted a choice selection of the most beautiful California girls available. He would fly us to Vegas, provide a luxurious suite for each of us, and pay for all the shows, dinners, and gambling our little hearts desired, plus $2,000 a day. It sure sounded marvelous to me. I happily agreed to go.

But now she was saying that all the plans had suddenly been changed. It appeared Sheik Smith could not risk being seen in Las Vegas with other women—something about a messy divorce. Instead we would party in New York.

It was Easter weekend, and it sounded like a delightful way to spend the holiday. And after I partied with the sheik, I figured I could visit my family in upstate New York.

Traffic had thinned out after the morning rush-hour on the 405 freeway to the airport. Victor dropped me and my four bags at the American Airlines departure terminal. Although it was a beautiful warm day in Los Angeles, I was wearing my new white fox fur–trimmed coat.

Rosanne was in her usual frantic coked-out state when she met me at the counter where I was picking up my prepaid first-class ticket. She introduced me to two other girls who were also traveling to New York for the sheik. They already had their tickets and were waiting for me.

Ashley was a strikingly beautiful, tall, light-skinned black girl in her early twenties. Thigh-high five-inch-heeled boots protruded from beneath her full-length black mink coat. A cloud of soft black hair framed her delicate features, and two dazzling diamond studs adorned her ears. The front of her coat opened slightly to reveal a marvelous cleavage. On anyone else the ensemble would have looked tawdry, but on her it was wonderfully exotic.

I already knew the other girl, Rita. I had worked with her several times before. A full-time journalist and a part-time call girl, she was a lovely petite brunette with a warm smile.

Rosanne told us there would be ten of us altogether, but only four of us were her girls. The sheik's man in New York, Garth, had arranged for several madams to supply their best girls. The three of us would be on this flight. The other one, a Caroline, would be on a later flight.

We were met in New York by a fleet of limousine drivers. Garth, the man in charge, was a very young up-and-coming ass-kissing gopher, and this was his first major assignment for the sheik. He did not want anything to ruin it for him. He was extremely upset when he thought Rosanne had sent only three girls. Somehow he assumed I was in charge and asked me where the other girl was. I told Garth she was supposed to arrive on the next flight from L.A., but I made it clear she was not my responsibility.

There were nine of us ladies and five limousines. Rita and I rode in the purple limo. At every stop light people tried to see through the darkened windows, wondering who was inside. Our parade of limos pulled up in front of the famous Helmsley Palace, shortly before 8 P.M. The valets jumped to attention and helped us out of the cars. All our luggage was assembled in the lobby. We were given our room keys and white envelopes with instructions. We were to go to our rooms and await a call from Garth.

Each of us could have our own suite in the new, exclusive tower of the hotel, but Rita and I wanted to share one. We had so much to talk about. We were both writing books, although I don't know when Rita found the time, between her work as a call girl and writing freelance articles for various national magazines.

The tower has its own exclusive elevators, and we were escorted to our suites on the forty-third floor. When the bellboy opened our door, I gasped. I had been working for over a year now and had been exposed to elegant palatial hotels and homes in Beverly Hills. I knew this was an expensive hotel, but I was not at all prepared for the luxury of the room.

On top of the beautiful mahogany desk was an arrangement of two dozen beautiful, flawless crimson roses. Next to it was a wicker basket containing two bottles of Dom Perignon. A note with the flowers read "Welcome to Our World."

Rita and I walked over to the window to enjoy the magnificent view of the city. We looked out past the glittering lights in the dark ribbon that was the East River where a bright full moon was just clearing the horizon. The twinkling stars in the cloudless indigo sky rivaled the sparkling lights below.

When the bellboy left, I put the chain across the door, and Rita and

I ran into the bedroom. It was huge, done in soft rose, pink, and cream, and dominating the room were two of the biggest beds I have ever seen, covered with beautiful matching floral bedspreads.

Next we inspected the bathroom. It had everything, including pink silk bathrobes! The rose-colored marble tub looked like a small swimming pool, and there was a telephone beside it.

The trip had been long and tiring. I was feeling gruesome, so I took a quick bath. After drying my hair I began to unpack. We were both wearing nothing but our underwear and Rita was getting ready to jump in the tub when there was a knock at the door. I thought it must be one of the other girls because I had heard them squealing and running up and down the halls. It sounded like a girls' dorm at college.

I left the chain on the door and opened it a crack. Standing outside was a short bespectacled man; his mouth was wide open, and his gaze was fixed on my cleavage.

He stood there stammering: "Uh, uh." He scratched his head. Although the chain was still across the partially open door, he could clearly see us in our skimpy lingerie.

"Um, girls, I have a present for you from the sheik. I am his personal secretary. Um, uh, here!" He thrust an envelope containing our first day's pay through the door opening, never raising his eyes from the level of my chest.

"Why, thank you," I said politely, taking the envelope out of his hand. Rita was sitting on the bed taking off her panties.

"What's your name, Mr. Personal Secretary?" I asked. Rita was now completely naked as she prepared to take a bath.

"Bob. Um, my name is Bob." His face was bright red, and he coughed as he spoke. He was so obviously uncomfortable, his voice came out barely above a whisper.

"Well now, Bob, I'm Norma Jean and this is Rita. I do hope the sheik will be pleased with us. Do tell him we thank him for his generosity."

He just stood there with his mouth open. "Well, I must be going. I have to inspect, er, visit the other young ladies. By the way, would you please be dressed by nine-thirty and assembled in Garth's room to meet the sheik?"

"Of course, Bob. And thank you for our present!" We giggled as poor Bob limped down the hall to the next room.

Rita took her bath, and I finished unpacking. We were dressed in record time and on our way to our first encounter with the extravagant sheik.

Garth was on the phone with the boss when Rita and I made our entrance. Each girl introduced herself. They were all great looking! Some were tall, some short, some big-busted, others more svelte, providing the sheik with a wonderful variety.

I found a place on the couch next to a well-developed green-eyed blond beauty who had introduced herself as Laurie. She was wearing an exquisite teal blue suede and leather pants outfit. Her long silky blond hair extended past her well-rounded bottom. She said she worked for Madam Alice and was also a model. She flashed me a very friendly smile.

One of the girls appointed herself hostess and offered everyone champagne. I declined and instead took a glass of tonic water. She had just proposed a toast to the generous sheik when Garth came over to me and asked to see me alone. I followed him into the hallway, where he informed me I would have the privilege of being the first to meet, that is to say, became intimate with the sheik. It was an honor. I was the oldest in the group!

Garth escorted me to the two-story penthouse chambers permanently reserved for the sheik on the fifty-first floor of the hotel. He announced me to the sheik, who was upstairs, and then left me alone.

A long spiral staircase in the hall led to the second story. For those who might not want to walk there was also a small bronze-doored elevator, and out of the elevator, right on cue, stepped Sheik Smith.

He was much shorter than I had expected, slightly chubby, and balding. He had big, beautiful Middle Eastern brown eyes, almost camel-like in their size and trimmed with long black lashes, and a thick mustache under a bulbous nose. He was not unattractive but certainly no Valentino. Although he had mastered the command of the American dollar, he had no great command of the English language, at least not with women.

"Shall we go upstairs?" He took my arm and pressed the button for the elevator. Not one to waste much time on foreplay, I gathered.

He followed me into the elevator. We made the short trip in silence. He took my arm and walked me past the staircase and silently pointed to a empty cavernous room that turned out to be a closet. It was easy to see how one could mistake it for a dayroom—it was furnished with a couch, chairs, and table. One entire wall was covered with a smoked-glass mirror.

As I undressed I checked my hair and makeup in the mirror and admired my newly acquired allover tan. I had recently discovered tanning salons.

Very self-consciously I entered the bedroom. The sheik had changed from his western-style suit to a more comfortable flowing jeweled Arabic robe. I could smell his very expensive cologne from the doorway.

"What is your name again?" He walked around the room lighting incense and candles, as though we were about to engage in some sort of sacred ancient ritual.

"Norma Jean."

"Nornnan Gee?"

"No. Norma Jean."

"Well, Normaa Jeean, can I offer you some liquor, cocaine . . ."

I hesitated to answer. I was afraid of offending him by refusing his hospitality.

". . . or something else?"

I smiled but declined politely.

Standing just inside the doorway, I was trying to look as seductive as possible. The sheik finished his ritual, walked over to me, and began stroking my hair. Then he started kissing me in a very slow, sensual way, and I was beginning to think this might be a lot of fun.

I followed him over to the enormously oversized bed, covered by an exquisite chinchilla fur spread. He put his arms around my naked body and slowly and deliberately lowered me to the bed.

He placed his very hairy chubby body on top of mine. Moving his hand gently down my breasts, across my stomach, he finally reached my vagina, into which he stuck a short, pudgy little finger. Before I was sufficiently lubricated, he stuck his little penis inside me. Stroke one, two, three, it was all over! With nary a groan, moan, or sigh, he achieved orgasm.

Still on top of me, he casually looked down and asked, in his cultured accent, "So, you are from Los Angeles?"

It was all I could do to refrain from laughing. This man, this Arab billionaire, was paying me a small fortune to enjoy my company, and this was to be the extent of our conversation? Without further small talk, I got dressed and joined him downstairs.

While we were in the bedroom the other young ladies were assembled in his penthouse living room. Some of them were admiring the original art adorning the walls between the enormous windows overlooking the glittering city below. The others were just casually talking among themselves. Ashley, the beautiful black girl, was in her room with a headache. She never did get to meet the sheik. Garth, anxiously pacing the floor, stopped and watched the sheik for an indication of his mood.

The sheik smiled benevolently and introduced himself to each of the girls, asked their names, and gallantly kissed their hands. After the introductions he looked around the room at all the eager faces and said, "I am so glad you have been able to join us. I hope you enjoy your stay with us, and if there is anything you want or need, anything at all, just ask Garth or my secretary, Bob."

It was the last time I ever saw our host, although the next morning several of the other ladies had the opportunity to collectively entertain him.

As he left the room I looked over at Garth's relieved face. Everything had gone well—flunky gopher had passed his first test.

Still in the sheik's suite, we began ordering all kinds of delicacies with delightful zest from the fantastic menu. We ordered enough food, caviar, and champagne for fifty people, even though there were only nine of us, including Garth. Caroline had still not arrived from Los Angeles.

Those poor room-service waiters! For the next six hours they ran back and forth, up and down, every time one of us thought of a new delicacy to try. Then, of course, we had to have dessert. And after that, more champagne. Even I, who seldom indulge in alcohol, was so impressed with the endless flow of Dom Perignon that I broke down and had a glass.

It was getting late, and we were feeling no pain. Garth had passed out behind the couch. Maggie, the tall, dark Mexican girl, laughingly suggested it might be fun to tip our hardworking waiters with something more than money. By this time we were feeling so good and so horny, it sounded like a great idea. We began stripping and threw our clothes all over the room.

When the four waiters returned with more champagne, we were all waiting for them behind the door. With fast fingers we locked the door behind them. We paired up, and each pair grabbed one of the blushing waiters and began to undress him. The waiters were only slightly reluctant.

Laurie and I picked a cute blond, blue-eyed hunk named Paul. We practically ripped off his clothes. Underneath his uniform he had a lovely golden-haired chest and tanned, rippling muscles. Laurie took hold of one firm bun and I took the other, and we seductively walked him upstairs away from the others. We found a quiet space on top of the stairs to attack our willing victim.

He was so excited by this unexpected gratuity that he didn't last much longer than the sheik, but he was certainly more vocal about his pleasure. The other waiters apparently hadn't lasted very long, either, because they were all getting dressed when we returned.

Garth was still passed out, and since I seemed to be the one in charge, the head waiter, no pun intended, asked me to sign the bill. I obliged gladly. I put down a very sizable tip as well. I'm sure we were remembered long after the cash was spent.

After our grateful waiters left, we gathered again in the living room, sitting around in various states of undress. I was on the couch next to Laurie. It was obvious she was flirting with me.

She had moved much closer to me and then was caressing the insides of my thighs. In an altered state of mind it was very stimulating.

She giggled and whispered, "Come upstairs with me. I have to pee."

"Okay," I moaned hoarsely as she pulled me up the stairs behind her.

In one of the bedrooms Laurie found a portable radio and turned it on. "Norma Jean, you wanna dance with me?"

"Well, um," I stammered. "I don't dance very well because of my bad back."

Laurie grabbed my arm. "Please don't go yet, Norma Jean," she urged. "Let's sit up here and watch the others get crazy." Innocently, she put her arms around my waist and leaned her head on my shoulder.

Maggie appeared at the top of the stairs. "Garth, telephone. It's that girl, Caroline. She's at the airport."

Poor Caroline. Not only had Rosanne given her the wrong flight information, but she had told her the wrong hotel. Caroline had been at the airport for hours, calling the other hotel, and of course no one there knew of our existence. Finally she was able to reach Rosanne in Los Angeles. Rosanne was free-basing cocaine and was out of it, but she managed to tell Caroline where we were.

Caroline had no money to take a cab to the hotel, and she wondered if I could find her someone to pick her up. I called the concierge and explained that one of the young ladies in the sheik's party was stranded at the airport. Could they please send a limousine to fetch her. When I spoke to her again, I made her promise to call me the moment she arrived at the hotel.

Meanwhile, Garth whistled to get the girls' attention.

"Okay, everybody, listen up. You can do anything you want tomorrow during the day, but I expect you to be back here by five o'clock. All of you may not have to join the sheik for dinner, but he wants you to be here so he can pick his companions. You got that? Any questions?"

Shortly after Rita and I returned to our suite, the phone rang. Caroline, our long-lost sister, had finally arrived; it was 3:30 in the morning.

With everyone safely accounted for, I thought it was time to go to bed. No more dancing with Laurie.

Before I closed my eyes I called my boyfriend in L.A. to say good night. I just had to share this wonderful, crazy day with him.

After four hours' sleep I woke with the sun in my face. I tossed restlessly for another hour and then decided to stop fighting it. I was in New York, it was a beautiful, warm, spring day, and I had money to spend. I was going to enjoy myself!

I threw my pillow at Rita. "Hey, wake up, sleepy head." I hit my target under the cover, and she began to stir. I showed her the clock. It was 8:45. "Rita, if we're going to see any of New York, go shopping, and be back here by five o'clock, we have to start now!"

Rita was dressed and out of the suite before I was. It took more time to set my long hair.

I made my way through the lobby. In the daylight the hotel was even grander than at night. I walked past all the little shops and checked out the artwork on the walls. The concierge greeted me warmly. Exiting through the glass doors into the bright, crisp New York morning, I found my way to the quiet side street where the limos and cabs parked.

Flashing a brilliant smile at the doorman, I asked, "Are there limos available?"

The doorman smiled back and shook his head. "Not at the moment, miss, but there will be soon if you want to wait."

I didn't, so he hailed a taxi for me. I felt cash rich that day and didn't care if I had to spend a little money.

The cabbie was a woman, as tough and as hard as they come. I asked her to take me to the Empire State Building, where I had worked so many years ago, before I went out to California to visit my aunt. In a gruff voice she said, "Right!" Off we went with a jerk and a squeal, as only New York cabbies can. The fare was under three bucks; I gave her a ten and told her to keep the change. She looked as me as though I was crazy. Her voice was much softer when she said thanks.

Outside the landmark building I noticed that not much had changed since my teenage years. Only the people walking by seemed more dazed and perhaps a bit shabbier than I remembered. The limousines were still lined up out front, awaiting their important passengers. Now I knew what it was like to ride in one!

I entered the building through the same door and with the same sense of excitement I had a million times before—years ago when I was young

and innocent. I was still a virgin when I worked there. I never could have
conceived of such a life for my future—not in my wildest dreams! Especially not when I used to spend hours in my room reading Christian
novelettes, dreaming of one day becoming a missionary!

One hot, muggy Saturday afternoon in 1963, at the beginning of summer
vacation, I lay reading on the lumpy bed in my very own bedroom, which
I acquired as the oldest girl when the family moved into the new house on
Moffatt Avenue. A woman from a nearby church called, wanting to know
if my mother had any female children in their teens who would be interested in working for two weeks at a Bible camp in Pennsylvania about
thirty-five miles away. Deer Trail Ranch, it was called, and its main
feature, besides being a Bible camp for young teens, was horseback
riding.

It was the answer to my prayers. I had just turned thirteen. Vacation
had barely begun, and already I was bored. Mother agreed to let me go,
and camp became a yearly summer ritual.

Going to summer camp every year was the only relief I had from the
pressures of my large family and the horrors of being looked down upon
by my peers. I escaped the cruelty of the upper-middle-class kids at
school by dropping out of the accelerated classes, but there was no
escaping the cruelty of the kids at church.

It didn't help me one bit to know I was a direct descendant of John
Howland of the Mayflower or of the Reverend Charles Chauncey, who
was the president of Harvard from 1654 to 1672. My uncle Edwin Eaton
was a historical buff who had painstakingly traced our family on the
Chauncey side all the way back to King Henry I of France, and back
beyond that to the emperor Charlemagne. On my maternal grandfather's
side we descended from the noble and once powerful Lyon and Porter
families. The family tree abounded with reverends and noblemen. These
things were unimportant to my mother then, and because of that I gained
no consolation from knowing my heritage. The kids at church thought I
was a poor little nobody, so I was basically a poor little nobody.

But no one at camp had the slightest hint I had a large, very poor
family, so I was able to develop a more outgoing personality. Most of the
kids accepted me—chubby, tattered clothes, and all.

The two weeks I had been scheduled to work as kitchen help turned
into an entire summer. I made myself indispensable to the people who ran
the camp because I did the washing and ironing, set the tables, washed

the dishes, made the coffee, tea, and Kool-Aid, and worked the snack bar after the evening service.

I also managed to fall off a horse three times, step on a razor and cut my foot open, fall out of the top bunk in my sleep and fracture my skull, and get my hand stuck in the washing machine wringer, breaking several small bones in my hand. Then I fell off the swing and fractured my skull again. When we went to the sister camp at a nearby lake, I nearly drowned attempting to learn to swim. I got poison ivy, was bitten by a snake, and developed a severe allergic reaction to a spider bite.

In all, the doctor was called to the camp no less than ten times on my behalf, and yet I was allowed to stay through the summer and even allowed to return the next two summers.

These summer escapes introduced me to elements in life I had never known existed. Many of the other kids who went to the camp, both as workers and as guests, were Puerto Ricans from New York City. I had never met anyone like them, and I became infatuated with the entire Puerto Rican population. I fell in love with Raul Ayala.

I felt I had been called by God to become a missionary, and my newfound love of Puerto Ricans made it clear my mission field was Puerto Rico. I imagined myself growing up, marrying Raul, and going off to the jungles of Puerto Rico to save all the lost heathens.

Raul was the object of my first girlhood crush. I tried to behave demurely, as befitted a young girl with a calling. I begged the Lord to forgive my sinful, wicked thoughts in which I vividly imagined Raul's strong arms around me and his hands doing wonderful things to my body. Every year I flirted with him, but my advances were met with disdain. He fell in love with some thin, blond-haired, blue-eyed girl named Celeste who wore contact lenses and had fashionable clothes.

I never captured Raul's heart, though my crush on him lasted for years. The first summer I went to camp, his parents and sister, Lou, came to visit him, and we became good friends. Years later it was Lou who convinced me to go to California.

When I turned sixteen, I was qualified to work at the religious resort for adults, Highland Lake Bible Conference, in Highland Lake, New York. That summer I managed to find myself a boyfriend. To me, Mike Pastronos was a Greek god. Tall, dark-haired, tanned, and muscled, he fit my ideal male image. He also wanted to be a missionary.

For whatever reason, this Adonis was actually attracted to me. I couldn't believe my good fortune. I vowed if I had the opportunity I would let him kiss me.

One afternoon we rowed across the lake and found a quiet, secluded inlet where we sat necking for hours. Soon passion overcame us. Mike convinced me we should find a cozy place to consummate our desires. We tied up the boat and walked through the woods. As we searched for a private spot, I stepped on a wasp, and it stung the bottom of my bare foot. Within minutes my foot was swollen to twice its size, and poor Mike had to row me back to camp as fast as he could while I chastised myself. I knew God had punished me just for thinking about committing a sin.

The last summer I worked at the camp, a missionary from South America was the guest speaker for a whole week. He became my hero and my mentor. I told him my goal was to become a missionary, too. Patiently, he listened and gave me fatherly advice. One afternoon he suggested taking a boat ride so we could spend several hours together without being interrupted.

We rowed to the same secluded spot Mike and I had found, and suddenly his whole personality changed. His breathing became labored, his voice grew strained, his words were slurred. His hands were sliding up the inside of my thighs as he leaned over and tried to kiss me.

"Oh, Norma, honey! It's so lonely in the mission field. My wife is almost never with me. I really need someone to help me get through the terrible loneliness! Come on, honey. Let me put the word of God in you. I know you want it, baby." He unzipped his fly.

"Reverend Farland! What's the matter with you? What are you saying?" I thought maybe he was trying to test me to see if I believed strongly enough to be a missionary.

"Oh, baby, God expects men in my field to be tempted by desires of the flesh. He put women like you on earth to take care of men like me. You are a woman of God. I am a man of God." He kept trying to force one hand further between my thighs while the other was groping my breast. "Trust me. It's okay if I use your body to get rid of my passions so I can carry on God's work."

I pleaded with him to stop it and to take me back to camp. He finally realized the only way he was going to get into my pants was to rape me, so he gave up. Angrily, he rowed us back to the other side of the lake in silence.

When we got back to camp, he hung his head apologetically and tried to offer an explanation. He said he had been under a terrible strain for such a long time. He asked me not to mention what he had done to anyone. He begged me to forgive him.

When I returned home from summer camp, it was time to get back to the reality of life and return to school. Since I had met the Puerto Rican kids at camp, I became infatuated with all things Spanish. In my first year of high school I transferred to Binghamton Central High, even though it was on the other side of town, just so I could take Spanish.

It was a long walk every day in the rain, snow, and sleet of the fall and winter months, but it was worth it. It was thrilling to attend the same school as Rod Serling of "Twilight Zone." His former drama teacher, Helen Foley, was also mine. I adored her because she made the written word come alive. Her class was one of the few happy moments of my high school days.

Since dropping out of the accelerated classes, I studied so little in high school I barely graduated in 1969. Despite my poor academic record I had been accepted at Philadelphia College of the Bible. I still wanted to become a missionary, but I was beginning to question the religious dogma.

I decided to postpone going to college for a year until I resolved my doubts. My friend Valentina had been accepted at King's College in Briarcliff Manor, New York. Until classes started in the fall she was spending the summer with her grandparents who lived in the Bronx. She invited me to go with her, and I gladly accepted. Her Russian grandparents, who spoke very little English, graciously opened their home to me. It was the first summer since becoming a teenager that I didn't spend at Bible camp.

My second week in New York, I landed a job as a file clerk at Robert Reis and Company, a small manufacturer of men's underwear whose offices were on the seventy-second floor of the Empire State Building. The pay was low, but it offered on-the-job training and good benefits. Working in a world-famous building was very exciting for a small-town girl, and I enjoyed watching the gawking tourists who visited *my* building.

The summer flew by very quickly. Having a job and being self-sufficient improved my self-image, and I began losing weight. By fall I had gone from a size sixteen to a more manageable but still chubby size twelve. As I continued to lose weight, I began to feel even better about myself, and it became a positive cycle for increasing my self-esteem.

In the fall Val went off to college, and I remained with her grandparents. They invited me to rent the spare bedroom. Even though they didn't understand me, we got along fine.

Like millions of New Yorkers, I commuted to my job by subway. At the same time every morning I ran down the steps of the old house, up

Dyre Avenue, past the delicatessen where I sometimes bought my lunch, and down the wide stone steps of the East Gunhill Road station to catch the express train to Manhattan.

The first snow had fallen and the strains of Christmas music were in the air when I first noticed a handsome young man standing near the area of the platform where I usually boarded the train. Without trying to appear too eager, I did my best to make him notice me. It took him two weeks to observe my not-so-subtle flirtations and finally approach me. His name was Ritchie. We talked all the way into the city. After a few more mornings of polite conversation, he invited me to a movie.

I was eighteen years old and had never been to a movie. All my life, my mother had warned me against going to the movies. I vividly remember a religious tract she gave me when I was eight or nine years old. Its title was "I Got Pregnant in Technicolor," and it claimed that women who went to the movies got pregnant.

I went to the movies and began the quick descent on the path of evil. More than anything else the memory of that tract and its outrageously erroneous information led me to question everything else I had been taught.

Even though Ritchie and I never dated beyond that movie, and we certainly never had an intimate relationship, he provided me with the first opportunity to test my theories about right and wrong. I went to the movies and did not get pregnant!

As I became more proficient at work, it become more difficult to stay focused. I liked my coworkers even though they teased me about being shy and having strange notions about religion and the world. But being fond of my coworkers wasn't enough to keep me from deserting my post.

My friend Lou from summer camp had gone to California for a religious retreat. When she returned to New York, she called me one bitterly cold day in early January 1970 and asked me to meet her for lunch. We met in Woolworth's cafeteria on 34th Street. She told me about the new life she and the other Puerto Rican kids had found in California, in some sort of church. I wasn't particularly interested until she told me the temperature was seventy degrees the day she left California. So when I saw the opportunity to take a break from my job and go to California for a vacation, I jumped. Not literally, of course, as many people did from the Empire State Building . . .

*   *   *

I looked at my watch and realized I had spent enough time lingering in the past. I had to get back to the hotel and get ready for dinner with the sheik.

The forty-third floor was very quiet when I arrived. No one else had returned. I filled the tub and poured in bubble bath. Rita would be back any moment, so I left the door unlocked. I turned on the radio, undressed, and then, leaving the bathroom door open so I could hear the music, lowered my weary body into a tubful of velvety pink suds. There was a knock at the door. "Who is it?" I yelled. When Laurie answered, I yelled for her to come in.

She came into the suite and looked around. "Where are you?"

"In the bathroom."

She opened the bathroom door and saw me in the tub. "Oh, I'm sorry. I didn't know you were taking a bath. I'll come back later."

"No, you don't have to go. I was just getting out anyway." As I got out of the tub I reached for the plush pink bathrobe hanging on the door.

"Oh, here, Norma Jean. Let me help you dry off." Laurie quickly grabbed a towel and started drying my back before I could slip on the robe.

She looked at my face in the mirror. "Gee, you have a beautiful body. Such nice, firm, beautiful breasts."

I blushed. "Thank you, Laurie."

"And your skin is so soft." She gently rubbed her hand across my back. She dropped the towel and began kissing my shoulders. I moaned. I hoped to God Rita wouldn't show up right now. Laurie's arms came around me, and her hands softly cupped my breasts. Her fingers caressed my nipples.

"You smell so nice." She was gently biting my ear. I just stood there, closed my eyes, and traced the back of her hand with my fingers.

"I want to touch you all over," she whispered. Laurie sensed I was not unwilling for her to continue with her advances. She turned me around and kissed my mouth.

I dropped the robe and put my arms around her. We were deeply engrossed in each other—hugging, kissing, caressing—as she pulled me into the bedroom. I sat down on the bed while she seductively unbuttoned her pale lavender silk blouse, revealing two large beautiful mounds of pink skin, barely contained by her expensive Dior satin bra.

She slid out of her matching Dior slip and stood before me, her fingers caressing her own mound underneath her French-cut panties. Slowly she removed her stockings, then her bra and panties, exposing a flawless female form with a silky thatch of blond curly hair, which glistened ever so slightly in the late afternoon sunlight.

She licked her lips as she knelt down beside me. She gently pulled my hesitant legs apart and buried her beautiful blond head between my thighs. Her warm wet mouth teased the insides of my legs, and she ran her long nails across my stomach, reached up, and pinched my nipples ever so slightly.

She moved up beside me and began to suck on my breasts. Her mouth was so wet, her tongue so quick, I lay there writhing with pleasure, not knowing which way to turn. She slid her hand down between my thighs and gently probed me with two fingers. With her thumb she caressed me, making me nearly beside myself with desire. Sensing I was about to climax, she put her sweet mouth on my swollen clitoris, gently coaxing out the most wonderful, exquisite orgasm.

I pulled her head, screaming with pleasure. I wouldn't let her move her mouth away from me. I was going to explode again. My body gyrated with her mouth. Wave after wave of orgasm passed through my body. I was in ecstasy.

As I came down, she slowly moved up my body, her tongue flitting softly over my belly, the outsides of my breasts, up my neck, and back to my mouth. She held me in her arms and stroked my hair. "You're so beautiful. I love making love to you." I lay in her arms, purring like a kitten.

Then I put my arm around her tiny waist. I was just beginning to explore my sexual attraction to other women. It was awfully nice to feel the softness of another female, and this was very much a soft, feminine woman.

I needed to taste her sweetness. I began to explore her beautiful body with my fingers, as she had done with mine. She began to sigh and wiggle. I certainly hoped I was doing it right. I did unto her as she had done unto me, and she seemed to be enjoying herself.

She grabbed my hair and called my name over and over. She arched her back and moaned with pleasure, her hips undulating to the rhythm of my tongue. At last she cried out as she gave in to the passion of the moment, coming in my mouth with all the fluid they say women don't have. Forcefully, she moved my mouth away before I could try to bring her to a peak again. She pulled me up beside her, hugging and kissing me. We snuggled and giggled and petted each other like two innocent children who knew no shame in enjoying their own bodies.

At last we turned on our sides, saw the clock, and realized how late it was. Reluctantly we got dressed, kissed each other, and she went down the hall to her room. In half an hour we expected to be summoned for dinner with the sheik. Smiling blissfully, I put on my makeup.

Assembling in Garth's room at five o'clock, we were all anxious to share our day's experiences. But before we had a chance, Garth told us which lucky young ladies were the sheik's evening entertainment. Everyone else was dismissed.

Since I was not on the sheik's menu that evening, I planned to go out on the town with my friend Sam. I invited the other girls to join us. Sam was practically panting when I told him eight of us would accompany him. We all decided to eat in the hotel restaurant before going on an all-night revelry. I made reservations for nine at eight.

Sam had already arrived at the restaurant and was flirting with all the girls when Rita and I joined them. Laurie was sitting on his left, and I seated myself on his right.

When it started out, it was a perfect evening. Dinner was fabulous, and the girls really soaked up the champagne again. Remembering my slight hangover that morning, I declined.

After everyone had ordered dinner, Garth appeared. There just wasn't room at our table for him, so he had to sit at a table by himself. He looked unhappy.

During dinner Garth came over to the table several times and rudely informed me that the sheik would not pay for my friend's dinner. I told him my friend had asked for a separate check at the beginning of the meal. Garth sulked back to his table. To our relief he soon finished eating and left.

At the end of the meal the hostess came over and asked which one of us was Norma Jean. When I indicated I was, she whispered in my ear, "There is a woman downstairs named Rosanne, and she is demanding to speak to you. We did not let her in because she appears to be influenced by a mind-altering substance."

I dropped my napkin on the floor. What in the world was Rosanne doing here? I looked at the hostess. "What do you want me to do?"

"Please follow me. You can use the phone over here to call the lobby." She escorted me to a house phone.

Following her past several other tables I noticed men and women gaping unabashedly at our little harem. Picking up the phone, I was connected with the lobby. The manager at the front desk courteously called to Rosanne. She was behaving most unladylike.

"Norma Jean, what on earth do you think you are doing having a man join you girls for dinner? The sheik is going to be really pissed off if he finds out!''

Now I knew where Garth had gone. I started to answer. ''Rosanne, nobody told us we couldn't—''

She cut me off. ''You should have known better. Arabs are very jealous. You bitch, you are going to spoil this whole thing for me. And I heard one of the girls didn't even go up to meet the sheik—she was in her room with a headache. What do you mean by letting her get away with that? What do you think you ladies are getting paid for anyway?''

I was mad. I was not getting paid to be the group leader. I had to pay Rosanne the full cut for this adventure. I don't know what made her think I was going to take charge for her . . . for free!

''Look, Rosanne, I am not their boss, you are. It's not my job to look after anyone here. And Garth knew full well we were all going out with my friend Sam tonight. I asked his permission this morning. He's just pissed because Laurie was flirting with Sam and wouldn't pay him any attention.''

Rosanne's voice raised several decibels. In the background I could hear the manager asking her to keep it down or he would throw her out. I hung up the phone.

I calmly made my way back to the table and explained to my friend he would have to leave, to save us from any more trouble. He understood completely and graciously bid us all good night.

As I signed for the dinner check I told the others, ''I don't know what the rest of you guys are going to do this evening, but I'm going back to my room. And oh, by the way, Rosanne is here in New York, and she's on the warpath.'' She had certainly spoiled the evening for me.

The manager called my room and told me Rosanne was in such an antagonistic, apparently drug-induced state, they could not let her stay in the hotel. She had noisily huffed out of the lobby and registered at a nearby hotel. She began to hound me every five minutes by phone.

''I want everybody to bring me the money they owe me right now!'' she screeched in my ear.

''Rosanne, you still owe me seven hundred dollars from those credit card calls I took two weeks ago. I don't owe you anything,'' I replied stubbornly.

''Well, I don't care how much I owe you. You get your goddamn ass over here and pay me—now! You'll get your money when the credit clears the bank!''

Furious, I hung up on her again.

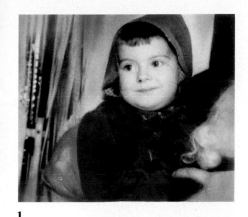

Here I am at one year old, the fourth child of a very religious and proper family in Binghamton, New York.

1

My high school yearbook picture, taken before I started losing weight and discovered contact lenses.

2

3

A lineup for inspection at the Hollywood Division station of the L.A.P.D.—all spit and polish on the surface, with a lot of hanky-panky, both off duty and on.

4

5

I was nicknamed ''The Bionic Arm'' for writing more tickets than anyone else in my division. I couldn't believe that anyone would knowingly park illegally—I certainly had a lot to learn!

An older but wiser me in the 1978–79 yearbook for the Rampart Division of the L.A.P.D.

I much preferred my new
"uniform"—an elegant
Adolfo—to my drab navy cop
clothes. Here, I am dressed to
attend a party with a well-heeled
client.

When news got around that I was
writing a book about the force, I
was set up by the L.A.P.D. and
busted for "pandering."
According to the Assistant
District Attorney Richard Weber,
who prosecuted my case, "there
is no distinction between Norma
Jean's crime and that of an
armed robber. . . ."

8

My "crime" was "soliciting Penny Isgro to lead a life of prostitution," although the Los Angeles District attorney candidly admitted, "not too many customers would go for a girl of her description (which sounded like your typical linebacker)."

9

Guilty as charged. "I want you to have a taste of prison," said Judge Aurolio Munoz, who presided over my trial.

10

Victor, my friend and lover, became my husband the night before I was sent to the California Institute for Women at Frontera. Meanwhile, the L.A.P.D. had confiscated my manuscript.

11

Out of prison on probation in 1986, I tossed my hat—and almost everything else I was wearing—into the political arena, campaigning for lieutenant governor of California.

Election night. I garnered over 100,000 votes—not bad for my first time out. Someday, I may just win.

For the first time in twenty years, my entire family—Mom and all fourteen kids—was reunited in Binghamton, after my father's funeral. Some of my brothers and sisters still prefer to remain anonymous, even when I dress conservatively.

14

"Pandering is a worse crime than rape or robbery," proclaimed prosecutor Harry Sondheim, who filed an appeal of my probation. Of course, the L.A.P.D. knew I had begun working on my book again.

15

Back in the California Institute for Women for eighteen months, some of which was spent in solitary confinement.

16

"Free Norma Jean!"
Supporters protesting
my latest imprisonment.

Free at last. I was finally able to
finish my book and work for the
rights of prostitutes everywhere.

17

She called me back screaming and cursing. I hung up again. The phone rang incessantly, but I refused to answer it. Rosanne's behavior really made me angry. While I tried to calm down, Rita returned to the room, and Caroline was with her.

Caroline seemed very upset. She sat down on my bed and cursed the sheik and Rosanne. "Damn it all, Norma Jean! Do you know what that cunt Rosanne has done?" Caroline started crying. "Because I didn't get here with the rest of you last night, Garth says I'm not going to get paid at all. He says I should be happy I have a place to stay."

Rita continued the story. "Rosanne forgot to tell Caroline about the change in flight plans, so Caroline missed our flight. Rosanne told Garth it was Caroline's fault, and even though Caroline isn't getting paid, Rosanne still wants her cut."

Well, if Rosanne thought I was supposed to be in charge, then I would just take charge. I called a meeting. Everyone else had returned to their rooms after dinner. Rita and Caroline went down the hall and rounded everybody up. When they were all assembled, I said, "I don't know about you, but I've had about all I can take from Garth. Caroline hasn't been paid, and I don't think it's fair. Garth is too young to be handling this kind of assignment. The rest of you can do whatever you like, but I'm leaving."

The decision to leave was unanimous. I phoned Garth with the news. He panicked. "You can't go! The sheik is expecting you to stay until Monday. What will I tell him?"

"Tell him he doesn't own me, and I'll have dinner with anyone I like."

Garth sounded sheepish. "Oh, I just told Rosanne that because I was mad. He really doesn't mind. Please don't go. Can we talk about this?"

"There is nothing to talk about!" I hung up. It seemed as if I was always hanging up on people. A few minutes later a contrite Garth appeared at the door. He seemed very eager to make it up to us and tried to bribe us with a few extra goodies. I told him Caroline hadn't been paid at all, and as far as I was concerned, until she got paid his promises were nothing but hot air.

This game went on until three in the morning. Rosanne kept trying to reach us, but no one would speak to her except Garth, and he couldn't convince any of us to stay.

Caroline never got paid. We had our suspicions that Garth pocketed her share of the money. Caroline got even. While Garth was busy trying to convince us to stay, she called room service and ordered thirty bottles of Dom Perignon and several bottles of Finlandia Vodka. She uncorked all the champagne and managed to drink a great quantity of the vodka as well. All night long she called room service, ordering thousands of dollars' worth of caviar and other delicacies from the twenty-four-hour kitchen. By morning she was a mess and her room was a disaster, but she was definitely in better spirits than she had been the night before.

In the morning I made arrangements for a flight to Binghamton for me, and I booked Rita and Caroline on the flight back to L.A. The three of us decided to take the same limo to the airport because our flights left at about the same time.

As we left the stately Helmsley Palace a little less stately than when we had arrived, I signed very generous tips for everyone who had waited on us during our stay. Rita, Caroline, and I gave the delighted bellboys a kiss. The stiff-lipped doorman smiled as the three of us left in the limo.

Caroline shared the bottle of Finlandia with the limo driver, and both were completely polluted by the time we arrived at the airport. Rita promised she would look after Caroline on their flight to L.A. At the terminal we hugged each other good-bye and promised to remain in touch. We did, and years later we are still friends.

12. TRUTH AND CONSEQUENCES

Once upon a piglet, in old upstate New York,
Was born upon a May day, a little pound of pork.
Her hair was red, her eyes were green; her momma said,
she sure looks mean.
Mean she wasn't, but 'twas true, into a chop of pork she grew.

With a host of other siblings, piglet was born and raised.
That they made it thru their childhood left everyone amazed!
One bathroom in a house too small for each and every child
It is a wonder that grown up they didn't all run wild.

Now, AS I GAZED, out the window of the tiny commuter plane to Binghamton that bounced up and down in the wind, I thought about what I would tell my family about my career change. When I began working I knew I had to tell them the truth. I didn't want them to discover it from friends or neighbors who might see me on a TV show.

When I first started working as a prostitute, I didn't know there were other women, such as Margo St. James, the founder of C.O.Y.O.T.E. (Call Off Your Old Tired Ethics), who were fighting for our rights. Eventually I discovered them, but I had already realized that sex laws violated a woman's right to choose. I had planned to become a public spokesperson for decriminalization of prostitution and become outspoken against police corruption. Since my bogus arrest for "keeping a disorderly house," I had already been approached by some members of the media for interviews.

If I were arrested for prostitution, I did not want the cops to have anything to hold over my head. Often when a woman is arrested, the police threaten to tell her family if she gives them a difficult time. This is usually always effective. It would not be used against me—I would tell them myself.

My father hadn't spoken to me for years, so what he thought wasn't important to me. My brothers and sisters might not understand or approve my decision, but knowing them, they would probably think it wasn't any of their business. And that's exactly how they felt. Mom was quite another matter. I doubted she would be pleased to hear that not only did I look like a whore, but that I had become one.

When the taxi pulled up in front of the familiar shabby old green house on Moffatt Avenue, a tear rolled down my cheek. It was not a tear of shame, remorse, or regret but one of sorrow that my mother might be hurt by what I had to tell her. If it had been possible, I would have spared her this pain.

I hadn't told Mom I was coming home. When she saw the taxi pull up, she came running out to greet me and threw her arms around me in a tight hug. "Oh, it's so good to see you! What are you doing home, honey? How long are you staying?" Mom always asked a million questions at once.

"Only until Monday. I had to go to New York City for a couple of days, so I thought I'd come to see you."

"Well, I'm glad you're home, and for Easter, too! I'm cooking a ham for dinner tomorrow, your favorite!"

I kept my arm around her and looked at her with tears in my eyes. "Mom, there is something very important I have to tell you when you get some time. Not now, though."

Her eyes grew wide for a minute, as though saying, "I think I already know. Please don't verify what I suspect."

She smiled and said, "Sure, honey. We can talk tomorrow sometime, after dinner."

My baby brother Joe put the luggage in the guest room, which used to be my bedroom. While I unpacked she chatted away as she sat on my lumpy old bed with torn sheets.

"Ma, do you need anything at the store? I have to get a few things."

"Can I go to the store with you? I have to get Joe some sandwich meat for his lunches."

We trudged to the Binghamton Plaza several blocks away. Even though it was spring, heaps of ugly leftover black snow were still in the parking lot.

As we walked through the aisles, I told her to get anything and everything she wanted, and I would pay for it. I loaded the basket with goodies she could never have afforded to buy for herself. She was like a kid in a candy store. It made me feel good to be able to buy things for her and to see her so happy.

Mom's eyes grew wide when she saw the hundred-dollar bill I pulled out to pay for the groceries, but she remained silent. Since we had walked to the store, I decided to splurge and take a taxi home so we didn't have to carry all those groceries.

The delicious aroma of ham filled the house when I woke the next morning. Mom was at church until one o'clock. She left me a note asking me to check on the ham and put the peeled potatoes on to cook at noon. After I took care of the potatoes and ham, I set the timer for an hour and went into the unbearably quiet living room. Silence seemed strange in the house where so many of us had grown up.

Mom's comfy reclining rocking chair in the corner was filled with loose photographs, spilling out of her album onto the floor. I picked them up, put them all on the couch, and sat down in the rocker. I sighed. How many times had I sat in this chair on Mom's lap when she rocked away the troubles of my world.

Before I knew it, with the gentle rocking motion of Mom's chair, the fragrant smell of cloves and ham filling the air, and the warmth of the spring sunshine on my face, I became very relaxed and began to drift.

Ringggg . . . rattle . . . rattle . . . I pulled the pillow up over my ears. The darn alarm clock on Daddy's dresser always went off at 6:30 on Sunday mornings. Even from the back bedroom of the old two-story Victorian house on Chenango Street I could hear it—ringggg . . . ringgg—until my mother woke up and finally shut it off. I don't know how my father ever slept through it, but he always did.

The coal-burning stove outside the bedroom I shared with my sisters in 1960 crackled and snapped as Mom raked the coals and tried to light the burners. The smell of freshly brewed coffee and burning coals soon filled the morning air. Mom knocked at the bedroom door.

"Okay, girls. It's time to get up and get dressed for Sunday School. Who's going to be first in the bathroom? Norma Jean, come on, get up. Ruth, Grace, get a move on."

Lucky us. The girls were always the first to be awakened. The boys got to sleep an extra half hour while we girls brushed our teeth and scrubbed our faces. Everyone already had the weekly bath on Saturday, so on Sunday morning the traffic in and out of the bathroom was swift and steady.

Breakfast around the big oak dining room table was loud and quick.

"Pass the toast," my brother Dave yelled.

"What do you say first?" Daddy picked up the platter of crisp, burnt toast and held it up in the air, well out of reach of our little grasping hands.

"I don't know. Pass *me* the toast?"

Laughter around the table.

"Say please! Where's your manners?"

"I ain't got any!"

"David! Where's your grammar?"

In chorus the rest of us yelled, "She's upstairs!" Mom had already passed on to us her warped sense of humor. Paronomasia is the inherited compulsion to tell very bad puns.

Mom snapped, "Douglas, put that toast down. You're already had two pieces. Let somebody else have another slice!"

"But I'm still hungry."

"Ma, why can't we have scrambled eggs on Easter Sunday?"

"We had them last week. Philip, go blow your nose. Norma Jean, I thought I told you not to wear that dress until I mend it. Go change it right now. Quick!"

"Oh, Mom!" I procrastinated long enough for her to forget her command.

"Mother, when are we going to have bacon again?"

"When the cows come home," Dad answered for her.

"Oh, Daddy, bacon doesn't come from cows!"

"Yeah, well, money doesn't grow on trees. Bacon is expensive. Besides, since it's Easter we're having ham for dinner."

"Oh, boy!" A collective yell of joy around the dining room table. Ham was everyone's favorite.

"Okay, girls, it's your turn to clear the table. The boys wash the dishes. Come on, hurry up. It's almost time for Sunday School."

Loud groans from both groups as another Sunday breakfast concluded.

After breakfast I stood on tiptoes to reach the mirror in the bathroom as I finished getting dressed for church. I was wearing a secondhand dress bought by my mother for seventy-five cents at the Salvation Army thrift store. It was torn on the side and Mom said she was going to fix it, but she never found the time.

I fastened a large safety pin over the worst part of the tear. It wasn't even close to the dainty flowered dress I had wanted, but what little money my father made as a factory worker had to be spent on diapers for the new baby. Every year there was a new baby, so I never got a new dress for Easter. Ultimately there were fourteen of us kids.

I had found some discarded bright orange lipstick on the sidewalk near the K mart in the shopping center that was on my way to school. In defiance of my mother's strict rules regarding makeup, I stood there that Sunday morning applying the "devil's tools" to my face. I knew it was a horrible color and did not match my dress, but it was lipstick nonetheless.

Pop called us to attention. It was time to line up for the march to church. Just before we left the house, little sister Grace gave me away. She spotted the forbidden lipstick and began to holler, "Ma, Ma, look at Norma Jean!"

"Shh, be quiet, Gracie!" I tried to focus her attention on something else. "Look, your shoe is untied."

"It is not! Ma, look, Norma Jean is wearing lipstick!" Gracie yelled at the top of her squeaky little voice, which I often wanted to silence by strangulation.

My mother grabbed my arm. "Let me see your face, Norma Jean!" She sounded stern. I looked my four-foot seven-inch mean mother straight in the eye, which wasn't difficult since I was as tall as her already. "I wanted to look pretty for Easter. I don't have a new dress!" I pouted, tears rolling down my chubby cheeks.

Mom grabbed hold of both my arms and pulled me out of the lineup and into the bathroom. She handed me a wet washcloth. "You wipe that makeup off your face right now, young lady! You aren't too big to take over my knee and spank! No daughter of mine is going out of the house looking like a whore!"

My mother always carried out her threats, so I obediently scrubbed my face.

What I remember about church was that there was far too much of it, far too often. On Sunday we were in church all day. First there was Sunday School, then morning worship service. On Sunday evenings there was junior choir practice, young people's church, and then the evening worship service. Monday night was Pioneer Girls (a Christian version of the Girl Scouts). Wednesday night was prayer meeting night, Friday night was missionary night, Saturday night was young people's night. More often than not, other spontaneous meetings were scheduled on the nights in between.

Sunday School on Easter and Christmas was different from regular

Sunday School. On those special days the children got to attend church upstairs with the grown-ups.

Calvary Baptist Church was a fairly new building, replacing the old one that had burned down when I was still too young to remember. The hymn books were left over from the old building and still smelled of fire. The wooden pews were narrow and uncomfortable but well waxed, and we discovered it was easy to slide back and forth on the pews when everyone's heads were bowed and eyes were closed in prayer. It was many years before I realized the minister wasn't talking about us when he condemned "backsliding" sinners.

The only thing we were allowed to do on Sundays, beside attending church, was read or engage in family-type entertainment.

We did not own a television set because our mother did not believe in it, so the Wright children became extremely adept at entertaining themselves in other ways. Sunday afternoons, while Mom and Dad napped, we put on skits that would make the Little Rascals blush. Since Mom and Dad never gave us any real sex education, what they failed to tell us, we made up ourselves.

There was no evening meal on Sundays, only a snack before we went back to church. It was never enough to get me through the night. I had so little energy and I got so sleepy! It seemed as if I always fell asleep somewhere between the last song and the evening sermon.

The annoying ringing of the stove timer finally penetrated my deep reverie, and the dreams and memories of my past vanished in the crashing reality of the present.

I checked on the ham once again, and of course had to cut off a slice to taste test. Being a taste tester was my favorite job as a kid. That, and making whipped cream out of the cream floating at the top of the milk that was delivered twice a week. Everyone said I made the best whipped cream, except the one time I whipped it too long and turned it into butter.

My least favorite job was washing dishes. I could see by the stack in the sink that my siblings living at home had inherited the same loathing of housework. I remembered when all of us had to take turns setting the table, clearing the table, and washing the dishes. No one was exempt, and the chores were rotated so no one got stuck doing more work than the others. Our dad always laid down the law when it came to cleaning the house, using his heavy leather belt to reinforce the point.

One hot summer night it was my turn to wash the dishes, but I snuck away right after dinner to play with my friends. Daddy had denied my request to switch nights with someone else, but I figured by the time I got home someone else would have washed the dishes and I would simply take his or her turn.

When I got home a little after ten o'clock, I had a surprise waiting for me. The dishes from dinner were piled high, waiting for me, plus Dad had taken all the silverware, dishes, pots, and pans from the cupboards and piled them alongside the dirty dinner dishes. Not only did I get a whipping, but I ended up washing the dishes every night all summer long. While the rest of the kids went down to the park to play softball after dinner, I was stuck in the kitchen. And I'll always remember the welts left on my legs by Dad's heavy belt.

But Dad was no longer around to delegate the household chores anymore—because of me.

When I was four years old, I always looked forward to the baths Daddy gave me. He had a special touch Mom didn't. In fact, his touch was quite pleasurable. He gently rubbed my tummy, thighs, and bottom, which brought marvelous sensations. His fingers tenderly massaged my "puddly" as he slid the soap around my baby nipples. Daddy and I were so close during those times. He made me feel so special—I was Daddy's little sweetheart. I enjoyed the immense pleasure his caresses brought me and the special attention he paid me.

After my bath Daddy would take me out of the tub and powder me and tickle me. "Honey, do you want me to kiss you down there?" When he put his mouth between my thighs, tingling feelings went through my body. I didn't want him to stop. Then he would play with my little nipples and suck on them while I giggled and squirmed on his lap. I wanted Daddy to play with me.

Daddy said, "Honey, I don't ever want you to tell your mommy or your brothers about this. You are my very special girl, and we don't want them to feel bad. Promise it will be our special little secret, okay?" I was pleased to have something of my own I didn't have to share with my brothers. My first sister didn't arrive on the scene until I was five.

We continued to play our little game until I was seven or eight. When I was very young, he only fondled me, but as I grew older, he introduced me to his sex organ, which he called his big stick. He would ask me to touch the fleshy thing between his legs, which grew big, hard, and bone-like when I rubbed it. I don't remember if he ever had an orgasm, but I know he never tried to put it inside me.

Whenever we were alone in the house, day or night, Daddy would approach me. As I grew older I began to resent his advances, not because of any sense of wrongdoing but because he became frustrated with his guilt and then took it out on me. After a tender loving scene in which I was his darling little girl, he would hurt me for no apparent reason. His favorite method of punishment was whipping me with the buckle end of his wide leather belt.

When I started school, I was often sent to the nurse's office because the teacher noticed large welts and bruises on my arms and legs. The nurse sent notes to my mother, questioning the cause, but my mother explained I had been a bad girl and my father had punished me. Most of the time I had done something to deserve being punished because I was a bratty kid, but I learned that most frequently Daddy whipped me immediately after our intimate moments. Cause and effect. Thereafter, when he approached me, I expected he would also hit me when it was over.

I truly don't know if my mother was aware of what my father was doing to his daughters. I like to think she didn't know about any of it until the time she wrote to tell me she had discovered he was molesting one of my sisters. She said she didn't know what to do.

I was twenty-two by this time, but knowing the trauma his abuse had caused me, I decided to return home and have my father thrown out. None of the usual government agencies, such as the police department, would do anything about him unless there was a corroborating witness to the fondling. I could not be the corroborating witness against him because the statute of limitations had run out on his crimes against me. Finally, the Child Abuse Center in Albany, New York, was able to issue a temporary restraining order to keep him from living at home. He would be able to return to the family in eighteen months.

Fortunately for my sisters' sake he did not want to return home. Unfortunately for my mother's sake, the court did not order him to pay child support, so she went on welfare for many years, until the last of her children were grown.

My young brothers who were still at home did not know what my father had done to my sisters and did not understand why I came home and had him kicked out. They resented going on welfare and blamed me for it.

*   *   *

Now he was no longer at home, and my mother wasn't strong enough to carry out her threats if the kids disobeyed her. She was too tired, too tiny, and too frail to put them over her knee and spank them. So the dishes and other household chores largely went undone until someone needed a glass or a plate, and then a solitary setting was washed. Mom tried to keep the house clean, but with so many of the kids still at home, it was hopeless.

Late that night, when everyone else had gone to bed, Mom and I had our talk. I didn't want to spoil the pleasant time we were having by making Mom unhappy. But on the other hand, I couldn't leave without putting my cards on the table. I suppose I could have called and told her over the phone, but it was better that I did it face-to-face.

We were sitting on the couch in our pajamas. I was wearing an orange chenille robe and a pair of heavy socks. It was April, but it was still chilly at night. My face was covered with Noxzema, and I couldn't have looked less like an expensive Beverly Hills call girl. But I was, and I had to tell Mom as gently as I could.

On her lap was her photo album. "Did I show you the pictures Grace sent me of her and Kelly? And here, look. Ruth just sent me some of Michelle and Chris! Chris is getting to be such a big boy now!"

"I know, Ma. Look, we have to have a serious talk."

"I know, honey. It's just that I want you to know I'm praying for you, whatever it is. If you would just give yourself to the Lord, He will help you work it out and—"

"Mom, you know how I feel about that. We could discuss it again if you want to, but I don't think you do." I started crying. "Look, Mom, I'd do anything in the world not to have to hurt you, and I know this will. But I have to live my own life and make my own decisions and do what I think is right."

She put her arms around me. "I know you do, dear."

"Remember when I had my last accident, when you were out in California with me and I said I was never gong to go back? And you asked me what I planned to do, and I told you I didn't know? Remember all the things that were going on in Hollywood when I worked there, and I was angry and said somebody ought to tell the whole world? Well, I have decided to tell the whole world, Mom. But there are things I decided to do to make a living while I wrote about the cops, and I don't think you'll approve. I'm not asking you to approve or disapprove. I'm just going to tell you about them so the police can't use them to prevent me from writing my book."

Mom was crying, too. "Honey, you don't have to tell me anything."

"Yes, I do. I don't want you to find out from somebody else. I expect to go on television and admit what I have been doing. Somebody else might see me and call you. I don't want you to find out that way. I want you to hear it from me—the truth and the reason behind it."

She was shaking her head. She already knew. She must have suspected something when I sent her money even though I was supposed to be out of work.

"Mom, please listen to me. I am still the same person I was before, and you have to understand I would never do anything that would hurt other people or that I thought was wrong. You and I disagree on what is right and wrong, I know, but . . . Mom, I'm a call girl now, all right, a prostitute. I have no problems calling it what it is because I don't think it's wrong!"

There, it was out. I was waiting for her to slap my face or yell, but she didn't. She just hugged me tighter.

"Honey, I still love you."

"And I still love you, Mom." We sat holding each other for a long time. Neither of us spoke.

Finally, Mom broke the silence. "We'd better get some sleep. You have a long trip home tomorrow."

We never brought up the subject again. She watched most of the talk shows I did, and she even wrote a letter to the local newspaper once.

Letter to the Editor, *Binghamton Sun:*
LOVE DOES NOT NEED ABSOLUTE AGREEMENT
I have had quite a number of calls regarding the article in your paper on Saturday, October 19, about Norma Jean Almodovar. I would like to make a general response.

You have seen Norma Jean on the television news; you have read all about her in the paper; perhaps you have seen or heard her on talk shows. She is my daughter, and I love her very much, and God loves her more. Knowing her from birth I feel qualified to say I know the many events in her life that have led her to the present time. I understand what she feels she has to do to get people to understand what is going on in high places.

Religious people will judge her. Religious people will shake their heads and wag their tongues. Religious people will not be concerned about her as a person, nor will they realize that, given the same circumstances, they might be in the same position.

Christians will join me in prayer for her and for others who take the dangerous position that it is all right for each person to do that which is right in their own eyes.

So while I most heartily do not agree with my daughter's philosophy, I still love her and will never cease to care.

Mrs. H. Wright

Mom and I are still close. I call her as often as I can afford to, and even when I can't. I know it hurts her to watch me on TV, saying the things I do. I have asked her not to read this book, not because I am ashamed of anything I have written or done but because there is no need to reinforce the pain she already feels. She knows where I stand, and I know where she stands. I love her, but I will not live my life for her.

13. You Can't Make a Silk Purse Out of a Sow's Rear

There once was a woman named Penny
Who looked like she never got any.
On top of all that, she was tall, old, and fat,
And her number of suitors weren't many!

Then along came a friend, namely me,
Whom she told of her sex fantasy.
But, to get her ass laid, it was I who paid,
And they took all my freedom from me!

Well, I did fifty days in the jail
For which I couldn't even post bail!
And no way to appeal it—the judge signed and sealed it,
And sent me away with a wail!

But, now comes the truth, so you see,
Even now I might not be free.
Three, four, six years is the sentence for doing the penance,
But what did I do? You tell me!

The moral of story is this:
Do not help an old friend who insists!
But if she does, shoot her. You'll get out a lot sooner.
'Cause that's the way life fucking twists!

SINCE MY ARREST the year before I had more of an aversion to cops than ever, and I tended, emotionally, to lump them all together as bad, evil, and corrupt even though I knew, intellectually, there were far more good cops than bad.

I was still undergoing psychological therapy for my stress and anger toward the police department since all my coping mechanisms seemed to have shut down. I could not even talk about the police without breaking into tears. In fact, I started crying at the slightest provocation.

My therapist suggested that it would help me recover if I tried to reestablish some relationships with my former coworkers. I needed to see them as individuals and not as a collective whole. I made a list of the few I once considered honest and who had some integrity. The only one I could locate, after several phone calls, was Penny Isgro. I never socialized much with my peers, but Penny was friendly and as close a friend as I had in the department. I also thought her philosophy of life might be similar to mine.

Penny had spent several years working as a secretary in Internal Affairs before she transferred to Traffic. She was an older woman, tall, and overweight. In her first week of training as a traffic officer she broke her leg learning to ride the three-wheeled motorcycles.

Some of her classmates found out I made dolls and asked me to make one for her—a little traffic officer doll with a broken leg. They presented it to her while she was on six months injury leave.

When she finally returned to work, she was assigned to light duty in the office because her leg still caused her pain. I saw her one day in the office, and she introduced herself to me.

"Aren't you the lady who made the doll?"

"Yes. Did you like it?" I smiled.

"It is darling, but I had a little accident. Could you fix it for me? I'll pay you."

I assured her I would.

Then she said, "You're very pretty. You ought to be in the movies or something. You're wasting yourself working for the police department."

I was flattered. After that I made it a point to say hello to her whenever I stopped in the office.

After I had been transferred to the Hollywood division, I still had to go downtown to pick up my paycheck and I occasionally ran into Penny. One day she was just getting out of her car, and she walked with me to the office.

"You know, Norma Jean, you get prettier and prettier every time I see you. I sure wish you'd try to get into acting or modeling or something. My husband is in show business, and he might be able to help you."

I blushed and gave her a hug. "Thanks, Penny, but I don't think I'm ready for the big time yet. Besides, if I left, who would Captain Pitfalls have to pick on?"

She laughed. "Well, if you ever decide to get into the business, I'd love to be your agent. I think we could make a lot of money, and we could both leave the aggravation of this job."

It was June 1983 when I contacted Penny. She was surprised to hear from me. "What's this I hear about your arrest last year for prostitution? Is it true?" There was no hostility in her voice, only curiosity.

"It's true I've become a call girl, but I was arrested for keeping a disorderly house. I can't afford a maid yet, and they caught me with some dust on the coffee table and some dishes in the sink."

We both laughed. She said, "Come on, what's it all about? Why are you in *that* business?"

"Well, Penny, after my last traffic accident I decided I couldn't and wouldn't return for any more b.s. I decided to do what I do best—screw!"

"And they pay you for that? I do that all the time, but I didn't know there was good money in it. Do you work the street?"

"Hell, no. I decided if I was going to do it, I was going to start at the top! I'm a call girl!"

We chatted for a little while and then agreed to continue our conversation over a drink some night after she got off work. In the latter part of June we set a date to meet at El Torrito, a popular Mexican restaurant at Fisherman's Village in the Marina, near her home.

I arrived a few minutes early and found a nice front table in the bar area. I ordered my usual 7Up and some appetizers. She had not arrived by the time I ordered my third soda. A half hour later a large woman with dark hair walked from the back of the bar to the front desk. I saw her and said, "Penny? Is that you?"

The woman turned around and smiled. "Norma Jean? Where have you been?"

"I've been right here. I got here early. Where have *you* been?"

She laughed. "I left work early, and I've been sitting in the back. Wow, I didn't recognize you at all. You sure look different!"

"Thanks! I've let my hair grow, and I can afford nice clothes now, instead of jeans and T-shirts."

"You look much happier, too, than the last time I saw you down at Central Traffic."

We moved to her table and for the next two and a half hours caught up on all the latest gossip. Of course I spared no details about my new career—my rich and famous clients, the hilarious stories, and the book I was writing.

"Yeah, We all heard about your book. What's in it?"

"What did you hear about it?" I was curious. I had assumed the book was an issue to the cops, but I didn't know how interested they were.

"Oh, you know, that kind of stuff gets around. Why are you writing a book anyway? I didn't know you could write anything but parking tickets!"

We laughed. "Penny, when I left the department, I was so angry with what was happening, I was even writing a book before I left. It was just a way to get all the anger out of my system. You know what they say: The pen is mightier than the sword."

"Wow! Are you going to name names and everything? Be sure to spell my name right if you use me in your book!"

"There is no point to naming names. I don't want to spend the rest of my life in court, being subpoenaed to testify against cops who just get a slap on the wrist, *if* they get convicted! I mean, look at Ron Venegas. After he admitted he and his dead partner Jack Myers committed over one hundred burglaries on duty in their police car, he got on the witness stand and testified against twelve others, none of whom got convicted. And the only sentence he got was a sixteen-month suspended sentence and three months probation! Thanks, but no thanks."

"Yeah, wasn't that something! Can you believe it? And that poor prostitute, Sandra Bowers! She was also supposed to testify against the cops but was found stabbed to death a few weeks after Jack bit the dust. Norma Jean, do you think it was a coincidence?"

"Sure it was!" I said sarcastically as I took a sip of my soda. At times like that I wished I drank something stronger.

"Aren't you afraid something might happen to *you?*"

"I hope nothing happens to me. That's why I'm trying to get my book out as fast as possible. Right now I'm working on a chapter about kinky cops. If you ask me, the cops I dated were kinkier than any of my clients."

Penny laughed. "Yeah, I know what you mean. I've dated several cops myself."

"I thought you were married!"

"I am, but I fool around. My husband is always gone, and I get lonely. I was dating a motorcycle sergeant for a while. Now I'm seeing a man I met while I was directing traffic downtown. He's a jeweler. Look at the rings he's given me!" She showed me her hand, covered with diamond rings.

"Whew, Penny! They're beautiful! But what do you tell your husband? Doesn't he get suspicious?"

She laughed. "Nah. I tell him I saved up the money working overtime. Remember all the overtime we can work during the summer, with the Dodgers and the Greek Theater and the Hollywood Bowl all going at once?"

"Don't you know those rings are a form of prostitution, Penny? The law defines prostitution as a lewd act for money or other consideration. But what the hell is a lewd act?"

"I could tell you about a lewd act. A captain who is no longer with the department used to commit it *while at work!*"

"Tell me about it! That's just what I need!" I said excitedly.

"Well, you're gonna *love* this one!" Penny proceeded to tell me about a captain who masturbated with a live chicken. Someone who didn't like him found out about it and arranged to film the captain's office secretly. The next time the captain ordered out for chicken, he got caught; he retired shortly afterward.

"That's a dynamite story! Do you have any more I could use for the book?"

"Well, I gotta think about it, Norma Jean. You know, I have a friend who just retired from working Internal Affairs after twenty-five years. Her name is Gertrude. I bet she'd have some stories for your book."

"Oh, that's wonderful. I guess I could pay her for every story I use in the book, and you, too. But I can't afford to pay at the moment. If I was working harder as a call girl, I could afford a secretary. That's what I need now."

"I worked as a secretary before I became a traffic officer."

"That's what I'd heard. Maybe when I get my book sold I can hire you as my personal secretary, and you can kiss the police department and all the weird cops good-bye!"

"Hey, they're not all weird." She laughed.

"Yeah, I know, but . . . anyway, can you imagine the two of us going all over the world on a book tour? We'll leave the boyfriends and husbands at home and paint the world red, so to speak."

My therapist was right. I was beginning to feel better already!

"Penny, would you work as my secretary when I can afford your services?"

Penny smiled. "Norma Jean, just how much money do you make as a call girl?"

I took a sip of my drink. "That depends."

"On what?"

"I don't see many clients. Maybe one a week, maybe five."

"Do you see any movie stars or politicians?"

"Oh, sure. I have several famous clients. But most of them are just very rich men, heads of companies, lawyers, people like that. I only work enough to pay my bills, buy some new clothes once in a while, go out to dinner once a week, and pay my taxes."

"You pay taxes?" She looked amazed.

"Not because I want to but because I don't dare not to. I can only fight one war at a time. The police are all I can handle. I figure if I go public, the I.R.S. will come after me, and I'd better be covered."

"So how much do you make?"

"Anywhere from two hundred to five hundred an hour . . . and up. But out of what I make I have to pay the madam a forty percent cut."

Penny shook her head. "You do all the work and she gets forty percent? Why don't you become a madam?"

"I have too many other things to do. Being a madam is like being in management . . . a supervisor or something. You have to be on call all the time. I don't have time for that. I'm too busy writing the book, composing poetry, making dolls, drawing cartoons . . . and screwing my boyfriend."

"I was going to ask you, why does your boyfriend let you work as a prostitute? Is he your pimp?"

"Victor is not my pimp! It's just a myth that all or most prostitutes have pimps. Victor 'lets' me work because there isn't much he can do to stop me. He doesn't own me! I'm over twenty-one, and I chose this occupation with my own free will. It's what I want to do."

She leaned toward me confidentially and said in a low voice, "Norma Jean, I've always fantasized about being a high-priced call girl. If I was still young and attractive and I knew what I know now, I'd make a million dollars. I love sex, and it sure would be nice to do it for a living. I envy you in some ways because you are doing what you want to do."

I didn't know what to say. I wished I could tell her she wasn't old and unattractive, but she had lived the good life and, unfortunately for her, her face and body showed every year of it.

I tried to smile as I stuttered, "Well, uh, Penny, if ever I find anyone who might like your type, I'll let you know!"

She laughed, and we finished our drinks. It was time to go. She walked me to my car, and we parted with the understanding that we would stay in touch. She would call her friend Gertrude for her stories, and I would keep her posted on my new career and the progress of the book. I promised as soon as I could afford her, I would hire her as my secretary, and I would take her away from the police department, which we both agreed was a miserable place to work.

"Don't forget to call Gertrude," I reminded her as I got into my car.

"Okay. And you be careful! Don't got out with any strange fellas!" Penny waved.

"Nah. I don't go out with cops anymore!" I laughed as I waved and drove off. Little did I know that the next time I would see my "friend," she would be wired for sound!

Very early in my career as a prostitute I worked for the Clara Lane Escort Service, a legitimate escort and dating service founded by the late Clara Lane in the early thirties. In her later years she decided to sell the nationwide service to some investors. I wanted to see if working for a legitimate service was as glamorous as an article in *Cosmopolitan* magazine made it out to be. There weren't that many calls for legitimate escorts, however, and I soon gave up.

The manager of the service, Spike, and I became friends because we were both poets. We often read our new poems to each other over the phone. He knew I was working as a call girl.

One day I got a call from Spike. "Norma Jean, I have a young lady here named Catherine Mills who came to our service hoping to get involved in your line of work. I told her we are a legitimate service, and she wanted to know if I knew anyone at all in your profession. The only one I know is you. Can you help her?"

At the time I was ignorant of the pandering law, which is defined as "encouraging a person to commit an act of prostitution." It would apply to him in referring her to me, and to me in referring her to a madam. Naively, I thought that since I was not a madam, I was not breaking the law. I told him I would give her the name and phone number of my madam.

Catherine Mills came to my house on a Saturday afternoon in June, just before my meeting with Penny. A tall, thin, fairly attractive blonde, she wore a feather earring in one ear. She said she was twenty-one and wanted to work as a call girl, catering only to female clients. She claimed she had some experience but did not elaborate.

I told her I would call my madam, and if she was interested, I would give the madam Catherine's phone number. But that was all I could do for her. She said she understood. It was a very brief meeting.

She seemed serious about going into the business and was attractive enough, so I gave my madam a call. As I expected, the madam was interested, but she was very busy and didn't have time to meet Catherine at the moment. She asked me to tell Catherine the madam would call when she had a chance.

Looking back, I can't believe I was so trusting and naive. Since I didn't feel the tiniest bit of guilt concerning what I was doing, I was very open about talking on the phone. Back then I couldn't imagine any of our phones being bugged. I left a long, detailed message on Catherine's answering machine and gave her some advice about what to do in the meantime if she needed work. I suggested she try other escort agencies since most of them were operating as prostitution services.

A few days after I left her that message, I got a call from her. "I need to talk to you right away. Can I come over? It's very important!" When she arrived, her face was ashen. I offered her a glass of water.

"What's up? What's the problem?"

"I . . . I didn't tell you the whole truth about myself."

"Oh?"

She coughed. "My dad is a state senator, and he had my phone bugged. When you called the other day, he found out about the madam and you. He told me to tell you and the madam not to call me anymore or you'd be in a world of trouble. I'm sorry, Norma Jean."

I sighed. I didn't know whether to believe her father was a senator (he was) or that her phone was tapped (I now think it was), but I certainly wouldn't call her again, and I told her so.

I never saw her or heard from her again, but I am still feeling the effects of those telephone conversations. It is my belief and the belief of my private investigator that because of that incident, my phone was later tapped. I am sure the vice squad was just waiting for some reason anyway since my arrest the year before, and the good senator provided them with that reason.

If my phone was tapped, it may well have been illegal. My attorney tried in court to get the police department to release the information, but the D.A. said we had to go to federal court. We never did. However, part of my lawsuit against the police involved the allegation that illegal wiretaps were used to gain access to information, such as my meetings with Penny. With the wiretap in mind, the rest of the events that occurred made sense.

*   *   *

Several weeks later Liz introduced me to a couple of very interesting men—her friend Bob and his friend Harry.

Bob liked younger, nubile women, but Harry liked women around my age, although he preferred them tall. Unfortunately, she told me, they were cheap and wouldn't pay more than $100. (I later found out why: Bob and Harry saw many girls in a day, and if they paid the going rate for each girl, they would have gone broke.) If I would see them and get them off her back, Liz said she would forgo her usual fee of forty percent. They kept calling her and every other madam they knew for more girls, more girls!

Bob and Harry were a strange team. Bob, an oil millionaire active in Republican politics, looked surprisingly like the late William Holden. He even had pictures of himself and William Holden in their younger days; they could easily have been twins.

Harry, short, dark, with a thick accent, owned and operated a successful gas station in Beverly Hills. Autographed pictures of TV and movie stars hung on the walls of the garage. Harry also claimed cousinship to the then-incumbent governor of California.

Every Saturday afternoon Bob and Harry met at Bob's Century City office to conduct a session of steamy sex with a stream of cuties who were supplied by every madam in town. Sooner or later, if you were a working girl in this town, you were sent to Bob and Harry, provided you were either young enough for Bob or old enough for Harry.

I met the dynamic duo one Saturday in early August, and sat and chatted with them for quite a while. I ultimately did have sex with Harry on the floor in the other office, which was quick and nothing exotic. I did not have sex with either of them again after that afternoon encounter. While I was the right age for Harry, I wasn't tall enough. But Bob and I became friends. He took me to lunch several times, to the marvelous Bistro Gardens in Beverly Hills. He introduced me to many people he thought might be interested in my book. He became like a second father to me, a real sweetheart, because he liked me—and not because, as the D.A. later claimed, I found a tall, older woman (Penny) for Harry.

In the meantime I had been calling Penny to find out if she had made contact with her friend Gertrude. Once I reached her, we had a curious conversation. At first she was very distant with me and sounded a little frightened. She had not yet reached Gertrude, but she would keep trying.

Then she said something that startled me: "Norma Jean, you will be careful, won't you? I mean, try not to get caught!"

"Yes, Penny, of course I'm careful. I don't enjoy being arrested. Why do you say that?"

"You know they might be trying to set you up?" She hesitated.

"I know they might, Penny. They aren't too happy with me." I laughed. Not that it was funny but it was true. Those vice cops and Internal Affairs guys were definitely unhappy that I wouldn't let them look at my manuscript the night I got arrested.

After I talked to her that day, I began to think about all the nice people who were helping me while I wrote my book: Harry had tuned my car at no charge; I wasn't making lots of money then because I spent so much of my time working on the book. Penny wanted to help me with stories, and she was worried about me. I had some neat new friends and some very nice old ones. I really wished I could do something nice in return.

And then an idea hit me, just like in the cartoons when a little light bulb goes on over one's head. Why not fix Penny up with Harry? I thought it was a wonderful idea.

First I called Harry to see if the idea interested him. I described Penny, and he started laughing. "Is this a joke?" he said in his broken accent. "I would have to put a paper bag over her head."

I was persistent. "Harry, you'll like her. She has a great sense of humor!"

He was unimpressed. I didn't want to lose him on this. How often would I find a guy who might consider a woman like Penny? Even if I had to pay him to see her, it was only a hundred dollars. Surely having Penny contribute stories to my book was worth that.

"I have an idea, Harry. Would you see her if you didn't have to pay for it?"

"What do you mean, I don't have to pay for it? She gonna come for free?" Harry had plenty of money but was cheap. He didn't want to spend his own money to see someone he didn't want.

"No, Harry. I will give you the money to pay her with. That way you won't have to pay her yourself."

"Okay, all right. I'll see her. But you owe me a favor!"

"Okay, I owe you a favor. Thank you! I'll give her a call right away. When can you see her?" I breathed a sigh of relief. I was going to make Penny's fantasy come true even if it was more trouble than I expected. But I had no idea just how much trouble it would end up being!

I was in a splendid mood when I called Penny. She wasn't in the office so I left a message for her. She had not returned several of my other calls, either, when I had called her about Gertrude. She had said something about going on vacation in late August, and I figured she might still be gone.

During the trial she testified that when she returned from vacation, there were at least fifteen messages from me. This may very well have been true, but not all of them were regarding Harry. Except for the last one or two, all my calls to her were about the stories she was getting for me.

When I finally reached Penny in the first week of September 1983, she had just returned from Hawaii. I welcomed her back.

"So, what's up, Norma Jean?" Penny's voice sounded very distant and flat.

"I was just calling to find out if you were ever able to reach Gertrude. And I have a question to ask you." I was beside myself with excitement. "What if I had a friend who liked big, older women. Would you know anyone who might like to see him?"

There was a long silence at the other end. Finally she laughed nervously. "Oh, Norma Jean. You're such a kidder! Look, I have to go. The supervisor is calling."

Several days later Penny called me back. As it turned out, she was wired, and in order to get my confidence, she had to try to make it appear as though she needed convincing.

I was typing in my workroom. The phone rang. The following is a condensed version, *word for word,* of excerpts from the court transcript of our conversation recorded by the police. Ordinary human conversation is frequently disjointed and punctuated with "ums" and "ahs," which makes it look very strange when transcribed!

"Norma Jean? This is Penny." [She certainly sounded friendlier than she had the other day.]

"Hi, Penny. How are ya?"

"I'm beat!"

[I laughed.] "You're beat. Who beat you up? Listen, that's my field of endeavor here. What are you getting into it for?"

"What do you mean, it's your field of endeavor? God, you are funny. . . . You know . . . anyway, I was . . . I have a special assignment . . . and I'm working Dodger baseball tonight. . . . Anyway, listen, I couldn't talk the other day . . . and I didn't want you to think I was crazy . . . cutting you off like that and, you know, acting crazy and laughing, but I . . . figured, well, that was the thing to do and . . . what the hell were you talking about, Norma Jean?''

"Okay, well, I . . . this is a hypothetical situation because, see, I don't wish to stick myself into any trouble. A friend of mine . . . loves to enjoy the company of much older women. . . . I'm not old enough for him. . . . He likes women in their late thirties, late forties, and even fifties . . . who are tall and big.''

"Where could you find a girl like that?''

"I don't know. . . .''

"Is there, uh, money involved?''

"Uh, yes. That's all yours and, um . . . since I'm not in the it's   uh   friend to friend thing, you know. . . .'' [It should be noted that nowhere am I asking her for a percentage as a madam would have, especially since *I* am paying for it.] "And it's . . . one hundred . . . and I'm sure he will fall in love with you. So I am sure he will see you frequently if you were interested.'' [I said that because I didn't want her to suspect that I had to offer to pay Harry the money to get him to agree to the date.]

"[C]an I ask you another question? Is he weird?''

"No . . . not at all, he is extremely nice.''

"I mean, he's not going to beat me up or . . . tie me up . . . well then, I don't want anything to do with it!'' [We both laughed.]

"[H]e's extremely nice. He will be at his friend's office. . . . It's quiet.''

"[T]hey won't hear me screaming, will they? I have this fear that this guy likes a big girl because he wants—''

"Oh, no! He'd be the . . . one . . . screaming because you would be the one. . . . If you want to, you can borrow my whips and stuff, but I don't think he's into that.''

"Thanks a lot! He might take them away and use them on me. . . . Oh . . . what was it he wants to do? Do you know?''

"Well . . . um . . . nothing that you haven't done before.''

"[S]uch as . . .''

"Well, what haven't you done? Well, I mean it is . . . it is the normal ordinary thing that you would find in a normal ordinary adult relationship. Nothing beyond that.'' [This was my crime of pandering.]

"Nothing, then . . . I don't have to be afraid and . . . bring a switchblade hidden in my high heel or something. . . . The only thing is, Norma . . . do I have to go up and ask 'em . . . are they gonna give me the money . . ."

"No . . . you don't have to do a thing. . . . Everything is taken care of. These are gentlemen. . . . I don't work with anybody that's not a gentleman, and it's discreet."

"I was surprised you called me at work . . ."

"Well, I just wanted to ask you, and I had no way to get a hold of you at home. . . . [I]f you are interested, that's fine. If you're not, that's fine, too." [It was no skin off my nose if she didn't want to go through with her fantasy.]

"What do they have, a bedroom up there?"

"No. They just have it fixed up so they have . . . you know . . ."

"I mean . . . how can you have normal sexual relationship without a bedroom?"

"On the floor."

"[H]ow about on the barbecue?"

"No. . . ."

"Listen, I just thought of something. If this were to develop into a career for me, right . . . it definitely would come to be a part-time job, right."

"Uh-huh."

"[B]ecause how many people would go for that description? . . . I mean, it sounds like your typical linebacker."

"Listen. Your career is going to be as my personal secretary."

"You know what? . . . I thought . . . oh, she doesn't want me to be her secretary anymore, she's got other things. . . . What does he consider a fair price for my services . . ."

"Well, he's . . . cheap when it comes to cash. He . . . likes to buy gifts as well as, you know, fixing your car and stuff like that. But as far as like . . . um . . . being there, it's one an hour." [The other half of my crime—encouraging a person to commit a lewd act for money or other consideration.]

"One what?"

"Hundred."

"One hundred dollars an hour! . . . You're kidding! . . . You got a stop watch? . . . How long can I stay?"

"No . . . you only stay for about an hour. . . . If you want to stay longer, that's fine."

"Then that's my own—no overtime. . . . Okay, now this is normal sex, right? . . . If it were anything kinky, it would be more?"

"Exactly! If it's kinky, it's two hundred and fifty an hour."

"That's what I'm afraid of . . . that they'll get me up there and say don't we owe you a hundred dollars . . . here's two hundred and fifty. . . . I'm in this building screaming, and they'll say, Isn't she fun."

"No . . . Penny . . . they can't do that."

"Oh . . . okay. So it's kind of an honor thing. . . . You know, I don't like to put you on a spot or anything . . . but were any of the cops weird?"

"When I was screwing 'em?   Oh, yeah!"

"Really?"

"Yeah . . . most of the cops were weird in that, to me . . . in that . . . I mean, 'cause . . . they didn't appear to be weird to me then, because I didn't know any better. But they would arouse you, you know, wine you, dine you, get you home, arouse you, insert, withdraw, and that's it! And there you lay, and to me that's weird. I mean, you know, they don't do anything to you. They just leave you there."

"Huh."

"And that used to be the most frustrating. . . . They used to have different things, you know, that they would want to do which didn't turn me on and, you know, but, uh, you know . . . different strokes for different folks."

"[D]ifferent strokes? You know what? . . . Different strokes is right! [W]hat about . . . uh . . . you got anything else?" [She meant other clients who would be interested in her. Of course there were none. I tried to be diplomatic.]

"Well . . . see . . . the only . . . you're just . . . you're perfect for Harry. . . ." [Note that I make it clear that this is the *only* date I can arrange. I had worked so hard to get Harry!]

"Yeah, tailor-made . . ."

"Because you're just exactly what he wants."

"Norma, you could send him one of the Raiders with that description."

"Yeah—but they're not women."

"Oh, that's true. . . . So we're just talking about, with Harry, we're just talking about normal, missionary type of sex . . . and I know I'm going to go to bed with this guy for one hundred bucks . . . but what do you do when you walk in? . . . You just say, 'Hi, I'm Penny,' and lay down on the floor?"

"You sit down and you talk and you visit and you entertain them with your wit and your charm."

"Listen . . . the stories I like, they might send me home."

"I rather doubt it."

"You know, I'm gonna go down to Dodger Stadium and almost get killed in the dark with these guys [irate Dodger fans]. . . . If the Dodgers lose, they're gonna be throwing their beer cans at me."

"Uh huh . . . that's why I do what I do. It [traffic work] just wasn't worth it."

"Norma Jean, can I tell you the truth? . . . I wish you'd never left."

"Well, I had to. . . . I couldn't go on anymore like that. I just couldn't do it. . . . You know, you get to a point in your life and you say, hey, wait a minute, it's not worth it to me. I'm not making enough to be this angry and this upset. . . . It's just not worth it to me. And my life has changed so much. I'm doing so many things I always wanted to do and never had time for. I'm buying things I never could afford. I'm going places. I go to lunch at the Bistro in clothes I never could have afforded."

"Uh huh."

"And . . . there's just no way for me to describe how much better it is . . . and how much different it is and . . . how sorry I am I didn't do this when I was twenty-one."

"Um . . . listen, they're gonna come in here and get me because I have not taken my dinner."

"Okay, you go eat your dinner and call me next week. Okay?"

"Okay. Bye, Norma."

On September 13, Penny called and asked if she could stop by my house the next afternoon for more details. I was busy but agreed to cancel my plans so I could stay at home to talk with her.

She came over on Wednesday evening just after six o'clock. Victor was in the other room as we sat and talked. It was hot in the house, so we finally went into my bedroom, which was air-conditioned, and sat on my big brass bed. We talked for three hours. I gave her the most intimate details of my sex life with Victor, not knowing she was recording it all.

There was a stuffed walrus sitting on my bed, and I told her about going to Marineland and watching the walrus mating. She laughed when I described to her how a walrus is hung. I told her that a male walrus has a prehensile cock with feelers on the end that comes out of its body to find the female walrus's love box. Unfortunately, not very many civil servants have heard the word "prehensile," so when it was transcribed for the court it became "pretty handsome cock."

Penny seemed curious about so many things. Several times she asked questions that made little warning bells go off in my head. Unfortunately, I didn't pay attention to them.

After three hours of intimate conversation, Penny decided it was time to leave. Walking her to the door, I noticed she had some threadlike things hanging down from the front of her dress. I pointed them out to her, and she quickly ran down the stairs. I still hadn't made the connection.

Friday night, September 16, Penny called me once more. Victor and I were fooling around, and I was in a very good mood. I had no idea the next day my whole world would come crashing down on me. When the phone rang, I rushed out of bed to answer it, but my answering machine came on before I could turn it off.

Answering machine in my voice: "Well, hi, there. I'm sorry once again to inflict you with this inhuman machine, but there is a really nice person who might be listening, and so if you—"

I grabbed the phone. "I'm here."

"Was that you singing?"

"Yeah, I was frantically trying to reach the phone."

"Oh, are you busy?"

"I was playing with my boyfriend. . . . We were laying on the bed doing obscene things to each other."

"Oh, I'm sorry I called. Do you want me to call back later?"

"That's okay. You've heard of coitus interruptus."

"Oh, I've not only heard of it but . . ."

We joked around for a few minutes, but my instincts told me something was wrong with this whole situation. I sensed she was not being herself. I finally asked her the question that had been nagging me for a while.

"I know this doesn't make any sense to you, but it makes sense to me."

"What is it?"

"You wouldn't set me up, would you?"

"Set you up? . . . You mean like a setup? . . . Explain to me what it is."

"Well, you wouldn't"—I cleared my throat—"put vice onto the situation."

"Would you do it to me?"

"Hell, no!"

"I thought you would. In fact, when you called me, I said, 'Oh, no.' "

"How could I do it to you? It wouldn't make sense for me to do it to you. You're not in what I do. To trap you into doing this . . . that would make no sense."

"Norma Jean, I'll tell you what—"

"I don't think you would, but . . . I'm very careful. . . . They have to have my number, and they have to have my cooperation first. And I don't plan to do anything stupid. The most stupid thing I'm doing is doing this with you. But you're a friend and . . . I trust you . . . and I would like to see . . . somewhere down the line you quit the police department and not do what I do but work for me as a personal secretary. . . ."

"I know you [are] probably uh . . . nervous about people and all that. But don't worry about that."

"Okay. And . . . you will have a good time."

"If I don't, will they give me more money? Can I get a refund? Can they get a refund?"

"Sure! . . . Satisfaction guaranteed!" We both laughed.

"Okay. Well, I'm gonna do everything possible and make it, I'll tell you that! . . . So, anyway . . . listen, how about if I call you back about five-thirty?"

"Yeah . . . it'll be perfect."

After I hung up, I had a strange knot in the pit of my stomach. I knew there was definitely something amiss here, and I didn't know what to do about it. I did not know the laws about pandering or that I was breaking a law by trying to fulfill Penny's fantasy. Yes, I knew solicitation for prostitution was (and is) illegal but I thought prostitution per se was not. There was no law on the books at that time that prohibited such activity by specific ordinance. I reasoned since I wasn't soliciting but instead was paying for this date, I wasn't committing a crime. I was wrong. The act of encouraging a person to commit an act of prostitution is a felony in California.

After dinner my girlfriend Sarah called. She had received a call from Chester Davis, a famous Hollywood actor who was one of our favorite regular clients. Sometimes we saw him alone, but more often than not we saw him together.

Chester lived in Bel Air, a few mansions away from Hugh Hefner. He is a tall, good-looking actor in a hit TV series. He loved to watch two beautiful women together, and I think Sarah and I were his favorites.

I dropped off my car at her house. It was a hot summer, and Sarah had an old Jaguar convertible. When we went on calls together, we went in her car.

"Hi, sweetie." I gave her a kiss on the mouth. No matter how often we worked together, I still missed her in between. I stroked her hair as she drove. It was so soft and pretty!

On his front steps awaiting our arrival in an expensive, beautiful blue silk robe given to him by a very famous actress, Chester was very happy to see us. We had a lovely three-way kiss, and he hugged and squeezed us both until I thought my ribs would crack.

"Calm down, Chester!" I laughed. Chester was always so horny!

He offered us both some of his "precious" cocaine. Neither Sarah nor I used drugs, drank, or smoked. He knew we would decline, but he always offered.

He took our hands and led us into his huge master bedroom. He had pictures of himself and his various leading ladies all over the walls. He had been to bed with most of them, or at least that's what he told us.

Sarah and I undressed each other for him, and we were wearing identical red lingerie, garter belts, stockings, and heels. We looked at each other and laughed. We had not planned this, but it often happened.

The three of us sat on his bed and began fondling one another. Chester's hard penis was poking through his robe, and Sarah reached over to lick it. I pulled her breasts out of her low-cut red lace bra, and began sucking gently on her nipples. She sighed appreciatively.

After a moment we all decided to shift positions. I pulled down her little panties while she took off his robe, uncovering his hairy chest. What an erotic delight! This handsome hunk and my beautiful, sexy Sarah! What a treat!

Still playing with her breasts, I dove down on Sarah and buried my tongue in her wetness. She was as horny as I was. While I played with her, she deep-throated Chester's hard penis. She moaned and groaned her pleasure as she writhed under my firm grip. When she had come several times, it was time to reverse positions.

Chester helped me up on the bed and began stroking my breasts. He slid his penis in my mouth, and Sarah began her magic on my waiting body. She knew how to drive me crazy! When I was ready to let go, I grabbed her head and pulled it into me as far as it would go. "Sarah, honey, don't stop!"

Chester stood up beside the bed and watched the two of us make love to each other. "You are beautiful, my ladies!" He masturbated while the two of us had our pleasure, then he had his orgasm. He went into the bathroom and brought out a warm towel and gently washed us off. He was so thoughtful!

Sarah and I cradled each other for a few minutes, kissing, and stroking each other's hair, while Chester went to his office for money. When he came back, we pulled him down onto the bed with us and giggled while we hugged and kissed him.

"Ladies, you wore me out! I am going to fall asleep on you!"

"Are you trying to throw us out? If you want us to leave, why don't you just say so, Chester!"

He walked us to the front door, where he put $500 into each of our purses and gave us a kiss on the cheek. "You ladies are the best in the whole world. Thanks. Let's do it again soon!"

Driving back to Sarah's house, we giggled like two schoolgirls. "Ah, what a life! To make love to you and get paid for it. I just love being a call girl."

"Me, too, Norma Jean. It beats the hell out of being a secretary!"

As we got off the freeway and headed toward her house in Encino, Sarah asked, "Norma Jean, would you mind very much if we stopped at the store for a minute? I have to get some paper towels, and I don't want to go out again after I get home."

"Of course, Sarah. I should get some things, too. Victor is out of coffee, and I need some paper towels, too."

"Oh, what brand do you use? I always get the store brand since they're cheaper, but I go through an awful lot, so maybe I'm not saving any money in the long run."

"I always buy Job Squad. They are real heavy duty! We use them for everything around the house!"

I looked over at her and laughed. "Here are are, two high-paid call girls who just had sex with *the* Chester Davis, and we're sitting here talking about paper towels? We can afford any kind we want, and you're talking about buying a bargain brand. Do you realize how funny that would sound to some poor waitress who gets two lousy bucks an hour and a pinch on the butt by Joe Shmoe in his polyester suit? I mean, nobody would believe we sit around and actually talk about ordinary stuff like paper towels!''

She chuckled. ''You're right, nobody would believe it. But they sure would believe we were call girls!''

''We don't look like hookers, Sarah!''

As we pulled into Ralph's parking lot on Ventura Boulevard, she grinned at me. ''No, we don't look like hookers, but we sure look expensive!''

14. COCKROACHES INTO THE NIGHT

Marching across the swamp to the north
And across the great void on the right,
The comrades linked arms as they marched forth
Like cockroaches into the night.

We'll take her by storm, cried the bug-eyed rat,
And we'll leave not a strip on the bone.
Does she think she'll ever survive all that?
'Cause we will never leave her alone!

Thus Ms. Piggy's world was so crudely invaded,
Intruded upon in her most private affairs.
They pillaged her papers, her poems they degraded,
And laughed as they dragged our poor pig down the stairs.

◇

WHEN I WENT to bed that night, I had a very strange and chillingly prophetic nightmare: The cops were in my house, tearing through my belongings, and then I was arrested and dragged off to prison. I woke drenched with sweat. It was seven o'clock in the morning, Saturday, September 17. I couldn't shake the feeling that something was wrong, and it wouldn't let me go back to sleep. If I was being set up by Penny, then perhaps I could still salvage things by calling it off. I later realized I was wrong again. Pandering does not require the exchange of any money or keeping a date. It is a felony simply to encourage a person to commit an act of prostitution.

I called Harry. He wasn't in so I left a message on his answering machine: "Harry, it's Norma Jean. I know it's kind of late notice, but I think we'd better call off your date with Penny. I think she's setting me up. If she calls you, tell her one of your kids is sick or something and hang up. When you get this message, call me, okay? Thanks, Harry."

Several hours later, as I was sitting on the couch reading the news-

paper, Harry called me back. I explained to him again that I thought
something was going on and that he should cancel his date with Penny.
He was upset because he had turned down several other invitations for his
Saturday playtime, so he had nothing else lined up.

"Harry, I'm sorry it didn't work out. I just don't want to take any
chances, and I sure as heck don't want you to get into trouble because of
me."

Harry reasoned that because of his cousin, the governor, he would
never get into any trouble. The governor later denied that Harry was his
cousin. Harry never did get into any trouble.

Harry asked me to call Penny and cancel for him since he didn't have
her phone number. I agreed to call her. I dialed Central Traffic. Yes,
Penny was working today, but she was on a special assignment. They
would pass along the message for her to call me.

When I put down the phone, I felt worse. I went to my workroom and
got my client file and some other papers with phone numbers. I took them
into the living room and tried to find a place to hide them. "Let's see, if
I were a vice cop looking for a little black book, where would I look?"
I scanned the room. There were obvious places I definitely did not want
to hide things. I looked at my sewing machine in the corner. Ah, the ideal
place. I reached under the machine and gently tucked away those valuable
names, dates, places, and fees. I felt reasonably sure they would be safe
from the cops.

I was very nervous and obviously wasn't thinking clearly because I
never thought to hide my manuscript, the very thing they'd be after.

I paced all morning, feeling tense, anxious, and angry. When
Victor got out of bed, he was surprised that I had been up for hours.
I told him I thought something was going to happen. He laughed.
"Nothing's going to happen, honey. You haven't done anything except
try to fulfill a friend's sexual fantasy." He was as naive about the law
as I was.

We decided to run errands that afternoon. I took a bath and got
dressed in a short-sleeved black silk blouse and tan slacks, with a black
bra and panties underneath. I put my hair up in a ponytail. For some
reason I took off all my jewelry—ankle bracelet, belly chain, delicate
heart wrist bracelet, and tiny diamond earrings—and hid them. If anything happened, I wasn't going to be wearing anything valuable for the
police to steal.

Just as we were about to leave, the phone rang. It was Penny, returning my call. From the transcripts again:

"What's up?" [She sounded out of breath.]

"Listen, I . . . Harry was calling me frantically all day 'cause he has no way of getting hold of you. His daughter is sick, and he can't meet you."

"Well, I'm glad you called me . . . because I was just getting ready to leave."

I apologized for the delay in getting the message to her. I told her I had been trying to reach her since eight o'clock that morning. I didn't know what had taken her so long to call me back.

"So what do I do now?" [She sounded disappointed.]

"Um . . . well, did you take off time from work?"

"Yeah, I'm off now."

"I don't know what to tell you. I wish you'd a called me a little earlier, 'cause I've been trying to call you for so long. . . ."

"On Saturday we all hide from the supervisor, don't you remember?"

"I try to forget all that, you know. I mean it's so nice to be away from there."

"Well, actually, I was kinda sitting in a movie, Norma Jean, and I didn't hear the Code-One and, oh, God, everybody came running up, you know, and said, 'They're looking for ya.' So I says, 'The heck with it. They just want me to sit in the office anyway, so I won't answer.' "

Penny was thoughtful for a moment, then asked if she could drop by. After all, she explained, she had taken off from work and now had nothing to do. Unfortunately, I was on my way out the door to run errands. We said good-bye. I breathed a little easier, but not much.

Ten minutes later there was a knock at the door. It felt like my heart had stopped beating. I took a deep breath and walked down the hall toward the front door. Looking through the peephole, I saw a black woman in civilian clothes. I didn't see anybody else with her.

"Who is it?"

"I'm looking for Norma Jean Almodovar."

"Who's calling?"

"It's the police. Open the door, or we'll break it down!" Just like in the movies!

I should have made them break the door in, but instead I opened it. Seven cops with their guns drawn came bursting into my home. Right behind the black female cop were Fred Clapp and Alan Vanderpool.

Fred Clapp waved a warrant in my face. "All right, Norma Jean. I have a warrant for your arrest."

Just then Victor came into the living room from the kitchen. He didn't know they were cops; he only saw seven people in civilian clothes madly waving guns. For all he knew we were being robbed. He yelled at them to get the hell out before he called the cops. One of the men laughed. "We *are* the cops, asshole!"

One of the others grabbed Victor's arms and shoved him onto the couch. After seeing I was not armed, the cops put away their guns. Then Fred Clapp approached me. "Okay, Norma Jean, where is your workroom?"

"What for? Do you have a search warrant?"

He grinned broadly. "Yeah, sweetheart. We got a search warrant this time!" He shoved a piece of paper under my nose.

Officer Alan Vanderpool, in his request for an affidavit for a search warrant, told the judge; "Based on the matters related in this affidavit, your affiant has formed the following conclusions. Norma Jean Almodovar is currently acting in the manner of a madam. . . . This opinion is based on sexual terminology used by Almodovar such as: 'Head'—Street terminology for act of oral copulation. 'Laid'—Street terminology for act of Sexual Intercourse. 'Kinky'—Street terminology for perverted sex act." The irony is that I learned this so-called street terminology from the cops!

It was a search warrant, all right, but there was no specific mention of a manuscript anywhere. I looked at it and then back at Fred. "Just what I am being arrested for?"

"I think you should ask Penny that."

Fred dragged me into the workroom. "Okay, where is it?"

I stared at him blankly. "Where is what?"

"You know what, bitch. Do you think it's fair to embarrass seven thousand cops just because you had a few bad fucks?" He spit the words out angrily.

We both knew he was referring to the manuscript. I glared at him with hate-filled eyes. "You're damn right I do! What are you going to do about it?"

"You'll see." On top of my desk were folders that contained the reference material for my book. He grabbed them and threw them on the floor. Then he started opening my desk drawers and taking out every piece of paper that had writing on it. He searched through the trash can and took out crumpled pages I had discarded. He smoothed them out, then called for Alan.

In the meantime a sergeant had been assigned to keep Victor at gunpoint on the couch to see that he didn't interfere.

Alan found a paper bag in the workroom and began dumping the pages of unfinished manuscript into it. He and Fred laughed and joked over it, reading each page before they dropped it into the bag. They really got a kick out of the name change list, which revealed both the real names and the names I had used in the book.

I had had about all I could handle. "Why are you taking my manuscript?" I yelled.

Alan winked at Fred. "We need it as evidence."

"Evidence of what, you bastards? It's evidence that I'm writing a book, that's all. There is nothing in your search warrant about my manuscript! You have no right to take it! Whatever you are arresting me for, it has nothing to do with my book."

Fred laughed. "Well then, honey, if it doesn't have anything to do with the arrest, me and Alan will *personally* return it to you on Monday morning. Won't we, Alan?" He grinned at his partner.

Alan's glasses were slipping down his sweaty nose. Large dark stains were forming on his shirt under his armpits. "Yeah, we'll bring it right back to you so you can finish the story of being a whore!"

"Well, I'd rather be a whore than a cop. You are sick perverts, peeking in other people's bedrooms!" My earlier anxiety had been replaced by indignation. I was as mad as hell now. Alan searched my bedroom and came back with my diary. He was reading it and laughing. He showed a page to Fred, and Fred laughed, too.

"Tsk, tsk, Norma Jean. You are a horny little bitch, aren't you?"

I felt my face flush. I glared at the two of them reading, violating my private, innermost thoughts and feelings. I felt as though I had been emotionally raped. My diary contained things I don't even tell Victor! After this it was a long time before I could write in my diary again.

I said things to them that not not repeatable. I must have been making quite a bit of noise, because Victor, sounding angry and frightened, yelled to see if I was all right. One of the other sergeants came into the workroom and attempted to threaten me: "Listen, Norma Jean, if you don't behave yourself, we can leak this arrest to the press! Then your mama will find out her little Norma Jean is nothing but a hooker!"

Having already told my family about my new profession, I wasn't at all bothered by his threat. They began to realize that I wasn't afraid of the media, either.

This threat might have worked with others. Having one's family find out is a fear the cops have preyed on for years, and it gives them enormous power of extortion over a woman. I knew several working women who had annoyed the cops; the police retaliated by telling the neighbors they were living next door to a whore. One prostitute told me that she was arrested *after* she had performed oral sex on the police officer, so she filed rape charges against him. She had her stomach pumped at a rape clinic, and semen was found in her stomach, providing evidence against the officer. She was told by Internal Affairs to drop the charges, but she refused. After the police exposed her profession to her neighbors, however, she didn't have a place to live. Ultimately she was pressured into dropping the rape charge in exchange for having the prostitution charge dropped.

Alan wrote a receipt for the property they were stealing. They didn't call it stealing, but it amounts to the same thing. The Los Angeles Police Property report, DR.#83-0212252, dated September 17, 1983, describes my confiscated property as including: "1 telephone bill, 1 rolodex clear plastic misc cards [my family Rolodex, not my clients], 1 envelope, manila, w/ misc papers written notations, 1 envelope, manila, containing 2 beige folders, 1 red with written and typed notations." This was how they described my manuscript!

Alan threw a copy of the property report at me. I looked at it and exploded. "You son of a bitch! I will never get my manuscript back with this shit! What the hell are 'typed notations'? That's nearly four inches of hard work in there, and you call it 'typed notations'? You swine!"

After they finished pillaging my workroom, they marched me out to the living room where the officers did a cursory search of the rest of my apartment. Since they found what they had come for, they did not bother to look for my client list. In fact, they completely ignored the sewing machine. At least my clients were safe!

One of the officers told Victor that my bail would be set at $5,000 and that he could bail me out after seven that evening. As I walked with them down the street to their car, I expected them to read me my rights, but they didn't—not ever at any time during the whole ordeal.

Once again I was dragged through the hallways of Central Station, past many of my former fellow workers. This time they knew I was coming.

"How's your book, Norma Jean? Am I in it?"

Fat chance, asshole. You'd have to be interesting to be in my book.

Upstairs I noticed some new autographed centerfolds on the walls. "You guys have been busy, huh?" I remarked to Fred.

"Sit down and shut up, slut!"

"Hey, just because I wouldn't date you years ago is no reason to get vicious. You never were my type. And I demand to know what I am being charged with!"

Alan looked at Fred and smiled. "Why, you tried to lure a poor, naive woman into prostitution, Norma Jean. You should be ashamed of yourself!"

My mouth dropped open. "What poor, naive woman is that? Penny?" I laughed. The idea that I had "tried to lure" this old, unattractive, overweight woman into my profession was comical to say the least. It certainly wouldn't be profitable for me to *pay* men to see her!

Fred opened the paper bag that contained my manuscript. He dumped it unceremoniously on his desk, picked up a page, and began reading it aloud to the other officers. "Look at this chapter, boys! 'This Little Piggy Went to Market!' Isn't that cute!"

They all laughed. "Hey, that's pretty clever. Anybody in the book that we know, Fred? Like me?"

He read several more lines from the first page. "Hey, Norma Jean, is this 'Liz' Betty McFarland?" We just arrested her. I hear she is a real nice madam to work for. Is that true?"

"Fuck off, Fred."

"Hey, is that any way for a lady to talk?"

"I thought you said I wasn't a lady, Fred. Make up your mind."

"Oh, this is hot! It ain't exactly *The Happy Hooker,* Norma Jean, but it's not bad."

Alan began filling out his reports. I looked at the clock. It was 6:30. According to what they had told Victor, I could be out of there within a half hour. I tried to be patient. I should have known better than to believe a word they said. Hadn't I learned anything from my days on the L.A.P.D.?

When I first joined the L.A.P.D. I learned the police had a habit of waiting for a Friday night or a holiday to arrest someone who had especially annoyed them. That way they could keep the person over the weekend, using a variety of excuses to postpone the release. At first I thought it was very clever. When they used the ploy on me, it wasn't very humorous.

When eight o'clock came and went and I still had not been finger-printed or booked, I began to get a little impatient. I heard a loud clomp-ing coming down the hall. "Gee, what is that, a hippo?" I asked Fred sarcastically. It turned out to be Penny, of course. She thumped into the room, saw me sitting in the corner, and abruptly turned away. I was shocked for a moment, but before she got more than few feet away, I managed to regain my composure and ask her loudly, "What the hell did I do to you that you could do this to me, Penny? I just tried to fulfill your fantasy. And the worst part is *I* had to pay for it."

She stopped for a moment but did not turn around. I think I hit her where it hurt; at least I hope I did. That was one date I've paid for and paid for and *paid* for! Penny never answered me. She joined Alan and Fred for a few minutes and then she left, using the other door so she didn't have to pass by me again.

Finally, very late that evening, Fred and Alan took me to Sybil Brand for booking. They dropped off the paperwork with a tough-looking dep-uty and wished me farewell. "We'll be seeing ya, Norma Jean. Take care. Stay out of trouble now. And good luck with that book." They both laughed.

The deputy bitch who was booking me looked at my false eyelashes and said, "Are these yours?" as she tore them viciously from my eyes. Goddamn, that hurt! I asked her to please save them because they were a brand-new pair. Smiling wickedly, she took a property envelope and dropped them in. Then she smashed them and sealed it tightly. "There now, they're nice and safe," she growled.

Sybil Brand hadn't changed much since my arrest the year before. In fact, I don't think it had been cleaned since then, either. The holding tank still smelled foul. Graffiti covered the walls, the open toilet in the corner overflowed, and the pay phone was out of order. I was certain Victor was already at the front desk waiting to bail me out.

What I didn't know was that I was supposed to be kept in jail until my court arraignment, which had been scheduled for Tuesday. Throughout the night, as I was showered, checked for lice, given a body cavity search, given some bedding, and taken to the general ward for sleep, it was beginning to dawn on me that I was in deep trouble. I stayed awake all night waiting for my name to be called; the call never came.

The next morning I got my first taste of breakfast as a guest of the county. The bells went off at six o'clock, and we were all supposed to get up, make our beds, and get dressed. I watched the other women and mimicked their behavior so I wouldn't get into trouble with the guards.

After we passed bed inspection, we were ordered to line up. We stood there while the cell blocks were called one at a time. Two by two we marched silently to the main dining room.

It was difficult for me to walk because the red plastic slippers I had been given were torn, and my feet kept sliding out of the sides. I tried to shuffle but it slowed me down, and the guard yelled at me to keep up with my line partner.

Breakfast was inedible. I offered my hot cereal to anyone at my table. My partner told me that wasn't done. She saved me just in time; the guard walked by our table, eyeing me suspiciously. I pretended to take a bite. It worked. She walked away.

After breakfast the cell block had to be cleaned. I was certain I would be released at any moment so I volunteered to help clean the showers, a job that would be done first. I finished, and my name still hadn't been called. I checked with the guard. No bail yet. I began to panic. I knew Victor would be able to get a bail bondsman to post my bail. I had met a wonderful bail bondsman the year before, and we had kept in touch. I knew he would post the bond! So why was I still in jail?

Lunchtime came. I wasn't able to shuffle down the long corridors again, so I asked the guard if I could stay behind. I was locked in the dayroom until everyone returned from lunch. I paced the room, annoyed because the phones were turned off until after lunch. When the women returned from lunch, the phones were turned on again. When it was my turn to use it, I dialed my home number. It was busy. I tried again, still busy. One of the other women yelled at me, saying it was someone else's turn to use the phone. I ignored her. At last the phone rang and Victor answered.

"Honey, it's me." I was ready to cry.

"Sweetheart, hold on. I'm going to get you out of there; it's just taking a little longer than I thought." He tried not to let me hear the anger in his voice. "They've had some problems finding your paperwork, and when they finally found it last night, they told me the night officer had gone home already. This morning, they said the computer was out of order."

I started laughing. "The paperwork was lost? And the night officer went home? What time was that?"

"Well, I called at two-thirty, and they told me she had already left for the night, that no one would be released until morning."

"That's very interesting since they were still calling names at four o'clock! And the computer was down? You don't say!" Now I knew what had happened. "Honey, I think you'll find it almost impossible to get me out of here before Tuesday."

He sounded very, very tired. "Darling, I won't let them do this to you. I'll get you out of there this afternoon."

Victor had called my attorney the night before and he had contacted my friend the bail bondsman. When the police didn't cooperate and it appeared as though I was not going to be released, Victor called a D.A. friend of ours, Ralph Nesmith.

When he called Sybil Brand, they told him I could not be released until at least Monday. He made it clear he was a D.A. and wanted me out of there immediately, not Monday. He was told I would be released on my own recognizance if he would vouch for me. He did. He called Victor back and told him I would be released within a few hours. When several hours passed and I had not been released, Victor called him back. Ralph talked to Fred Clapp, who assured him I would be released momentarily.

"Momentarily" stretched into the next morning, and when Victor called Ralph at nine and told him I hadn't been released yet, he was furious. Ralph called Sybil Brand and was assured I would be released by eleven. I believe if he hadn't called that last time, I would not have been released that day.

At 3:15 that afternoon my name was finally called, and I was taken to the property desk to get my clothes, which had been misplaced. They were found an hour later, and then I was sent to the front desk to have my jail bracelet removed. Coincidentally the woman who cut the bracelet off had gone to lunch, and I was told to wait until she returned. When she finally returned an hour later, it took her half an hour before she got around to cutting off my bracelet. She had other things to do first, I was told.

It seemed like an eternity before I was finally on the outside. I had no money so I called home collect. Victor was so upset he didn't dare drive to pick me up; instead, Sarah came to get me, in record time. I was damn glad to see her car coming up the hill.

We drove in silence; I was afraid to say anything because I couldn't trust my voice. She didn't know what to say, how to console me or comfort me. Within a week I would be bailing her out of jail. In all the time she had worked, she had never been arrested. Suddenly, a week after she came to pick me up, she was busted!

Victor rushed to open the door, and he held me tightly in his arms. He smothered my face with kisses. "My darling, my poor darling. Are you okay?"

Through chattering teeth I told him I was fine. I couldn't stop shaking.

After Sarah went home, Victor and I had a good long cry. The first time I had been arrested couldn't begin to compare with this nightmare. I was so paranoid, I wouldn't even talk out loud. We wrote each other notes just in case we were still being bugged, and then we burned them.

He saw a suspicious-looking van parked outside. I shouted at the van just in case it was the cops: "You bastards! You can't stop me from writing a book. I don't care how many times you arrest me. You picked on the wrong person. You're going to be sorry you did this!"

15. LIFE GOES ON

Tragedies befall you
And you think life's at an end.
Misery with misfortune
Seems to be your only friend.

You just want to get far away—
Let trouble know you're gone.
Amazing as it seems today,
You find that life goes on.

THE NEXT FEW MONTHS were painful and confusing for both of us. I tried to get my manuscript back from the cops. Contrary to their word, neither Fred nor Alan showed up on Monday (or ever) with my manuscript.

I had to get a good lawyer to find out just how much trouble I was in. I decided to retain Richard Chier. We hit it off right away because he disliked cops, too, and he really fought hard against this kind of outrage. he did a fine job of representing me, but due to his overloaded schedule, he had to drop my case just before it came to trial. In the meantime my life went on, and I still worked and tried to reconstruct the book, which seemed to have become my life's quest. Not only would I rewrite the incidents of police corruption that occurred when I was a member of the L.A.P.D. as well as the adventures of my life as a call girl, but I decided to chronicle how the law was used to persecute me and discredit my book. Fortunately I had some wonderful clients who stood by me through the rough times.

Many of the clients of a Beverly Hills call girl are the bored husbands of female stars and powerful women executives. The wife's career keeps her occupied, so the husband, who may feel neglected or in competition with his wife, spends his lonely afternoons being consoled by my sisters in the business. I had my share of these men, the most memorable of whom was Lawrence Dean.

Larry's wife was the powerful head of a fashion empire and was once herself a beauty queen. Financially Larry had no need to work, although he always had several "projects" in the works to keep him out of trouble. A tall, good-looking, athletic type, Larry could have gone into show business, but he wasn't that ambitious. Gray at the temples, with a full head of thick, curly black hair, he looked distinguished enough to be a politician. But Larry just wanted to play.

I was introduced to Larry through Liz, and she was very happy he took a liking to me because it took him off her hands for a while. He had been pestering her with his persistent calls for a new girl to play with.

Right after we were introduced he began calling me at all hours, demanding I come and play with him. I had to set some ground rules so he would not become a pest. I liked him and wanted to see him but not every minute of every day. I had other things to do and other clients. If I let him get away with it, he would behave like a spoiled child, so I didn't let him.

Larry thought of himself as a stud in bed, but in reality he was not very good—which was fine since I was not with him for my sexual pleasure. He was amusing, though, because he called his penis Uncle Albert. When he was about to climax, he'd say Uncle Albert was about to attack Pearl Harbor. He would pull out of me, get on top, take off his condom, and pretend his penis was a fighter pilot dive-bombing over my body. He would make noises like a machine gun, aiming his penis at my vagina. Then he would shoot his semen all over my belly, which he called my navel base, as he demanded total surrender.

In the afterglow of his orgasm I once asked him, "Why are you bombing Pearl Harbor? You aren't Japanese!"

He picked up his exhausted tool and showed me the top. "See the head here, where the hole is? Mine kind of slants off to the side, like Oriental eyes. And when I was a kid, the school nurse made fun of it and said I was probably a Japanese spy. I told that to the first girl I ever fucked, and she laughed and said, 'So dive on my Pearl Harbor, kamikaze pilot!' "

Ever since, Larry got turned on by reliving that experience. I decided to enhance his fantasy by learning a little about fighter pilots, using key words to provide him with maximum verbal stimulation. He appreciated the effort because it showed him he was important to me.

After I stopped working I ran into him one night while Victor and I were having dinner with some friends. He was with his wife, so of course I did not rush up to him to say hello. When he passed our table on his way to the men's room, I smiled at him and said, "Bombs away!"

*   *   *

Many people don't understand that much of the work I did as a prostitute did not include intercourse. I even found this surprising when I first started working. As I have said many times, I started working as a call girl fully expecting hot, wild sex and nothing but. Yet the fantasies were harmless, some even cute. One client, Dick Brown, had a charming fantasy that took so little time, it was almost a sin to make him pay.

Dick, the owner of a very exclusive restaurant in Santa Monica, was a very busy man. Life in the fast lane made him savor every minute of his free time. Before he opened his successful restaurant he made money in real estate, and from his landlord days came his sexual fantasy.

He always saw two women at a time, and usually it was Sarah and me. Since he was too busy for a wife, we were able to visit him in his palatial bachelor home in Beverly Hills. Immediately on arrival we progressed to his fantasy. He would go outside and knock at the door as though *we* lived there and he was visiting us. He had come to collect the rent. Seductively we'd invite him in. Sarah led him to the couch, where we'd sit on either side of him and give him the bad news.

"Oh, Richard, what are we going to do? Norma Jean and I don't have the money to pay you right now." She suggestively lifted her skirt, letting him see the naked flesh above her garter belt. She placed her other hand on his thigh.

"You know we are just two starving artists, and things haven't been good this month. I knew we are three months behind in our rent."

"Maybe we could work something else out, Richard, until we can afford to pay you."

Sarah unbuttoned his shirt and began rubbing his hairy chest. His glasses steamed up. I played with the back of his neck.

"Uhhh, what did you girls have in mind?" He stammered, the bulge in his pants growing.

"Well, honey, we thought that maybe you would like a little, um, entertainment."

By this time Richard was sweating, groaning, and breathing hard. Sarah's fingers were gently caressing his extremely sensitive nipples. I was rubbing his thigh and trying to unzip his pants.

"What do you say, Richard? Can we interest you in alternative financial arrangements?"

He was rapidly reaching peak excitement. I pulled out his throbbing penis and ran my long fingernails up and down the shaft. His eyes rolled to the back of his head as he quietly moaned, "Ohh yeahhh!" and came in my hand.

"Oh, thanks, girls. That was wonderful. You are the best!" He kissed us and discreetly slipped the money in our purses.

Sarah and I were finished in ten minutes, fifteen at the most on days we really tried to stretch it out by improvising more dialogue. Never once did we get undressed, and when were ready to leave, not a hair was out of place, nor did our lipstick need a touch-up. Dick was a sweet man and a pleasure to service.

And it would be difficult, if not impossible, to catch (or spread) any kind of sexually transmitted disease working with clients like Dick.

Arnold Litzinger was a television scriptwriter and screenwriter of considerable merit. Several past and current popular evening television shows are products of his vivid imagination and brilliant writing skills. I was thrilled to have him as a client, and I am certain that just as he appears as a character in my book, I will appear as a character in some TV show he will write or has written.

As in Dick Brown's fantasy, Arnold's scene could not contribute to the spread of any sexually transmitted disease because there was no physical intercourse, only verbal interaction.

Arnold took great care in preparing for his dates by sending an entirely scripted fantasy, detailing every move, to the woman who was to see him. It had the date and time he wanted his date to arrive, what she should wear, various props she should bring, and what she was to say at the door. The rest of the conversation could be ad-libbed according to the story line.

Whatever part I was playing, the plot always developed the same. Although it seldom rains in California, except for a few weeks in the spring, for the purposes of fulfilling Arnold's fantasy, it rained every time.

At my appointed time, always wearing a dress with a garter belt, stockings, and high-heeled shoes, I stood knocking at his door in the pouring rain. He would open the door a crack and ask what I wanted.

"Hello, um, excuse me, sir. Can you help me? My car has broken down, and I need to use a telephone. May I come in?"

Second variation:

Seductively, "Hello, Mr. Litzinger? My name is Alice Murphy, and

I have written a script that I would like you to read. May I come in?''

Third variation:

"Hello. I'm looking for my friend Frank Doolittle. Is this 42259 Mulholland? It is so difficult to see the numbers in the pouring rain. May I come in?'' There were several other variations on the same theme.

Upon being invited in I immediately complained about being soaked to the skin. As coyly as possible I asked, ''Could I use your rest room and take off my wet clothes? Do you have a robe I can borrow?''

He would graciously escort me to the bathroom downstairs, which had a huge window that looked out on the pool and patio. The wooden shutters were arranged so that by standing right outside the window he could look in at me, but I couldn't see him. I was to take off my dress slowly and, looking at myself in the mirrored wall, narcissistically admire my body from all sides and play with myself, pulling down my panties and inserting my fingers into my vagina. After a while I would put on his robe and go into his bedroom, where he returned from standing outside.

"What took you so long? Did you have any trouble getting out of your wet things? I could have helped you if you asked me.''

"Oh, no, Mr. Litzinger. I was just trying to dry out my clothes. Shall we go back upstairs?''

He would sit in a chair across from the couch where I sat with the robe slightly open and my legs spread just enough to give him a titillating view past the top of my stockings.

"Nasty night out there, isn't it?'' Casually I rubbed my legs.

He coughed. "Oh, yes, very.''

"Would you mind very much if I stayed for a little while, until the rain lets up a bit?''

"No, of course not. Can I get you a cup of tea or something?''

When he returned with the tea, I removed the robe and was stretched out comfortably on the couch.

He pretended to ignore my scantily clad body.

"So what kind of script did you bring me to read, Miss Murphy?''

"Well, I wrote a screenplay about a woman who gets stranded in a strange man's house during a violent thunderstorm. The lights go out, and he rapes her as— Here, let me show you the best scene.''

I picked up a pile of papers on his coffee table and pretended it was my script. I bent over his shoulder, with my cleavage almost directly in his face, as I showed him a nonexistent scene in a nonexistent script while he pretended to ignore my blatant overtures.

I pointed to a line of print which actually read, ''Fine furs kept in our storage area,'' but I read it as, " 'He took her in his arms after she stopped struggling.' See, here is the best part, Mr. Litzinger: 'As the storm raged outside, the passion raged inside her body, and she willingly gave herself to him.' ''

"Yes, I see what you mean. That is a very interesting scene." He squirmed uncomfortably in his chair.

I stood up and stretched so my crotch was at mouth level. "I think my clothes must be dry by now. I'll just go downstairs and see."

Slowly parading past him, I smiled invitingly as I descended the staircase.

I went back into the bathroom and repeated my performance in front of the mirror. This time I sat on the edge of the bathtub and masturbated for quite a while.

Then I went back to his bedroom. "Are your clothes dry yet?" He was perspiring.

Now we had a confrontation scene.

"No, not yet." I pointed to the porch. "Tell me, Mr. Litzinger. Can you see into the bathroom from out there?"

"Oh, no, of course not. I was just out on the patio for a minute getting some fresh air. It has almost stopped raining."

"Well, I think you were peeking into the bathroom while I was changing clothes. You were watching me, you naughty boy!"

"Oh, no, no! Of course I wouldn't do that! Really."

"Well then how come you have a bulge in your pants?"

He looked down. There was definitely a swelling, and he put his hands over it. He kept shaking his head, denying it. "No, no, I wouldn't. I . . . Look here, Miss Murphy. I don't know why you'd want to accuse me of such a thing. I am a gentleman, and I wouldn't invade your privacy like that."

As he talked I pushed him toward the bed with my body. He fell backwards onto the bed. I stood over him with my legs spread. I unhooked my bra and let my exposed breasts fall out.

"Unzip your pants, you bad boy!" I demanded. "I want to see your erection! When I was in the bathroom, were you outside playing with yourself?"

He hung his head and very quietly said, "Yes."

"And did you get off watching me?"

"No, not yet."

"Then let me watch you jerk yourself off while I play with myself."

"Oh, no, I couldn't!"

"I said do it!" I grabbed a cane that was purposely left on the chair next to the bed. I gave him a light whack on the thigh.

"Okay! I'll do it. Please don't hit me anymore, Miss Murphy." His voice strained as his excitement mounted.

I whacked him several times as he stroked himself. "That's for being a bad boy and lying to me!"

It was all he could do to stop himself from coming, but we weren't finished with our little charade yet.

I sat down in the chair and spread my legs wide. "Stand up and let me watch you beat that thing off!" I ordered.

Obligingly he stood up, facing me, and proceeded to torture himself further until I finally allowed him to complete his orgasm.

"All right, naughty boy, empty your gun for me. Show me you're not shooting blanks!"

"Ohh! Ahh! Umm!" His eyes closed as he had his orgasm. Exhausted, he sat back down on the bed.

With practice I got to be very good with his fantasy. No kissing, no intercourse, nothing but lots of dialogue, and for that he paid me $300 an hour. That is what you call safe sex. You just can't catch AIDS *that* way!

Clients with clothing fetishes were equally safe from diseases. Most of these fetishes were foot fetishes, for which I never got undressed.

One of my clients, a doctor, was interested only in my feet being dressed up in high-heeled shoes. His arousal came from being forbidden to touch my feet. He crossed the room on his hand and knees, begging me for permission to smell them. Permission denied, I strutted my heels in front of his face, which was down on the floor.

While I strutted he played with himself, feeling torture and pleasure at my continued rejection of his request. Finally, I had pity on him and allowed him one brief touch. I took off my shoes and allowed him to feel the bottom of my "perfect" feet. That was all it took to make him happy. He had his release, got up, went to the bathroom to clean himself off, paid me $250, and away I went.

Sarah introduced me to an interesting couple from Santa Barbara whom I dubbed "the couple that wouldn't." I had the pleasure of going out to dinner with them several times, but I finally stopped because I felt it was a waste of my time and theirs. That woman wasn't ever going to give in, and I was tired of trying to pretend to seduce her.

Bob, her boyfriend, would call me a week in advance and make arrangements for us to meet at a fancy restaurant. Estelle was tall, attractive brunette with large almond-shaped eyes. Though she was in her early forties, she could easily pass for twenty-nine. And she had a dynamite body. During dinner Estelle would caress her hair and act seductive, and poor Bob always thought this time she would go through with it. He desperately wanted a ménage à trois.

After dinner we would go to their hotel, order champagne, and Bob and I would get undressed. Estelle would turn on the TV, sit in the chair fully dressed, and complain she was too full to play.

Bob would beg her, plead with her, get on his knees, try to persuade her to take off her clothes, but she never would. He wanted me to try to seduce her, but she stubbornly sat in the chair and said, "Get away from me. I don't want to play tonight."

I offered to make love to Bob by himself, but he wanted to watch the two of us together. That's *all* he wanted.

After a while I would give up, and Bob would, too. With a sigh of resignation he'd pull out his wallet and pay me for the entire evening.

I always felt bad for Bob because he drove all the way to L.A., paid for an expensive meal for three, rented a room at the Beverly Hills Hotel, and then paid me for the whole evening whether he fulfilled his fantasy or not. And he never did.

The time between my second arrest and the trial went by very quickly. With Richard Chier no longer on the case, I had to find a new attorney. Because of her reputation as a strong feminist lawyer, I went to see Gloria Allred. After meeting with her briefly I learned she did not do criminal cases, and she referred me to another lawyer, Martin Shucart.

Shortly after I hired Mr. Shucart I was contacted by the "Donahue Show" in Chicago and asked to be a guest. Margo St. James of C.O.Y.O.T.E. had told them my story, and the show's producer thought it might make an interesting program. Mr. Shucart did not feel it was a good thing to do, but since I was determined to go, he advised me not to discuss the case publicly. I listened to Mr. Shucart's advice and did not mention the case. Instead, the show focused on prostitution laws and how differently each state treated commercial sexual activity.

It was a big mistake not to discuss my case on the show. Instinctively

I thought I should have. People would have been outraged to learn their hard-earned tax money was being spent on something as ridiculous as this.

In addition to my first television appearance I was invited to be a speaker at a national convention in Las Vegas. An annual event usually held at the Hacienda Hotel, Bob McGinley's Lifestyles Organization convention was a chance for people with alternative life-styles from all parts of the country to get together. The highlight was always the last evening's Erotic Masquerade Ball.

I felt certain that as advocates of freedom of choice, the alternative life-style people would be sympathetic and supportive of my own personal choice, and I needed to know there were friendly people out there. And besides, Victor and I weren't averse to swinging when we met the right couple.

Although it is very hot in Las Vegas in the middle of August, the convention was the perfect getaway just a month before the trial. My lecture was well received by the group, which could not believe the charge against me was actually going to trial. It gave me hope that there are many Americans who think it is ridiculous to impose criminal sanctions on consenting adult activity.

Victor and I met a lovely couple who owned a restaurant in northern California. Barbara and Jerry both attended my seminar and then sat with us afterward at lunch. I knew Victor was attracted to Barbara, and so was I. The four of us decided we wanted to get to know one another better.

After attending all the obligatory functions, we separately made our way to their hotel room. In the beginning we were uncomfortable because it was our first time together. It took us hours to relax to the point of taking off our clothes. Sometimes I think it is much easier if you're working since there are no little games to play. One just comes in, gets undressed, and gets right to it.

After a while the ice was broken. Barbara and I went to the ladies room on the pretext of powdering our faces. Once there, we brushed against each other and then began touching. I took off my clothes and helped her undress. The two of us stayed in the bathroom long enough to make our mates curious.

"So there you are, you beautiful ladies. We wondered what you two were up to!" Victor came into the bathroom and began caressing Barbara's blond hair. Then he reached around and played with her nipples.

Jerry likewise began stroking my thighs. Barbara and I were engaged in a soulful kiss. We put our arms around each other's waists and felt the other's soft skin. She had creamy white skin, and it smelled clean and delicious. I kissed her neck as she purred in my ear.

The bathroom wasn't big enough for the four of us, so Jerry pulled me along behind him into the bedroom. Victor stayed in the bathroom for a few minutes enjoying Barbara's sweet, soft kisses, and then all of us were together.

Heavy sighs and loud moans came from every corner of the bed. It seemed as though someone was having multiple orgasms and at very frequent intervals. Maybe it was me. Maybe all of us. I was too busy feeling ecstatic to know where the orgasms were happening. I do know everyone seemed to be doing whatever felt good, and it all felt good!

Finally, everyone seemed satiated and totally exhausted. The bed was big enough to accommodate all of us, and we fell asleep in a big, happy pile.

I found out that despite my legal troubles, I could still enjoy life.

16. The Kangaroo Court

"I'll be the judge," the donkey declared.
"And I'll be the lawyer," the monkey, he roared.
"I'll be the D.A.," cried the thirty-pound rat
As he stood on the table and took off his hat.

The ostrich jumped in, saying, "I'll be the fuzz."
When asked why on earth, he said, "Just because!"
"You be the victim," they said to the elephant,
"And Miss Pig over there can be the malevolent."

"We must have a crime. What did Pig do?"
"Oh, what does it matter?" said the gnu.
"I know," said the elephant when the motion was made,
"Miss Pig over there tried to get my ass laid!"

In the Kangaroo Court, a crowd did assemble
To see if the Pig on the stand would but tremble.
Miss Pig sat so calmly, she held her head high.
"Not a thing did I wrong," she wanted to cry!

The D.A. pounded his fist on the table and roared,
"Miss Pig is a menace and ought to be gored!"
The lawyer and judge and the court did agree,
So they sent her to prison, sat down, and had tea.

CNN REPORT, SEPTEMBER 1984:

Two years ago Norma Jean Almodovar went from being a cop to a call girl. Now she's going to trial on a felony charge of pandering. Prosecutors claim that Almodovar called an old friend on the force last year and offered to help the friend become a call girl, too. But Norma Jean contends police planted the friend, wired for sound, to create an excuse for confiscating the manuscript she'd written about her experiences as a prostitute and a police woman.

Norma Jean is getting moral support from Margo St. James, leader of the prostitutes' rights group, C.O.Y.O.T.E. St. James calls her case an abuse of the pandering law. . . .

Norma Jean got into the law enforcement business in 1972, signing on as a traffic officer in the Hollywood Division. After ten years, she says, she was fed up with scandals on the force, dangers on the streets, and sexual harassment on the job. . . .

She's convinced it was what she was writing about sexual practices among L.A. police that got her marked as the target of a sting. . . . Norma Jean is rewriting her book. . . . For now, though, she's concentrating on making sure she doesn't have to watch the TV version of her life from prison. . . .

Brian Jenkins, CNN, Los Angeles.

Monday, September 17, 1984, a year after my arrest.

"All rise! The Superior Court of Los Angeles, Division Thirty-two, is now in session. The Honorable Judge Aurolio Munoz presiding."

The TV cameras on the side followed my every move. I tried not to look as miserable as I felt.

Penny, along with vice officers Clapp and Vanderpool, was seated at the prosecution's end of the table. She was dressed in a white blouse and black skirt and had on heels as high as mine. She appeared to have lost several pounds.

It had taken two days to select a jury. Mostly male, the twelve jurors and two alternates had assured my attorney, they would not be prejudiced by the fact that I was an admitted prostitute. Looking at their faces, I believed they would not.

The media was having a field day with my case. The Associated Press reported: "For ten years she wore a police uniform, but in her latest court appearance Norma Jean Almodovar had three-inch hot pink fingernails, spiked heels, and an ankle bracelet—trademarks of her new occupation as a $200-an-hour call girl."

Some of the newspaper said my hair color was purple, some said my nail polish was purple. None could agree on shades or lengths of either. For the record, my nails, painted in quiet, soft pink shade, were each one inch in length, and my almost waist-length hair was auburn. I had worn an ankle bracelet and spiked heels long before I had ever worked as a call girl.

It is ironic that I should become notorious for my long fingernails since I was a chronic nail-biter during my ten-year career on the L.A.P.D.

Despite the titillating headlines, I was glad to have the media at my trial. If I had tried to tell people what had happened and the press had not been there to see it happen, no one would have believed me! And I certainly forgive them for using sex to sell their newspapers. After all, I know better than anyone that sex sells!

And since sex sells, it is understandable why the press left any description of Penny out of their reports. The D.A. provided an adequate description of her in the appellate brief filed in 1985. They remarked: "Prostitution could only be a part-time job for Isgro, since not too many customers would go for a girl of her description (which sounded like 'your typical linebacker')." Further, they added, "A particularly vicious aspect [of the crime] is the fact that the victim's personal characteristics, *at best,* qualified her for only part-time prostitution, catering to specialized tastes (such as 'Harry's')."

Were it not for the members of the press who followed my case from its inception to its conclusion, I might not be alive today to write about it. One young lady who should have gone to the press with her story was Donna Gentile. Unfortunately and understandably, she did not want the publicity. A streetwalker from San Diego, her story made the headlines after her body was found, June 23, 1985. She had been beaten and strangled, and her neck was broken.

The *San Diego Union* reported: "Street prostitutes don't usually make headlines, but Donna Gentile did. She got a San Diego police officer fired and his lieutenant demoted. Then she was killed."

The San Diego edition of the *Los Angeles Times* reported in July 1985:

A woman whose nude body was found beaten and strangled in East San Diego County June 23 feared she would "disappear" because of her testimony against two San Diego police officers, according to a tape recording she made almost four months before her death.

Donna Marie Gentile, 22, a prostitute involved in the firing of one police officer and the demotion of another, made the tape March 13, the day she went to the County Jail at Las Colinas after being convicted of soliciting for prostitution.

"In case I disappear somewhere or is missing, I want my lawyer to give this to the press," Gentile said on tape. "I have no intention of disappearing or going out of town without letting my lawyer know first. Because of the publicity that I have given a police scandal, this is the reason why I'm making this. . . . I feel someone in a uniform with a badge can still be a serious criminal. This is the only life insurance I have. . . .''

Donna, like many other prostitutes in many cities, was being extorted by the vice cops for sexual favors. She simply got tired of it and made a formal complaint. One police officer was fired, but even though extortion is a felony, he was not prosecuted for it. Another police officer, a lieutenant, was simply demoted. The prostitute, guilty of a misdemeanor, went to jail. At the time of this writing, her killer or killers have still not been found.

Another prostitute who would have benefited by going public was Sandra Bowers, one of the key witnesses in the Hollywood burglary ring. Unfortunately, like Donna Gentile, her publicity came after her untimely and unsolved death. In 1982 the *Los Angeles Times* reported:

A prostitute who was to be a key witness in the investigation of the burglary and sex scandals plaguing the Los Angeles Police Department's Hollywood Division has been murdered, *The Times* learned Wednesday.

The paper went on to report how ''Sandra Bowers, twenty-six, was found in Hollywood's Crest Motel with her throat slashed and a dozen stab wounds in her back, and that she was the second witness in the ongoing investigation to die violently. The first policeman to be caught in the burglary scandal and the first to incriminate fellow offers, Jack Myers, was killed May 12 when he somehow lost control of his pickup truck and was hurled out of the vehicle, landing on his head in the middle of the Simi Valley Freeway.''

''At this point,'' Department Commander William Booth said, ''we are investigating the [Bowers] case with the belief she was the victim of her last trick. . . .''

It seems as though a lot of prostitutes who blow the whistle on cops end up this way.

At the beginning of my trial Richard Weber, the D.A., wanted to be removed from the case after I threatened to reveal that he and a friend of mine engaged in an illegal poker game every Wednesday night. The judge refused to remove him.

Every day, the courtroom was packed with reporters, my friends and supporters, and an odd assortment of groupies who spend their days as spectators at the criminal courts building. Victor was seated behind me and to one side so I could glance at him without too much difficulty.

In his opening statements D. A. Weber attempted to invent a new character for Penny, portraying her as practically a (fifty-year-old) virgin, naive and innocent as the driven snow. He told the jury I had tried to lure this poor, sweet, unsophisticated woman down the path to ruin, into a "lifetime of prostitution, shame, and degradation."

At the conclusion of the D.A.'s trip to never-never land, it was our turn to address the jury. My attorney stood up and said, "Your Honor, we wish to waive our opening statement at this time." This took me by surprise, and I looked back at Victor and shook my head.

Having waived our opening statement, the prosecutor now began his case. As his first evidence against me, D.A. Weber introduced the three hours of tape-recorded conversations between Penny and me.

The courtroom groupies had been waiting with anticipation to hear the supposedly lurid tapes. Rumors had been flying about their contents, and a story of what had happened at the preliminary hearing on December 16, 1983, fueled their anticipation.

On that date my case was heard before Municipal Court Judge Mary White; her job was to determine if there was enough evidence to hold a trial on the case. The tapes were then played publicly for the first time. On tape I referred to the size of my boyfriend's penis. My face burned as I listened. Everyone in court was laughing, and Victor had to leave. Suddenly the courtroom became absolutely still except for the tapes, which droned on and on. I turned around to see what had caused the silence.

Into the back row of the courtroom quietly marched a troop of thirty very young Girl Scouts, there on some sort of field trip. Their leader, busy making sure all the girls found seats, evidently wasn't listening to the content of the tapes. I looked at the stunned faces of the girls and realized they had heard every word. They were giggling and gesturing to one another. It wasn't a minute before the D.A. turned off the tape recorder, stood up, and said, "You Honor, I think it would be in the interest of justice if we took a short recess." He looked back at the Girl Scouts. The judge agreed.

The bailiff pulled the troop leader aside and told her this was a hearing for a well-known prostitute, and the tape recordings were more or less X-rated. She and the girls would have to leave. She was more than willing to do so. She turned bright red, gave me a long, piercing stare, and then marched the girls outside. They didn't want to go!

It took a while for the courtroom to settle down. The look of dismay on the girls' faces as they were forced to leave was priceless. The look on the troop leader's face when she discovered what she had stumbled into was even better.

Eleven months later, as I sat listening to the tapes again, I struggled to understand what motivated Penny to do this to me. Each time I saw her in court I found it difficult to look at her and keep from asking why she had set me up. But I was not allowed to. In fact, I had been warned if I attempted to communicate with her, it would be construed as harassment, and I would be arrested for that.

Whatever her reasons, the whole world now heard me discuss my private sex life with her. It was sheer agony.

Court reconvened on Wednesday, September 26, 1984. Penny was called to the stand. She was sworn in, and the circus began.

After the D.A. finished with his questioning, my attorney began cross-examining her. The *Los Angeles Daily News* reported in an article headlined "OFFICER TESTIFIES SHE WANTED TO STOP CALL GIRL'S BOOK" that a civilian traffic officer testified that she participated in the undercover investigation of a former colleague who became a prostitute because she wanted to prevent the call girl from writing an exposé on Los Angeles police.

> "I felt this [book] went a little beyond civil duty," said traffic officer Patricia Isgro during the third day of Norma Jean Almodovar's trial in Los Angeles Superior Court.
> "Our unit of traffic officers had enough problems with people on the street," she testified. "They do not need any adverse publicity."

The newspaper went on to note that "Isgro admitted on cross-examination by defense attorney Martin E. Shucart that she used graphic language in her discussions with Almodovar while 'playing a part to gain her confidence.' "

An understatement, to be sure. Actually, Penny was about to use the word "entrap" to describe what her intentions were when she noticed

Fred Clapp slapping his forehead. She decided to say "to gain her confidence" instead.

She openly admitted that she and the other police officers were attempting to stop my manuscript from being published. At that point many people thought my attorney would file a motion to have the whole case dropped. Penny was virtually conceding a First Amendment violation by the L.A.P.D.

Instead my attorney changed the subject and brought up her divorce. While he managed to get her to admit that she had lied about the time of her separation from her husband (in order to pay him a lesser amount of child support), this did nothing to challenge her credibility as the chief witness against me. At the end of his cross-examination the judge declared a fifteen-minute recess.

As I did at every recess, I went to Victor for a hug. My attorney motioned us to follow him out into the hall. We walked to the end of the corridor where we could be alone.

"Listen, Norma Jean. Umm . . . their case against you is very weak. This whole thing is silly."

"Yes, I know."

My attorney looked away as he said, "I don't think we should put on any defense. I think it would just hurt your case if I put you on the stand. We're just going to go back in there and rest the case."

As I stood in a daze looking at Victor. The clock ticked away on my options, and I thought of the letter I had received from my attorney not too long before. Dated August 1, 1984, Mr. Shucart informed me of case settlement discussions that had occurred. The position of the District Attorney was that jail time should be required but Commissioner Garfinkel proposed the following settlement:

1. I plead guilty or no contest to a violation of California Penal Code Section 266i (Pandering);

2. No jail or state prison time be imposed;

3. I be placed on formal probation for three years, with a specific condition of said probation that I obey all laws.

Mr. Shucart's understanding from Deputy District Attorney Weber was that, although they felt the sentence should be harsher, they would go along with it. Mr. Shucart wrote:

This will further confirm my advising you of above; indicating to you that it was a very acceptable proposal from my point of view; and that you should accept the same. As you know, you rejected the proposed settlement and the matter continues to be set for Trial at 9:00 A.M. on September 4, 1984 in Dept. 119 of the courthouse located at 210 W. Temple, Los Angeles, Ca. As we discussed we will now be making final preparations to try the matter. Thank you.

Now, standing in the hallway, holding tightly to Victor's hand, I felt confused and angry. If Mr. Shucart thought their case against me was so weak, why did he advise me to accept this proposal? If he thought we could win at trial, why would he suggest that I plead guilty? I had been offered a better deal earlier in the game when Richard Chier was my attorney and before it had cost me many thousand of dollars. The whole point of going to trial was to have my day in court! I wanted to tell a jury of my peers what the L.A.P.D. had done! If I accepted this proposal, the jury would never hear my side.

I tried to understand the significance of Mr. Shucart's suggestion to dispense with the defense. I had to believe he was acting in my best interest. I was already heavily traumatized, and I had to trust him. He was my attorney. I figure he must know what he was doing. My freedom was in his hands.

Victor shook his head and shrugged. I turned to Mr. Shucart. "Okay, if you think that's best. I would like to testify, but if you think I shouldn't . . ."

The judge returned to the bench. The prosecution, having finished with its case against me, rested. It was our turn to present a defense. My attorney stood up and said, "Your Honor, the defense rests."

The judge looked a bit surprised, as did the prosecution. I don't think they expected it to be quite that easy. The judge began the instructions to the jury. Court was recessed for lunch. The jury went into deliberations while the rest of us went to eat.

Victor and I walked to Eaton's Redwood House Restaurant on Second Street. It was early so we had no trouble getting a table. Nothing looked particularly appetizing to me, but I ordered something anyway. We both just picked at our food, saying very little to each other. We were just glad to be together.

After lunch we turned reluctantly to the courthouse, hand in hand. I tried to remain optimistic as we got into the elevator. "It's going to be okay, honey." I gave him one more long hug before we stepped out.

Outside the courtroom, which wasn't yet unlocked, the press was waiting impatiently, trying to get a story for the evening news.

"What do you think the verdict will be, Norma Jean?" The reporter from Channel 11 stuck the microphone under my nose. "Wasn't Penny your friend? Why do you think she did this to you?"

"Are you going to rewrite your book if you are convicted?"

"Are you naming names in the book, Norma Jean?"

"Are there any famous politicians involved in your prostitution ring?"

"Do you think you will go to prison?"

"You say the arrest was over your book. Why didn't you tell your side to the jury? Why didn't your attorney put on a defense?"

Victor tried to answer for me. I was so nervous, I couldn't talk to anyone. The video cameras recorded the moments before, during, and after the verdict for posterity.

The bailiff finally unlocked the courtroom. The press converged inside with their minicams, pens, and notepads ready to go. I took my place beside my attorney. We stood.

The judge took the bench. The jury filed in, expressionless. The jury foreman handed the verdict to the bailiff who handed it to the judge and then to the court clerk.

She opened it and read, "We, the jury, in the above-entitled action find the defendant, Norma Jean Almodovar, guilty of pandering." Three o'clock, September 26, 1984, I was a convicted felon. Sentencing was scheduled for November 14 at 9 A.M. After the jury filed out the judge told me I was to report to the probation department immediately and register as a convicted felon. Everyone left the courtroom.

I couldn't face the press. I couldn't stop crying. Mascara ran down my cheeks, and my face was all red blotches. While I sat blotting my eyes with a tissue the bailiff had given me, Victor went outside to deal with the press.

My attorney was also interviewed. "I think that we have spent a great deal of time with the jury in presenting the evidence, and I think the jury has given us their decision, which I happen to disagree with!" When I saw the interview on the news that evening, I was a little confused. Where was I when he spent a great deal of time with them presenting evidence? For that matter, what evidence did he present?

The jury foreman, Ron Kurtis, was interviewed. "It came down to just looking at the law on the blackboard. It was, you know, very obvious . . . unfortunately." The jury foreman seemed to be genuinely sorry they had no choice. By not testifying I had given them none.

Bailiff Hart let us go out the back exit. He put us on the judges' elevator and told us how to get out of the building without running into the media. I thanked him profusely. His kindness was the one bright spot in the whole trial.

Outside in the hot afternoon air my hysteria turned to anger. As we walked across the street to the county probation office, I kept shouting to passersby, "Hey, look at me! I'm a convicted felon!"

Holding my head proudly, I entered the probation office. I handed the clerk the slip of paper the bailiff had given me containing the information on my conviction. She took it and gave me a clipboard with a form. "You gotta fill this out before you can see the probation officer," she said in between chewing her gum and biting her bright red fingernails.

Under occupation I wrote WHORE in big, bold letters. I filled out the rest of the form and handed it back to the clerk. "Have a seat. You'll be seeing Probation Officer Wright." I refused to sit down in the filthy chairs provided by the county. My back was hurting, but I stood against the wall.

Over an hour later I was ushered into Mr. Wright's office. I tried not to exhibit anger, but it was difficult.

Probation Officer James Wright, no relation to my family, I'm sure, seemed to be a congenial person. I tried to explain my side and thought at first he was sympathetic. When I was given a copy of his probation report, however, in which he recommended four years in prison for me, I saw I was mistaken. He stated:

> Orally, in a conversation, the defendant appeared quite candid with the probation officer. She related that she is a prostitute and is not ashamed of her chosen profession as indicated by the way she listed her occupation on the application for probation form.
>
> She states she feels she is a victim of a systematic scheme by the police department to silence her and put her away because she was writing a book . . . which will expose scandals in the police department. . . .
>
> She states that she admittedly enjoys her work and that the only vice she has is that of sex and she gets great pleasure out of satisfying male clients. She related that her former employer, the Los Angeles Police Department's main concern in eventually attempting to secure a warrant to search her apartment was for the purposes of obtaining manuscript that she has written. . . .
>
> She relates on her previous arrest in which the matter was not prosecuted, the officers attempted to set her up and when the plan

failed they were unable to obtain a warrant to search her premises. She indicates at this time a new scheme was developed wherein her former friend, Patricia Isgro, was pressured by police into "setting her up" . . . and that in itself would give the officers reasons to obtain a warrant and search her premises in an effort to obtain . . . manuscripts. . . .

Defendant also related that at the time the police issued a warrant and searched her apartment during the time that she was arrested, they did not seize any materials that related to the business of prostitution but merely took her book manuscript. . . . She relates the manuscript had nothing at all to do with the trial . . . although the police indicated they were holding same for evidence.

She states to this date she has never been returned her manuscripts, and she firmly believes that for some reason or other they will "lose her manuscripts" and they will never be returned. . . .

She vehemently denies the fact that she is a madam as accused, states she has no pimp . . . does not solicit women to engage in acts of prostitution but merely works on her own. She states she refused a plea bargain in that she does not feel she is wrong . . . and would never plead guilty to anything she feels she is not guilty. . . .

The officer [Fred Clapp] related that in his opinion the defendant is guilty of attempting to solicit the services of victim Isgro for purposes of performing prostitution acts. . . . The officer stated that while he did not feel the defendant is a career criminal, he feels she is guilty in the present matter and should be held fully responsible for her actions. He further indicated that *the police department is resentful of the fact that the defendant has been given the limelight of the news media given indication that she is a former police officer* [italics mine]. He states there is no reservations regarding the defendant writing her book and that there has never been a scheme to set up the defendant to put her out of the community in an effort to stop her writing and publishing of a book that she plans to write. . . . He feels the defendant is deserving of whatever sentence the court may administer.

The defendant impressed this probation officer as an individual who has chosen prostitution as a profession with no shame. Despite such practices being not only contrary to the mores of our society as well as a violation of the law, the defendant's philosophy *is one of what consenting adults do in privacy is no vice* (emphasis mine).

Based upon her lack of prior record and the defendant's overall background, under ordinary circumstances she would be deemed a suitable candidate for probation. However, in view of the fact that the statute under which defendant stands convicted rules her ineligible for probation and mandates incarceration at the state level, the probation officer has no alternative but to submit a recommendation of denial.

Sentencing consideration

Factors in Aggravation:
1. the carrying out of the crime indicates premeditation.

Factors in Mitigation:
1. the defendant has no prior arrest convictions.

In view of the fact that the factors in aggravation and mitigation tend to balance, the mid-base term (four years) appears indicated.

Recommendation

It is recommended that probation be denied and the defendant be sentence to state prison. . . .

Respectfully Submitted . . . by James A. Wright, Deputy, Central Adult Investigations. . . . 10-22-84.

Four years for trying to help Penny get a date? Because there was money involved? If money hadn't been involved, there would be no crime. Robbers can get probation. Rapists can get probation. Even child molesters, in nonviolent situations, can get probation—especially if they're former police officers!

Former Hollywood division police officer Mike Casados was caught a second time having sex with an underage girl. The first time he had been caught was in 1982, during the scandal in which several other cops got caught as well. He merely received a six-month suspension. The second time, he got fired. As reported in the June 1986 *Los Angeles Times,* "A former Los Angeles Police officer pleaded no contest Monday to five counts of lewd conduct for sexually molesting a 15-year-old girl. . . . He was allowed to remain free without bail and is scheduled to be sentenced in Superior Court on July 15. Under terms of a plea bargain with the district attorney's office, Casados will receive *no state prison or county jail time, and eight other lewd conduct charges will be dismissed against him at that time* (emphasis mine). Police spokesman Cmdr. William Booth said an investigation was launched after police received complaints from the victim, who had been molested over a five-year period." This means that she was *ten years old* when he started molesting her!

The sentence in California for one count of pandering a consenting adult, using no force fraud or coercion, is a mandatory *three to six years* in state prison.

Former police officer Ron Venegas committed over one hundred burglaries while on duty with his now deceased partner, Jack Myers. Venegas was given a sixteen-month suspended sentence and three months probation.

After my interview with Probation Officer Wright, Victor drove us home. I alternated between hysterical laughter and outbursts of crying. "Darling, do you realize what this means? For the rest of my life I'll be a convicted felon. And the worst part is, whenever I tell someone what I was convicted of, they'll think I'm lying. I had to have done something worse than that to be a convicted felon."

"Honey, calm down. When you get your book published, you'll get even with all of them."

There was nothing he could say that would make me feel better. As we drove down First Street I grabbed the strand of beads on my neck and, in a wild burst of anger, hurled it out the window, but not before it broke, strewing hundreds of tiny beards all over the car floor. "Goddamn it, Penny. I hate you!"

When we got home, Victor tucked me into bed with little protest. Under the covers became my favorite place to escape from the rest of the world. Before I had succumbed to the soothing release of the sedative I took, I agreed to do an interview the next day with Channel 4 news, for the "Front Page People" segment.

The news crew and Kirste Wilde arrived at ten the next morning. Kirste seemed to be sympathetic and caring. I had a chance to say all the things Mr. Shucart had not allowed me to say at my trial. Those things were left out of the edited version on the four o'clock news, however. My only remaining comment was that I felt I was at war with the L.A.P.D. Kirste's closing comment was that I had lost the first battle for now.

Immediately after the trial I fired Mr. Shucart and rehired Richard Chier. Sentencing was scheduled for October 24, a month away. There were many things I had to do before then in case I was sentenced to prison. Richard Chier kept reassuring me there was no way that could happen.

Victor and I agreed we needed to get away. On Friday, October 5, we embarked on a memorable trip that took us to Carmel, Sacramento, Reno, and Las Vegas. We saw old friends, made new ones, and took a lot of pictures. We returned in much better spirits than when we had left. In fact, I felt so positive about the situation, I almost believed everything would turn out okay.

Then, thanks to my old friend Kay Rios, I still had a speaking engagement at the college in Fort Collins, Colorado. I left for Colorado on Thursday and spent four days with friends, blissfully ignoring reality.

I returned home with wonderful memories of beautiful scenery and words of comfort and love from my friends. I thought I was emotionally prepared for whatever lay before me, *even prison*.

17. TOMORROW I'M GOING TO JAIL

What bride isn't happy her wedding night
All lovely and decked out so fine?
And her waiting groom, a handsome sight,
Share a toast and sip the wine!

Shouldn't a bride be blushing and have not a care
The night she weds her man?
Together, forever, to have and to share
A life and a dream and a plan?

Surely most would agree that's the way it should be—
The ending, a sweet fairy tale.
But sadly enough, it's just not for me,
For tomorrow I'm going to jail!

VICTOR TOOK MY HAND and squeezed it. "Sweetheart, it's going to be okay. We've been through the worst already."

I looked at him without saying a word, not daring to tell him that I didn't agree. I had a gut feeling I was going to prison, although both attorneys assured me I wouldn't. "Trust us," they said.

Sentencing had been postponed until my new attorneys, Richard Chier and Ephraim Margolin, were able to file their motions on my behalf. I didn't expect to be in court very long, but it was still very difficult.

My former attorney, Martin Shucart, was there. It was a formality for him to request that the judge permit him to withdraw from the case. It was also a polite way to say I fired him. I looked the other way when he walked by. He stammered some unintelligible statement to Victor as he made his way out of the courtroom, something about getting more money, I think.

Richard Chier made the standard request for more time, and it was granted. I was to return on November 14 for sentencing. Mr. Weber, the

D.A., was visibly unhappy. He opposed the continuance, but the judge granted the motion.

I had bills from three criminal attorneys and no money to pay them. I decided to hold a fund-raising party the day before my sentencing. Victor was a member of the Masquers, a nationwide acting fraternity. They had a marvelous old building on Sycamore Avenue in Hollywood. The manager, Bob Duggan, graciously offered to let us use the place for just the price of drinks served.

Margo St. James, and Scarlot Harlot, a prostitute who wrote and starred in her own one-woman play, volunteered to help me organize the affair, and I called upon other friends and even clients to provide entertainment and food.

My clients in the food industries donated things like condiments, hamburgers, buns, and so forth. Many of my wonderful friends volunteered to cook the food and sell T-shirts, buttons, and books of poems. At the same time they tried to keep me from having a breakdown.

At one point during the event, as I walked up the stairs to the stage, I was so full of nervous energy I tripped and fell. I bruised my leg, and later when it was time to do my part in Scarlot's play, my leg was horribly swollen. The huge multicolored bruise was still there the next week when I was being processed in the county jail. One of the guards wanted to know if my "pimp had beaten me up because his money-making whore had got herself thrown in jail."

The event was not as successful as we'd hoped, but we did raise some money. Victor and I finally finished cleaning up around 2:30. Bob Duggan and Jack, the stage manger, were still around, waiting for us to finish so they could lock up. Since Jack had been helpful in staging the entertainment, we gave him fifty bucks. I knew he needed the money; he was an out-of-work actor.

He hugged me. "Norma Jean, thanks, but I can't take this from you." He took my hand and put the money in it. "You need this more than I do." He was crying, and he kissed me.

With that gesture the emotions I had been repressing all evening broke through, and I began to cry. That triggered tears from Victor and Bob, and soon we were all crying and hugging one another in an emotional display worthy of the best Irish wake.

Victor and I didn't sleep at all that night. The next morning we were exhausted but hopeful when we walked into the courtroom. Ephraim Margolin and Richard Chier had been in the judge's chambers with Judge

Munoz and the D.A., Richard Weber. When Richard Chier came out, I sensed something was very wrong.

"Norma Jean," he began in his singsong voice, his eyes avoiding mine. He looked uncomfortable. "I have some bad news. The judge is talking about sending you to prison for some kind of study." He shifted his weight from one foot to the other.

Judge Munoz was rumored to be one of the most liberal judges in the downtown Superior Court; he seldom sent anyone to prison. In fact, the last time I had been to court, I had witnessed him giving probation to a drug dealer who had violated probation a second time. Richard had told me we couldn't have gotten a more liberal judge.

Richard and Ephraim made their best presentation. The judge decided to set aside their motions and sentencing for the moment, and place me in prison for a psychiatric evaluation. A 12.03.03, it is called. He said such a study was necessary to determine the proper punishment for me.

The usual protests were registered on my behalf by my two attorneys, and they reminded the judge the holidays were soon approaching. The judge said that was why he wanted me admitted as soon as possible. They were able to get me one week's postponement to get my affairs in order, which the D.A. objected to!

The thought of going to prison was shattering, but I was grateful that I had a week's reprieve. Norma Ashby, the madam who had dated Daryl Gates' brother and who was also a prostitutes' rights activist and founder of the group CATharsis, had been thrown in jail the day she was sentenced to ninety days. The judge gave her no time to arrange for her daughter's care, settle her financial affairs, or cancel her appointments.

Outside the courtroom my friends shielded me from reporters. Victor gave them a statement, and somehow we made it to the car.

During the drive home I couldn't stop crying. Margo and Scarlot tried to comfort me, but I was beyond consolation. At home I tore off my clothes and crawled into bed. There was so much to do, but I had to escape the pain and anger, which had become so overwhelming.

The next day I called my mother. She wanted to be with me, so she took a flight and arrived the next evening. To come out to L.A. to see her oldest daughter go to prison must have been very difficult for her, but I was glad she did.

Monday, November 19, 1984—two days of freedom left and still so much to do. The court had told us that in order for Victor to visit me, we had to be married, so we planned to be married that evening.

Meanwhile, we went to the bank, where I signed documents giving him power of attorney. Then I had to buy the clothing that I would be allowed to have in prison. According to the sergeant in charge of admissions at the state prison, I could bring three changes of clothing, a robe, a nightgown, socks, underthings, and makeup, but the catch was that everything had to be brand new, with the tags still attached and the makeup in its original packaging. I asked him why, and he said it was just the rule.

In the afternoon Victor looked through the Yellow Pages for a wedding chapel while I bathed and dressed. "Wedding Chapels" are unromantically listed right after "Weaving and Mending Services." Years ago, when I worked briefly for Ma Bell, I always wondered who used these quickie wedding chapels listed in the phone book. Now I knew.

There was one close by on Wilshire Boulevard that didn't require couples who had lived together for two years or more to take a blood test for the license. I made an appointment for 5:30. Tactfully, my mother declined to join us. She had never approved of my relationship with Victor because of our age difference.

It was dismally cloudy and cool when we left the apartment, and the weatherman predicted it would rain. As we drove in silence to the chapel, I thought about the irony of this wedding. We were getting married only because the state was forcing us to—we had always felt that our lifetime commitment to each other did not require state recognition.

The chapel was tired and shabby, and smelled stale and musty, like an attic. Bouquets of wilted, fading flowers were strewn haphazardly around the room. On the walls were photographs of celebrity couples who probably had used the chapel to keep their weddings private.

At the back of the chapel an apathetic clerk who also served as the witness took our money and handed us forms to fill out. A little man in a threadbare black suit wearing a bad black toupee and wire-rimmed glasses introduced himself as the minister. Enthusiastically, he shook our hands. "I know the two of you must be very happy! Your bride looks so lovely!" He winked at Victor as we solemnly walked to the front of the chapel.

Neither of us responded, so he cleared his throat and proceeded to marry us. "Huhum. Shall we get on with it, then? Would you care for our lovely wedding music?"

Victor shook his head negatively.

"Well, do you have rings to exchange?"

We didn't.

"Okay, then, we'll do it without them."

As he recited the wedding vows to us, Victor and I held hands, the tears streaming down our faces. We gazed deeply into each other's eyes. For all the attention we paid to the minister, he might as well not have been there. Dazed, I thought I heard him ask me to repeat what he was saying, and somehow I managed. The words that came out of my mouth sounded so corny. Then it was Victor's turn. He squeezed my hands so hard I thought they would break. Slowly and very tenderly he repeated the vows to me.

Before the minister could say "You may kiss the bride," we were tightly locked in each other's arms.

Following the wedding we drove to Pasadena for dinner with our friends Ric and Margaret. We had told them only a few hours earlier that we were getting married. What they managed to accomplish on such notice was a wonderful surprise. The house was decorated with flowers, balloons, and streamers. They had prepared a turkey dinner complete with a wedding cake. Thoughtfully, Ric photographed everything. Victor and I posed somberly as we cut our cake. Those photos helped me get through some of the loneliest times in prison.

My days of freedom dwindled down to a few hours. On Tuesday night, in observance of the sorry occasion, we dined at Giuseppi's in Hollywood, our favorite Italian restaurant. It would probably be a while before I could feast on such exquisite pasta. I didn't think I would be allowed to order out in prison. Amazingly, the thought of going to prison in the morning did not dull my appetite. I indulged myself by ordering foods I would normally pass on. I figured I would have plenty of time to work off the extra calories.

When I ordered dessert, Romano, the headwaiter, was shocked. "Norma Jean, you are going to get fat!"

"I can eat what I want tonight. I am going to prison in the morning."

Romano scratched his head, looking very confused. Victor explained what I meant. "Oh, I am so sorry. What a terrible thing to happen to such a nice lady!"

We paid the bill, said our good-byes to everyone, and as we left I noticed that Rod Stewart, the rock musician, a frequent guest at Giuseppi's, was engaged in an intense conversation with Romano. As we approached our car, Romano came running up behind us. "Norma Jean, Victor, just a minute please." He was out of breath. "Mr. Stewart would like to know if you would join him for a bottle of champagne."

I looked at Victor and shrugged. Why not? It was late, but there was really no reason not to stay up all night. After all, I would have plenty of opportunity to rest in prison. We went back inside.

Romano introduced us to Mr. Stewart. The owner, Giuseppi, joined us, and we all talked and drank champagne until closing. It almost seemed like a normal celebration rather than the occasion it was. Everyone hugged and kissed me good-bye. Despite my overwhelming sadness, it was a night to remember. I doubt that many convicted felons are treated with such kindness and generosity—especially by a famous rock star—the night before going to prison.

Even though I'd had champagne, sleep was out of the question that night. How could I sleep knowing I was going to be away from the man I loved, away from my friends, and away from life for the next ninety days? Victor and I clung to each other tightly all night.

Before the sun came up I took a long, hot bubble bath, the last I would have for a long while. I sat in the tub, shaved my legs, and clipped off my famous long fingernails. The sergeant had told me that if I didn't, they would take them off for me. I don't think they would have been gentle.

At first I dressed demurely in a skirt and blouse, but then I changed my mind. I doubted there would be any press around for this court appearance so I put my long red hair into two neat braids that stuck out on either side of my head and decided that jeans would be as appropriate as anything for going to jail.

18. Pig in a Poke(y)

If you send a pig in a poke to the ''pen,''
You are apt to get a revolt now and then.
Beware if the pig that you send has a sword.
She just may decide that your ox should be gored.

If the sword that she has in her hand is a pen,
A mightier sword that your bullets can't bend,
When she's backed in a corner, her sword she will draw,
Nor will she be stopped though her flesh shall be raw.

The system picked on the wrong piggy to fry
And soon they will rue the day they did try.
The pen will by far do more harm than the sword,
For soon all will hear from the piggy that roared.

THE SILENCE IN THE HOLDING CELL was nervewracking. The cold cement seat was about a foot too narrow for long-term sitting, and sleeping on it was out of the question. I was alone for what seemed like hours.

To pass the time I read the graffiti on the wall and thought about the people who had passed through this place. I amused myself by trying to imagine what gruesome crimes they might have committed and whose lives they had ruined. From their scrawls I could see they were clearly as unrepentant as I was, but I didn't feel I had anything in common with them.

I tried to brace myself for the ordeal ahead. I was determined the sons of bitches would not win this round. Still, momentary anger overwhelmed me, and a hot tear or two sprang unbidden from my eyes and coursed down my face. This, in turn, made my nose run. I didn't have a thing to wipe it on except my sleeve.

After an eternity, a guard arrived and took me down the hall for booking. He picked up my pathetic bag of clothing before he unlocked the cell door. ''This yours?''

I sighed. ''Yeah.''

"What you in here for, honey?"

"I wrote a book." It was difficult not to be sarcastic, but it was true.

He said, "No, come on, I mean it. What are you in here for?"

I repeated I was there because I wrote a book that pissed off the L.A.P.D. He shook his head. He didn't seem to believe me.

"I got a live one here," he whispered to a female deputy sheriff, handing her my property bag.

The female sheriff shoved me inside a bathroom and did a strip search. She then took me into a small room where she filled out the paperwork on the clothing and cosmetics. It was the last time I saw any of it until I was released fifty days later.

The sergeant at the California Women's Institute at Frontera told me I would need some money to buy incidentals such as a toothbrush, toothpaste, and a comb, so I brought $50 with me. The deputy confiscated it and gave me a receipt. It was the last time I saw my money, too.

The deputy took me back to the holding cell, where I remained alone until late that evening when I was brought to a smaller holding tank with about thirty other women. I had been in custody since early morning, and so far I hadn't been given a thing to eat. I mentioned this in passing to the female deputy sheriff. Her response does not warrant repeating.

I leaned against the wall because there was no place to sit. I was given a once-over by all the women in the cell, some of whom appeared to recognize me from the trial publicity. One young black woman had the courage to ask, "Say, ain't you that cop-prostitute that wrote a book?"

The other women stopped talking and looked at me. I gulped. Would these women attack me for having once been on the other side? I looked her right in the eye. "Yes, that's me."

"Hey, all right!" She looked happy. I tried to smile. The other women weren't attacking, so I was relieved. Several of the women asked for my autograph. They scrounged around a found a dull pencil and tore a piece off someone's property receipt. The autograph I signed was slightly different from my usual signature; after all, some of these women were there for committing forgery!

I spent the rest of the evening listening to their stories of police abuse, which they hoped I would use in my book. Later, I tried to remember what they had told me, but I was so good at blocking out so much of what had happened that I forgot. But I have not forgotten them or the fact that they did not see me as a threat. In a situation that could have been disastrous, those women were good to me.

One of the inmates told me I would probably be taken to Sybil Brand for a few weeks before being transported to state prison. If she hadn't, I would not have known what to expect. The deputies told me nothing.

Around eleven the deputies finally came for us. We were shackled together like a chain gang and led single file to an old, decrepit bus that stank worse than the holding tank. Nausea swept through me, but there was nothing in my stomach to vomit.

Even though I had spent several hours unprotected in a cell with the other inmates, I was now given special treatment. The deputy seated me in the front of the bus because I was a "fish" (a new prisoner) and because I was an ex-cop. Behind me sat a young, scraggly, blond-haired woman who proudly recounted her most recent arrest and sentence. This was her sixth offense for shoplifting and forgery. She had been caught in Zody's Department Store stealing a coat she was going to give her mother for Christmas. It was too bad, she said, laughing, because it was a really nice coat! I asked what her sentence was, "Ten days," she replied. This meant, because of the overcrowded jails, she would be out in five.

The bus made several stops before we arrived at the Sybil Brand Institute. As we were preprocessed we were told to take off our shoes and socks to have our feet inspected. I was patted down, then put into the holding tank.

By this time my appetite was gone, so when the trustee (an inmate on good behavior with a good job in the jail) brought us each a cup of coffee and a dry bologna sandwich, I turned it down.

That was a mistake! The other women jumped all over me. "Bitch, why didn't you take it? You could have given it to one of us. You stupid girl!"

I never thought of that. I turned back to the trustee. "Okay, I'll take it," I called. But it was too late. In jail you are never given a second chance at food.

I was desperate to call Victor, but the pay phone was occupied all night by a black woman who had been arrested on a drug charge.

While I waited for my turn to be processed, I noticed that women who had arrived after me were being processed ahead of me. I finally got to use the phone. Victor said he had been sitting by the phone all day waiting to hear from me.

When I heard his voice, I almost lost control. "Hi, honey," I managed to whisper. "It's me."

"Are you all right?" The concern in his voice only made it worse.

I sobbed. "Uh huh." I tried hard not to break. The tears in my eyes were once again making my nose run. Just as I was ready to talk to him without my voice quivering, the deputy came to get me. It was my turn, I told Victor, and I hung up the phone without a good-bye. Another inmate grabbed the receiver out of my hand.

The record clerk asked if I had any medical problems. I made the mistake of telling her about my bad back, and I also mentioned that I had a terrible headache. She informed me that I would have to be taken to the infirmary if I wanted any aspirin.

There was no one to take me there at the moment, so as soon as I received the mandatory delousing shower and shampoo and my flimsy jail garments, I was put back into another holding tank by myself. Naturally, there was no phone. At about five in the morning someone finally took me to see the nurse and get some aspirin.

The night nurse was out on her rounds. I sat handcuffed in the doctor's office for another hour or so. The nurse finally appeared, looked at my file, and told me she could not dispense any medication, including aspirin, until after I had been seen by the doctor. "Fine," I said. "When will that be?"

"The doctor is off until after the holidays."

I almost choked. My head hurt so badly. I begged her: "Please, just one aspirin?"

"Sorry, I can't help you. You will have to see the doctor first."

"What do I do in the meantime?"

"I can fix an ice pack for you."

"Great."

It was decided that I had to remain in the infirmary because of my bad back. Besides, they could not find any room for me in the isolation ward, where I would have to be housed due to my special status. So I was placed where they put crazy women to prevent them from disturbing the general populace by screaming and carrying on.

My tiny cell had no bed, and I was given one sheet but no blanket or pillow. It was as cold as ice in there. There was no bed because the women who are usually put there sometimes try to kill themselves or set the mattress on fire. Instead there was a cold, hard cement slab to sleep on. Just what I needed for my bad back and headache!

Also, since I was in the infirmary, the garment I had been given earlier was taken away, and in its place I was given one of those little hospital gowns that opens in the back and doesn't cover anything.

I sat on my cement mattress, waiting patiently for the nurse to appear with my ice pack, but she never returned. I tried to fall asleep. I was cold,

I had a splitting headache, my back was killing me, my stomach was growling, and my mind was numb with anger.

Just as I thought I might actually fall asleep, I heard a blood-curdling scream. It sounded like someone was being murdered! Then the ranting and raving began. For the next four days some poor demented woman screamed incessantly, yelling and cursing life, God, the devil, whoever. Now and then the nurse came by and gave her a shot that would quiet her for an hour or two. It took several guards to hold her down for those shots. Mostly, though, the guards went by her cell to taunt her. She cursed at them, and they just laughed. Even when she was quiet the guards went by to get her going again. She was an older black woman named Gloria. She must have been suffering from religious guilt of some sort because her ranting generally came in the form of biblical quotes and in the tones of a hellfire and damnation preacher. Whatever demons she thought possessed her soul would not give her any peace and quiet. I didn't get any, either.

I was the only other infirmary "guest" for most of the time, but we did get a new inmate on Thanksgiving evening. She and Gloria exchanged insults, curses, and Scripture verses the whole night. At least I think it was night. There were no windows in the infirmary, and I had no way of gauging the time.

In addition to screams there was the loud clanking of prison doors, opening and slamming shut, all the time. The bells rang constantly. I tried to figure out what each set of ringing was for. There seemed to be a pattern to it. Ring . . . ring . . . ring. Pause. Ring . . . ring . . . ring. Pause. Ring . . . ring. Stop. Then the pattern would start all over again. Non-stop, at all hours.

On Thanksgiving morning breakfast was shoved through the tiny little opening in the heavy steel door, an appetizing entree of slush, mush, and blah! When the guard served it, I asked her what time it was. I must have been invisible because she didn't answer me.

Late Thursday afternoon (I think) a guard opened my cell, threw me a red cotton gown, and told me to put it on. I asked what was going on; she ignored me. She handcuffed my hands together and then chained me to her. She led me to the elevator, where all the other inmates were told to get off because I was a high-security case, and no one else could be on the elevator at the same time I was.

As the deputy led me down the hall, I begged her to let me have a toothbrush, a comb, or something that would make me feel almost human again. I was told I wasn't allowed those things in the infirmary because I might try to kill myself with them.

We finally reached the visiting room. It turned out Victor had finally made it through for a visit. He had been waiting in line for about five hours.

Since I was a high-security case, I had to be placed right next to the trustee in charge. I waited another fifteen minutes before Victor was allowed to come and sit on the other side of the glass. In some ways it probably would have been easier if I hadn't been allowed to see him at all because to be so close and not be able to touch him or kiss him was sheer torture. I tried to be brave, but I lost.

We were allowed a twenty-minute visit, and I couldn't sit there and cry my time away. I picked up the phone, and he picked up his. My mouth formed words, but my voice would not cooperate. I put my hand up against the glass window that divided us. He put his hand up next to it. Tears poured down my face.

"Honey, don't cry." His words made me want to all the more.

I'm still not sure how I made it through that visit, but it seemed like only seconds before the guard was telling us it was time to hang up.

When I returned to my cell, I found, much to my dismay, that dinner had been served, and I had missed it. No dinner for me that night—no turkey, no stuffing, no nothing! Breakfast had been so pitiful, lunch had been inedible, and now I was starving! I sighed in resignation, closed my eyes, and tried to sleep through the incessant noise.

Friday, November 23. Late in the day the guard came to get me. Victor had once again braved the long wait to see me for twenty minutes. He still didn't know I was being kept in solitary confinement. Neither did my lawyer.

"Hi, honey. How are you holding up?" He attempted a smile.

I told him I had missed dinner the night before and probably would again that night because I had been brought down around the same time. He promised to ask the sergeant in charge if there wasn't something they could do about holding my dinner for me.

When the trustee wasn't looking, I put my lips as close to the glass as I thought was sanitary. He did the same. I was glad for a change that there was a window between us! I hadn't bathed since being admitted into jail and having the delousing shower.

Saturday, November 24. Breakfast as usual. Nurse Smith served it that morning, and when she pushed mine through the little opening in the solid steel door, I tried to get her to talk to me, to find out if the doctor would be in that day. She ignored me completely. I know she heard me because she mentioned it to the guard.

Later that day, after Victor's visit, the weekend and night guard, a redhead named Officer Daly, took pity on me and let me take a five-minute bath. She even found a slightly used comb to give me and a new gown to wear. I felt like a new woman. And, bless her heart, she lent me one of her magazines.

Late Saturday night the guards decided I didn't belong in the infirmary. They tried to arrange my transfer to the isolation ward, but it was full. So back up to the infirmary I went, but this time I was taken to the other side where the cells had beds (for the maternity cases). For the first time in five days I had a blanket, a pillow, a comb, a toothbrush, some toothpaste, and even a small mirror above the sink where I could see a fuzzy reflection of my scraggly, pitiful-looking self. It felt like the Ritz Hotel!

The luxury was short-lived. Sunday afternoon, while lunch was being served, I asked the guard when I would be taken to where I was supposed to be, but like the others, she refused to answer me. When she came into my cell, she told me to get back in bed. Since I was not ill, there was no reason for me to get into bed. I asked for her name; she didn't answer.

As a prisoner I had the right to know the name of the officer giving me orders. Her sweater covered her nametag. I took a breath and repeated my request. She refused to tell me. My only recourse was to lift her sweater to see her nametag. It was the wrong thing to do. My hand froze in midair. My head hit the wall with a thud. She had long, bright red fingernails, and she dug them deep into my face. Her other hand was on my neck. I thought I was a goner.

"How dare you touch me, cunt! I'm not going to give you my name. What for? So you can tell '20/20' who I am? Don't you ever touch one of us again if you want to make it out of here alive!"

She pushed me onto the bed, then slammed the door behind her. Within fifteen minutes she was back. She rushed into my cell, grabbed my arms, violently pulled them back behind my back and handcuffed me. She took away my comb, toothbrush, and the $5 that Victor had given me. She pulled me by my hair out into the hallway and dragged me back into a cell in solitary. She was muttering obscenities under her breath, and when she slammed the door to the cell, she said, "Tell this to Barbara Walters, bitch."

About an hour later another deputy came to my cell. She was an older woman, a sergeant. She asked me my side of the story. I explained to her that I had been in the infirmary for the past five days. Then I explained that no one would tell me what was going on and that I had asked the deputy her name because she had been so rude to me. The sergeant saw I was nonviolent and said she would try to get me out of there.

In the meantime dinner came and went. I didn't get any because I was being punished. Also, I lost my visiting privilege that day even though Victor had spent the usual five hours waiting in line. When they told him he couldn't see me, they didn't tell him why.

Finally, the sergeant came back to my cell, handcuffed me, and led me to the isolation ward. I never did find out the name of the deputy.

I still had no pillow, but at least now I had a blanket. And what a cell! I looked around at my new home—a little cubicle about five feet wide and six feet long with a bunk bed, a tiny locker for clothes storage, a rusty commode, a sink, and a cute little picniclike table and chair. A standard isolation ward cell—no windows to the outside world, only the cheerless gloom of an olive green wall on the other side of a double set of bars. At least I was out of the "hole."

Monday, November 26. Five-thirty in the morning the blasting sound of the top rock-and-roll radio station in Los Angeles crashed through my restless dreams and pulled me with a thud back to the real world.

"Oh, shit! What the hell is that?" I almost hit my head on the bunk bed above me. I stuck my fingers in my ears, trying to block out the noise. The next thing I heard was the deputy of the morning, who looked and sounded like an army drill sergeant: "Okay, ladies. Rise and shine! Let's look lively! I want all of you up and dressed with your beds made! *I mean now!*" She passed once, twice, three times. By the third time I decided she meant business. I jumped out of my bunk, thinking the war had started.

Breakfast was served by two women in the unit, and it was no better than I had had in the infirmary. It consisted of lots of mushy cereal, maybe some rotting fruit, once in a while a piece of sausage, and now and then some runny scrambled eggs. Judy, the older woman server, introduced herself and welcomed me.

I quickly learned how the assembly line worked in isolation. There were twelve cells in a row on each side of the ward, twenty-four in all. No one was allowed out of the cell except for a shower or a visit. You had to be imaginative in order to engage in any form of effective communication. The bars were barely wide enough to fit your hand through, much less a hand with anything in it, but we managed. This is the way food, newspapers, and love notes were passed—that is, as long as everyone along the route was awake. But if there was a late sleeper or if the inhabitant of a cell had been taken out to go to court, well, the whole makeshift system fell apart.

For the next two weeks, until I was transferred to state prison, I learned the pattern of life in Sybil Brand. From the moment we were awakened until the radio was turned off and lights out was called at about 8:30, it was one struggle after another to (a) get a shower, (b) use the phone, (c) get some money from your account to buy little incidentals, and (d) get books to read. I am basically a shy, quiet type, but you can be sure by the time I left the unit I knew how to yell as loud as the next girl for my chance to take a shower.

The psychological games that keepers play on inmates are petty and cruel. I had more than my share because of who I was. For instance, when it was time for showers, the guard deliberately bypassed me in working her way up the line.

"Side A, cell number one, want a shower?"

Cell one responded affirmatively, as did cells two and three. I was in cell four. As I grabbed my towel and soap, standing ready by the electronically controlled door, the guard bellowed out, "Number five, ready for a shower?" Jesus, couldn't that bitch count? Four comes before five! I quietly tried to get the guard's attention. It was useless. The rest of the cells got their showers. I asked each of them to tell the guard that cell four would like to shower. They did, but the guard told them she had passed number four, and now it was too late. I never did get a shower on Monday.

By Tuesday I figured I couldn't retain my dignity *and* get a shower so I learned to holler. And holler I did, and I finally got a shower. Next on my list of things was to get a pencil and some paper. And then maybe a book to read.

The first few days I said very little, but listened to everyone and everything around me. I had to learn how to survive. I needed to know the language, to know what to do, and to know who did what.

The conversations were fascinating, especially at night after lights out. The guard was not at her desk, and the girls talked all night long. Now and then a guard would make the rounds and shine a flashlight in our faces for bed count.

Fragmented conversations went like this:

"Did you see the new guard they got in the visiting room? He's cute! Wouldn't mind if he brought me back up in the elevator!"

"Say, girl, I hear you're gettin' put in general ward 'cause you kissed ass to the sergeant."

"Don't be tellin' everybody such lies, bitch. I'll see to it you lose your visitin' privileges!"

"My asshole brother turned me and my old man in. Can you believe that flesh and blood would do that? Shit."

Soft black voice, singing to herself, "Want my man to want me . . . want to be with my man."

A more mature voice, authoritatively: "Shut up, girls. It's two-thirty!"

"Bitch!"

Silence for a few minutes, then whispers and giggles. A loud sigh. A toilet flushes. Then several.

A scream: "Guard, guard. I got a big cockroach in my bed!"

Everybody laughs. "Guard's not in here. Eat it, bitch. It's good protein!"

"Shut up!"

The front door creaks as the guard unlocks it. Silence for a moment.

"Guard, guard, I got a headache. Man, I need some drugs."

Giggles around the room. The guard raps on the bars with her baton. "That will be enough, ladies. Go to sleep." In a moment she is gone, and once again the whispers start.

I had finally heard enough and tried to sleep. The damned radio came on awfully early, and it was often left on well past lights out. The masochistic bitch in the control room probably thought it was as funny as hell to leave the radio on a station featuring sexual advice from Dr. Ruth for a group of women who couldn't get any sex (or weren't supposed to) and who were supposed to be sleeping.

Dr. Ruth's shrill, accented voice blared in an institution filled with horny women: "Vat should you do if your friend can't reach you in the normal position? Try putting a pillow under your little behind to prop you up. Dat will make it easier to hump you!" Titter titter. "Next caller, vat is your problem?"

From the ward: "Hey, Dr. Ruth, I need a vibrator in here! Or send me a man!"

Another voice: "You don't need a man, baby, you need my tongue!"

"I ain't queer!"

"How do you know until you've tried it?"

"That why you in here, Angie? You queer?"

"Aw, shut up. I'm in here 'cause my girlfriend says I hit her!"

"Why'd you hit your girlfriend, Angie? Was she cheating on you?"

"Hey, man, nobody cheats on me and gets away with it! I don't put up with that shit!"

A verbal fight broke out between Angie and another girl. Shouts and screams about sexual preferences echoed through the ward. Everyone was awake now. The majority yelled for Angie to shut up. Angie was belligerent. Nobody was going to push her around. Everyone was yelling, even me, and the noise was unbearable! Finally the guard returned and threatened solitary for everyone. Judy, the older woman who had befriended me, told her what was happening. Angie was taken away. After the guard left again, Dr. Ruth was still dispensing sexual advice. We were all still horny. The guards are a sick bunch.

Judy warned me I might be in Sybil Brand for several weeks before I caught the "train" to C.I.W., California Institute for Women. The train was actually a bus, but that's what they called it.

On Wednesday, one week after I had been incarcerated, the vendor cart came by. Victor had given me some more money, so I was finally able to buy shampoo, a comb, a toothbrush, and toothpaste. I also bought a candy bar, one of life's little treats. It had to sustain me for the weeks ahead when no treats of any kind were forthcoming.

19. NIGHTMARE HOTEL

It's no fun at all to be locked behind bars,
No fun being in a small cell.
Can't see out the window to look at the stars.
Yeah, being in prison is hell.

Got no one to talk to, got nothing to do.
I sit and count flies on my wall.
Time goes so slowly, and between me and you,
I'd rather not be here at all!

THURSDAY, NOVEMBER 29. I was awakened early by the guard. "Almodovar, you're leaving today. Get dressed." She stuffed the clothes I had worn to court through the bars.

Be still, my heart! For a minute I thought I was going home. I mean, the judge never told me what kind of study or how it was going to be done, or even where, exactly. But I discovered I was only going to the state prison.

After I showered and put on human clothing, the guard handcuffed me and took me downstairs. I was put in a small cell that was used as a drunk tank. I protested about the smell, so the guard took me to a closet outside the main holding cell and locked me in. Hours passed while all the other women who were being transferred to C.I.W. were processed.

One of the trustees brought lunch for the women in the large holding tank. My closet had a small window, and I watched as she handed the other women sandwiches and apples. I was hungry. Unlike the first day, I wouldn't have turned down a plain baloney sandwich now. I knocked at the window, but nobody heard me. Frustrated, I sat back down on the floor.

When the guard finally opened the door, the other women were already lined up in twos, handcuffed to each other, and shuffling to the bus. When it was loaded, the driver took me on board. He pointed to a seat at the back of the bus. "If you want to sit down on this trip, that's the only seat left." He gave me a sarcastic smile and shoved me down the aisle, then he turned and locked the bulletproof door between himself and the prisoners. I expect it was soundproof as well. I walked down the aisle and took my seat among the other women. So much for protective segregation. I was told I was being kept separate from them for "my own safety." That's why I was put in solitary in county jail and why I would be imprisoned in the special housing unit at C.I.W. Clearly, nobody cared if anything happened on the bus.

Several stops were to be made on our way to C.I.W. One was the California Rehabilitation Center, originally only a drug rehabilitation center but now used as a state prison for all lower-custody felons. It looked like a resort. The huge well-manicured lawns were emerald green, and it had a manmade lake, a golf course, and a huge tennis court. Mount Baldy loomed in the background, covered with snow. The buildings, a light tan color, were of Spanish architecture. I hoped the place I was going to would be as picturesque. It was, at least on the outside.

As we passed through the gates of C.I.W., I thought to myself, "This place doesn't look so bad. Sort of like a college campus. At least I'll be able to see the outdoors."

Once the bus had parked, I was separated from the rest of the prisoners. The sergeant to whom I had spoken about bringing new clothing came out to greet me. He took me through indoctrination and check-in. I was told to strip and take a shower, and then I was given a cursory examination by the nurse. After a thorough search, my clothes were returned to me and I was issued my new prison garb: three pairs of socks, three pairs of heavy-duty underpants, but no bra. I was told they didn't have any in my size. Weeks later, when Victor attempted to visit me, they wouldn't let him see me because I didn't have a bra.

The guard took me to the special housing unit, my new home, and again I was strip-searched. I'm not certain what they thought I could have smuggled in since the last search. I hadn't been let out of anyone's sight!

I was left in the custody of the guards, Officers Smith and Fulford. Officer Smith issued my sheets, blanket, pillow, soap, five sheets of paper, five stamps, and a pencil. Then she escorted me to my private suite. The good news was that it was slightly bigger than the one I had occupied at Sybil Brand. The bad news was that right outside my cell, straight across from the special housing unit, was a cow pasture and tons of hay. I am allergic to hay.

After I was tucked safely inside my new residence, the other five women in the special unit bugged the guard for information about me.

"What does she look like?"

"Nothing special."

"She's a two-hundred-dollar-an-hour hooker?"

"Well, I wouldn't pay it if I were a man!"

They whispered as though they thought I couldn't hear them. Every day I heard the petty, biting comments they made.

The women in this special housing unit were indeed special. Everyone except me was in there for murder!

There were six cells in the unit; mine was A123. Charlotte was right across from me. She had been involved in a robbery where a bank guard was killed. Ginny, who viciously murdered her boyfriend after he cheated on her, was next to Charlotte. The last cell on that side was occupied by Angel, a gang member who had been involved in a drug-related homicide. In the farthest cell on my side was Peggy, who had killed someone in a botched prison escape attempt, and right next door was a baby killer, Carol.

I never talked to any of them, and they only talked "at" me when they had something derisive to say. They also did plenty of talking about me to one another and to the guards. One day they decided that since I was a whore, I brought down the value of their neighborhood. The next day they theorized that the ex-cop whore was probably in there to spy on them. In either case they wanted nothing to do with me nor I with them. But it would have been nice to have someone to talk to.

Being in the special housing unit meant I had no privileges whatsoever. Even though I had done nothing except have the misfortune of once being employed by the L.A.P.D., I was in the unit usually reserved for women who had been on the "yard" and through bad behavior had lost their inmate privileges. I had no telephone privileges, no exercise privileges, no quarterly packages, and so forth.

My contact lenses had been in my eyes for weeks, and by now I was facing the possibility of a severe eye infection. Victor sent me a package that contained contact lens solution and a fresh pair of lenses. Because I was not supposed to receive any packages at all, the mailroom returned it. Victor mailed it back to the prison, called the warden, and threatened all kinds of lawsuits if it was not given to me immediately. When the mailroom lieutenant brought it to me personally, my cell block mates thought I was being given special treatment. They didn't drop the subject for the rest of the day:

"Hey, who does the bitch think she is? Don't she know how to read the rules? We can't have packages in here!"

"Ya don't have nothin' comin' to ya in here, whore!"

"I hope her eyes get infected and fall out. Then she could be the world's first blind hooker!" Laughter from the others.

Living in the special unit was like living in a Chevy Chase movie about a vacation where everything goes wrong. Your luggage is lost, the hotel turns out to be an abandoned cabin miles from civilization with no amenities, your cabin mates are all ax murderers, and the groundskeepers are the guards from hell. I kept hoping I would wake up from this nightmare.

Since I had been told that my clothing and makeup had been lost, I didn't have any little luxuries to make life easier. The other women had television sets or radios, but I didn't have anything, not even the means to shave my legs. At least I had paper and pencil, and I wrote to Victor every day. There was nothing else to do except use my imagination to keep him amused.

Thursday, November 29, 1984

My darling Victor,

Hi there, sweetie! Please give my love to everyone, okay? Tell them all to write! They will need my W# and bed number and the unit I'm in, special housing unit W209433SZ and bed #123. I hope everyone will at least write me!

My legs still need shaving, yuck, and so do my underarms! I will sure love a bubble bath when I get home!

Please send pictures! I need something tangible to remind me of my real world so I won't begin to believe this is it.

Later that week Victor sent me some of our wedding photos, which our friend Ric had taken. When they arrived and I saw my darling Victor's face, I started crying. My cell block sisters taunted me.

"Listen to that bitch cry!"

"Yeah, the poor thing. She probably misses her tricks!"

"More like she misses the money. She can't go shopping at Neiman Marcus."

I wish I could have told them to shut up, but I just sighed and kissed Victor's face. By the time I left, those pictures were terribly frayed and had curled up from the wetness of my tears.

With nothing to do but write letters every day, things got so boring I even asked the guard for some cleanser to clean up my tiny cell. Scrubbing the floor with an old toothbrush wasn't fun, but it did help pass the time between breakfast, lunch, and dinner room service.

After there was nothing left to clean, I sat scrunched up on my thin, lumpy mattress and mentally redecorated the pathetic, sparse cage. First I decided I would paint the gray concrete block walls a more palatable pink. Perhaps I would hang some pretty flowered curtains to cover the holes in the window screen, though that wouldn't keep the darn flies from getting in. I would definitely replace the small tarnished metal square over the sink with a real mirror so I could see how disgusting my face was becoming on this wonderful prison diet. Then again, maybe not.

The smelly, rusty commode next to my bed that, with the wooden top down, also served as my dining table and writing desk, would have to go. Its replacement would have to be enclosed for privacy. One shouldn't have to answer Mother Nature's calls while the guards watched.

The built-in wooden closet needed to be enlarged a bit, and perhaps a full-length mirror in front would be nice. Then I could see how fat I was getting. The sink on the opposite wall by the door was so corroded that I half-expected it to fall off the wall at any moment. Maybe it could be replaced by a marble one, with gold-plated faucets. Now that would be something to have in prison, I mused.

Naturally I would want a reading lamp over the bed so I could actually see while I read my letters. The overhead light was too dim to be of any use for reading at night. And last but not least, the narrow, uncomfortable cot that wouldn't even be welcome at summer camp had to be dumped for a more luxurious queen-size bed. In order to accommodate it, the whole room would have to be enlarged. I could start by tearing down the outer wall. But heck, if I got that far, I'd just leave! The guard brought me back to reality: "Almodovar, want a shower today?"

Anything to get out of my cell! But it puzzled me that I had to "bend over and spread 'em" to go to and from the shower that was just across the hall, not fifteen feet away.

December 1, 1984

My darling,

Already ten days have gone by—only eighty left to go! I am tired of swatting flies and squashing spiders who crawl through my food.

I have nothing to do here—can't even go for my meals! They push them through the cage door.

I have no one to talk to and don't know the time of day. I do have a window, so I can guess what time it is when it gets dark and when the sun comes up. Other than that, I am confined to my cell, except for a shower each day, with no sound but the chatter of other inmates who refuse to talk to me because I am a whore! And they are in here for murder! Can you imagine?

By the way, how is Sydney [*the Mayflower Madam*] doing? I hope they are treating her better than this!

Your glamorous wife! I am glad you love me anyway—all swollen-eyed and pale-faced and hairy-legged! Wouldn't my friends like to see me now! I sure hope nobody gets a picture of me like this and sells it to *Playboy*! Or *Penthouse*! Or uses it to blackmail me when I get home! "Hello, Norma Jean. Unless you want your husband and fans to know you look like a wild, hairy wildebeest, you'd better cough up some dough quick . . . and I don't mean squaw bread buns, honeybunch!"

December 2, 1984

So here I am again, always turning up like a bad—oh, shall I say it?—Penny! It is Sunday and I hope you are not too lonely. I know how you hate Sundays! Have you found another girlie to replace me yet? I hope not, my darling. I love you so much!

I will never be able to look at cows again without hating them! They will always remind me of this awful time in my life—and flies, too! I will forever be repulsed by flies. There are millions of them in my room. I have to sleep with the sheet over my head, else they might make a meal out of me during the night, and that would make for a very unglamorous and quite preposterous demise!

I am biting my nails again, honey. I'm sorry, but I have nothing else to do. I've been writing to you every night while I wait for the mail, but in between I chew them down to the quick!

So much for my infamous hot pink three-inch nails!

Finally, on December 6, the testing began. I was taken out of my cell to go across the yard, handcuffed to myself and to a guard on either side of me. I guess they wanted to be certain I wouldn't try to escape.

It was almost heaven to be outside my cell and see something other than a fence and cows in the distance. Even if I was under such heavy security, and everyone stared at me as though I were a mass murderess, I was getting a change of scenery. I welcomed a break from the monotony that was my daily routine.

The first interview was with Correctional Counselor E. Beattie. She seemed pleasant enough. During questioning she asked me why such a nice girl would try to force someone else into prostitution. She had a false notion that the charge of pandering had to involve some type of force or coercion. I was astounded that she hadn't read my file; if she had, she would have known that no coercion of any sort was involved.

On day two of the evaluation I was interviewed by staff psychologist Dov Arbel. Before he began his interrogation I was asked to take a Minnesota Multiphasic Personality Inventory test to determine my psychological fitness. When a copy of the report was later given to the judge, I learned that "the only significant aspect of the personality profile emerging from the test" was "a feature of being passive, submissive, constricted, and a fault-finding person. Otherwise, there were no indications in the test of any major psychiatric disorder or antisocial personality." Well, thank goodness!

Moreover, Dr. Arbel stated, "She appears to be sincere in attempting to express herself fully, clearly, and on occasion with unusual openness." Wasn't that what Captain Dills said about me, too? Only I don't think *he* stated it in such *positive* terms. And I don't think the captain considered me either passive or submissive.

With the study over, there was absolutely nothing to look forward to and no reason to be allowed out of my cell. I surmised I would not be seeing any more of the prison facilities, but I really didn't care. I just wanted to go home. I made a calendar for my wall, on which I marked off the days. If the judge's order was strictly adhered to, I had quite a few more days to pass here before I saw freedom again.

December 11, 1984

My sweet, darling husband,

Here I am, still sitting here waiting for the cavalry to arrive to rescue me. Not so much as a single soldier has come on the horizon yet. Oh, well.

The hair on my legs is getting so long that very soon you won't be able to tell one end of me from the other. If I stand on my head, you won't know it because my legs look like the top of my head.

As for my nails, well, I won't make you any sadder by telling you how awful they look, bitten to the quick.

Goodness, it's shower time again! And then comes dinner and then it's time for letters and then, after a completely empty, useless, wasted evening, it will be time to fall asleep again!

I didn't want to burden Victor with all my pain. Most of the time I managed to keep my letters from expressing the bitterness I felt. Sometimes, though, as the holidays drew closer, it became more and more difficult to conceal.

December 13, 1984

My beloved husband,

Another day is upon us, hip, hip, hooray! As the days peel by like the skin on my face, it brings us one day closer to being together. I am afraid with the holidays so close by that we can't expect the civil servants who control my immediate future to work hard enough to process me out of here before Christmas. I guess we can plan that I will be a guest of the state this Christmas through the New Year.

So, my love, how goes the Christmas madness out there? Are the milling throngs filled with the holiday spirit, peace, and good will toward their fellow man? Is society breathing a collective sigh of relief that this horrible, vile criminal is safely locked away, unable to perpetrate any vicious acts of fantasy fulfillment, pandering, or prostitution? Are the streets safer now for my fellow man to walk because I am put away this Christmas? Are the doors of their homes unlocked and protected with me in here?

Shall I sit here cheerfully and pretend it isn't happening? Oh, I am usually able to stave off the ever-present undercurrents of bitterness and anger; why, goodness, if they should become a permanent condition, my face would soon reflect it, and I would no longer be able to hold court with my esteemed clients. I would turn sour-looking like Penny, and someone might be forced to have pity on me and try to do me a good turn by arranging a date for me . . . and then they, too, shall land in the slammer for the heinous crime of trying to get me laid, and they shall wonder as I, Where the hell is justice? So to spare some other poor soul this fate, I shall try not to dwell on these thoughts too long or too often, thus maintaining my dignity and my future career opportunities!

If I didn't dwell on them once in a while, you might think my mind has altogether left me. I would sit here with an idiotic grin on my face and drool running down my lips, and the spirit you love so much would be long departed. So please grant me the pleasure of wallowing in this injustice once in a while!

In between my busy schedule of taking a shower, reading the limited selection of books available to me, and dining, I had taken to concocting stories about the ever-present, annoying fly population in my cell. If I couldn't get rid of them, I might as well use them to amuse myself. Sometimes I shared my anecdotes with Victor. I gave them all names and told Victor we played strip poker with a tiny little deck of cards. And then there was the story of Big Louie's unfortunate death and touching fly funeral.

Every day the guards gave me a new story regarding the whereabouts of my property. And every day it never arrived. I was beginning to lose hope of ever seeing it again. Christmas was now less than a week away. The guards told me that my husband could definitely come to visit me. It certainly gave me something to look forward to. I wrote Victor to tell him the good news. Then one of the guards warned me it was possible he wouldn't be allowed to visit me after all. The sergeant in charge of visiting had not yet sent the clearance notice to our special unit lieutenant. But he assured me there was plenty of time before Christmas.

My clothing and makeup were obviously not going to materialize during my stay at Nightmare Hotel. However, I erroneously assumed the money I had brought with me, which had been booked by the female deputy sheriff in the courthouse, was still on the books.

The one "privilege" women on the special unit had was ordering goods from the "canteen." While the other inmates on the yard had to stand in long lines when it was their turn to shop, we on the special unit merely had to order from a list, and then it would be delivered to our cell two weeks later.

When the list came around, I made my selections and impatiently waited for the delivery date. It had been a while since I had had any treats. A Hershey's Kiss would have been awfully nice right then. But all I got was my order sheet back with NSF (non-sufficient funds) written across it.

Christmas was being celebrated by everyone but me, it seemed. Still, in a few days I would finally get to see Victor, after being apart for over a month. It was difficult to contain my anticipation.

December 22, 1984

My dearest husband,

Hello, my darling. I love you. Well, it's almost Christmas. Are the crowds worse? I hope you don't have to go out anywhere. I hate to imagine you driving in all that rain.

It's Saturday afternoon, and in honor of Christmas the C.I.W. people are having a concert which is being broadcast to us segregees via a loudspeaker. Either the loudspeaker is warped or the group that is playing is as horrible as they sound. Still, it is music, and I haven't heard any in weeks, so I am bending an appreciative ear. But really, they are pretty awful. It sounds like the cows on the farm next door!

I understand the chaplain will be coming over here Monday night to hold Christmas mass for the young ladies of the Catholic persuasion. There is supposed to be some music, too, possibly some carolers. How nice!

Ah, the music is finally over. I was right. It was a group of the cows from the adjacent farm, in which case they were wonderful. Do you know how difficult it is to teach a group of cows to play musical instruments and sing?

Well, the guards still insist you will be here on Christmas. If that's true, I can hardly wait. Good night, my darling, from me and all my flies.

Christmas Eve day turned into a trauma zone in our unit. Angel, the killer gang banger, was supposed to be released after being incarcerated for ten years. Someone in R&R (records and receiving) had screwed up, and now it looked as though she was not going to be released until after New Year's. A verbal riot broke out. For some unknown reason the other women blamed the snafu on me! The problem was finally resolved, and at 3:35 Christmas Eve an ecstatic Angel walked out of the special unit a free woman. During a momentary spell of dementia I suffered delusions that somehow I, too, would be leaving that day. Thankfully, such futile notions passed quickly.

December 24, 1984

My darling husband,

I miss you like crazy and hope you are coming tomorrow. It is a beautiful day outside, although it is a bit cool. My poor little feet are freezing.

The good Father was here this morning to give these young ladies mass. Naturally, since I am not Catholic, I did not participate, but I guess my flies are, since they did. They all lined up at the door to receive communion and say their confessions. The Father gave them itty-bitty glasses of wine and a wafer. It was touching! The only problem was that they all got drunk, and they have been acting very strangely ever since. There I sat, smiling in wonder, spending my Christmas Eve 1984 in prison. So how is yours going, my darling?

No mail tonight. It has been "misplaced." I hope they find it by Wednesday! The last letter from you said you are definitely coming tomorrow. Boy, what a Christmas if you do!

Please give all our wonderful friends my love, thank them so much for keeping those cards and letters coming. I need these cards and letters so desperately. I just wish I could have gotten some mail on Christmas Eve. I am looking forward to seeing you tomorrow, my darling, but of course, by the time you get this letter, you will have come and gone! Next year we will do Christmas up right! Okay?

Christmas morning I was awake at the crack of dawn. My darling Victor was coming to see me today, and I wanted to look as civilized as I could without benefit of makeup, curlers, or human clothing.

I was too nervous to eat breakfast, so I passed on the food cart when the guard went through. Everyone got their showers before me, but today it didn't bother me. So what if these guards played their petty little games on me. Victor would be here soon, and everything would be all right. I sat on my bed as I did every day during this perpetual nightmare, biting my nails until they bled.

At around 9 A.M. Peggy's visitor arrived. Although I had no way to gauge time other than by hunger pains and unit activity, I had become adept at guessing the hour. Sometimes I would ask the guard the time to see how close I came to being right.

The visiting area for our unit was in the unit itself rather than in the normal visiting room. It was just outside the gate at the end of the hall, by the guard shack. Only one inmate at a time was allowed to have a visitor so it could be monitored by the unit guard. Each visit was limited to two hours.

I did some calculating. If Victor was here, I could see him by 11 A.M.

I sighed. Could I wait that long? Restlessly, I drummed my fingers on my "table."

Peggy returned to her cell. She was smiling as the door opened and then slammed behind her.

At eleven lunch came and went, and I did without that as well. I had the impatience of a lover who has been away from her loved one much too long.

What seemed like an hour passed. Where was Victor? I was ready any time he was. "Officer, has my husband arrived yet?" I called out to the guard on duty.

"Not yet. He'll be here. Don't worry. We'll let you know when he's here."

I went back to biting my nails. There really was nothing left of them and they were bleeding, but I persisted.

Carol's visitor arrived. It must have been nearly one o'clock. "No problem," I thought. "Visiting is until eight tonight. I still have plenty of time." Still, mentally I hurried Carol's visit along.

Carol returned to her cell quietly. This must be a painful time of year for her. I tried to comprehend what it must be like to know you killed someone else's child—not to mention several of them. I wondered if she felt any grief for the families. She would have plenty of time to think about it. She had been sentenced to three hundred years. I don't think she'll ever spend Christmas at home again.

I was beginning to get anxious. Where was my darling? Didn't he know I was beside myself with worry? I thought surely he would be there at the crack of dawn, as eager to see me as I was him.

Then it was dark outside. The food cart came by again for dinner. By this time I was hungry enough to get a plate of food, but I just picked at it. Dinner was cold cardboard turkey, papier-mâché mashed potatoes, and paste-flavored gravy. Mmm, my favorites!

There wasn't much room, but I paced the floor. Horrible thoughts filled my mind. What if something happened to Victor? Surely he would be here by now if he was okay. Every imaginable calamity crossed my mind.

Finally I knew visiting hours must be over. The guard came by with a special holiday snack. "It looks like your husband didn't show up after all, Norma Jean. Too bad! I know you were looking forward to it."

There was no way to call Victor to see if he was safe. I restrained the urge to bash my head against the wall to stop the anguish in my heart.

The next day I received all the mail that should have been delivered on Monday, Christmas Eve. In the stack was Victor's letter telling me that he had been denied permission for a visit and would not be there on Christmas after all. The prison post office had stamped it on Saturday, December 22. Even though all incoming mail had to be read by the unit staff, there was no reason to hold it until after Christmas.

December 28, 1984

My dearest husband,

It is Friday again. Not that time has flown or anything, but we are racking up those days. My cellmates want me out of here. I heard them say to the guard today, "When is that broad leaving? She's been here a long time. Isn't it about time for her to go back to Sybil Brand?" Well, I hope they are right.

Okay, so now what? Did you truly enjoy Big Louie's funeral? Well, maybe I can find a lady fly, and we can have a wedding. Oh, no, skip that. I am in enough trouble for trying to fix people up. I wonder how much time they would give me for trying to arrange a date for a fly?

I guess this is it, kid. I've reached into all the crevices of my mind to come up with something new, cute, or witty to say to you, but I'm afraid that, like Mother Hubbard, the cupboard is bare!

I feel you here, my darling. I know you are, in spirit. Good night, my hero!

Toward the end of my captivity, nearly all of my usually placid disposition abandoned me. The days, devoid of meaningful activity, were unbearably long, and the nights spent in sleep, not nearly long enough. But New Year's Eve was significantly easier to handle than Christmas. I saved a glass of warm, diluted, bitter C.I.W. punch from dinner to toast the coming year.

December 31, 1984

My dearest husband,

I hope to be asleep at midnight. If I am not I shall toast the New Year with you with a glass of water. I hope you are at home tonight so I can be with you when I close my eyes. If you are sitting on the couch looking out the window drinking a glass of champagne, please have a glass for me and send your spirit out to reach mine and we shall hold each other for a moment with our minds.

Here's to all of our hopes and dreams. May they all come true soon! Most of all, here's to you!

I don't think my flies will be able to come home with me. They held a meeting tonight and I told them about Vegas, but they decided if there were no cows in Vegas, they really didn't want to uproot themselves. They all have family out here somewhere, and I have promised to release them and give them some money for new clothes when I leave. Which is soon, I hope.

Am re-re-reading *We the Living* and *The Fountainhead,* and each time I do, I find gems I have missed, and they sure help give me courage and bolster my strength. I'm thinking particularly about Kira's speech to herself when she is walking home after trying to find someone to send Leo to the south: "It's not dangerous as long as you don't give up. It's war. You're a soldier, Kira, and you didn't give up. And the harder it gets, the happier you should be that you can stand it. That's it, the harder, the happier. It's war. You're a good soldier, Kira." I am sorry, my darling, I don't have enough courage on my own, but at least I can take strength where I can find it, and it keeps me together for a while.

Well, my beloved, I guess I will close for now. It's really cold in here and my hands are frozen, so I am going to sit on them. I love you so very much.

And then finally, on January 2, good news came. I was leaving that awful place the next day. I couldn't wait to put that sordid experience behind me. But, even when I was leaving, the guards couldn't resist playing psychological games, with which I had become so familiar.

The next morning the day-watch sergeant awakened me very early and asked if I had called my husband to come and pick me up. I was ecstatic. Did that mean I did not have to go back to Sybil Brand? As far as he knew, I was going to go home that day, he told me. I could hardly wait! Unfortunately, my joy was short-lived. When I was taken to the R&R, I learned that I was indeed going back to Sybil Brand, and no one knew for how long. I really should have known better than to believe the sergeant and get so excited about going home.

The bus trip to Sybil Brand was horribly long and boring. Once we arrived I was processed through the same way as a brand-new prisoner. Did I tell them about my headache and backache this time? Not on your life! There was no way I wanted to end up in the infirmary to see a goddamn doctor. This time I kept my big mouth shut! I guess I did learn something in prison after all.

20. When I Get Home

When I get home, I will shave my legs.
And when I get home, I'll have ham and eggs.
Oh, to be safe in my very own bed.
And into the arms of the man I wed.

When I get home, I will finish this book.
When it is done, and whatever it took,
I've paid the price dearly for speaking my mind.
But it's truly been worth it, I hope I'll still find.

JANUARY 8, 1985. The day started out in the same miserable way as the past forty-nine. I slept very little during the night because I was supposed to go to court in the morning. Awake long before the blare of the radio came over the loudspeaker, I was counting the minutes before I would start my journey back to Judge Munoz's court and perhaps back to my husband and freedom.

I waited for the guard to come to my cell and give me my clothes. She never came. I started to panic. I began pacing in my cell. Finally Judy, one of the other prisoners in my cell block, came by with breakfast.

"Judy, what time is it?" I asked her quietly. Some of the other women slept through breakfast, and I didn't want to wake them.

"It's breakfast time, Norma Jean," she said gaily. She was going home on Sunday.

"No, I'm serious, Judy. I'm supposed to go to court today."

"Are you sure? You're not on the officer's list today." She sounded as if she knew what she was talking about. My stomach dropped.

"Will you ask the guard please? My husband said my attorney had told him I was supposed to go back today." I was desperate and feeling very fragile. I tried to squelch the tears.

"Okay, hon. I'll ask her when she gets back. Here, eat your breakfast. If you're going to court today, you won't get any lunch." She shoved the runny breakfast gruel through the bars and passed me a shriveled orange.

I knew I couldn't eat, but I took them anyway. I sighed heavily. I was so impatient. Hadn't I learned anything in these past fifty days about patience?

Finally, I heard the guard coming back into our cell block. I yelled to her to see if she had found out anything about my court appearance. She had not.

Trying to find a way to amuse myself while I waited, I thought about what I would have to eat that night if I were freed. Ham! A nice big piece of juicy ham! And then maybe some English muffins with Cheez Whiz! Several of them! Yes, I thought, licking my lips, I'll pig out tonight and eat anything and everything I want. The hell with calories! Every imaginable food I had hungered for during the past fifty days went through my mind. My mouth watered with anticipation. Eat, eat, eat. That was the first thing I would do after I had a nice long bath and shaved my legs. Maybe I would eat while I took a bath. I looked down at the runny slop on my plate and shuddered.

After what seemed like hours the guard came to my cell. She didn't have my clothes with her. I swallowed hard. I didn't think I could take it if she told me it was a mistake, that I wasn't going to court that day.

"Almodovar, get your things. You're going to court after all. They just put you on the list."

"Where are my clothes?" I inquired meekly. I didn't want to risk having her keep me there for insubordination.

"You'll have to have the guard get them for you downstairs." She turned around and marched back to her desk.

I quickly gathered up my personal belongings and combed my hair. My face was an absolute wreck with all the stress of the past fifty days, I looked like zit city! It would have been nice to have some perfume and deodorant, too.

I had a whole tube of toothpaste, a new bottle of shampoo, and an unused extra comb and brush, which I definitely did not need at home. I put them inside my towel and tied the ends. On my way past Judy's cell I quickly stuffed them through the bars and whispered, "Please give these things to someone who needs them, Judy, and thanks so much for your help. Good luck when you get out." I shook her hand briefly. The guard was yelling for me to move my ass.

The guard that morning was the big, beefy blond woman who had yelled so loud at us the first morning I was there. In spite of her gruff exterior and mannerisms, she kindly wished me well and said she hoped she wouldn't see me again in there. Hell, I hoped so, too!

She stuck my belongings in an envelope and handcuffed me. We walked to the elevator, and she asked me what I planned to do when I was free.

"Finish my book and make millions of dollars," I replied.

She looked at me with a peculiar stare and said softly, "I bet you will make millions. I hope your book sells well. Don't tell them we're all bad because we aren't."

I looked her straight in the eye and said, "Yes, I know. I will tell them that."

She took me to the waiting cell and took off the cuffs. I was alone. There was even a clock on the wall and a pay phone. I hadn't known what time it was for fifty days. It was only seven o'clock in the morning, and nobody would be awake yet. Still, I thought, I could call my mother in New York. But wouldn't you know it? The phone was out of order.

Eight o'clock. I was still in the cell, pacing again. Women were being lined up outside the cell to wait for the bus to court. They were all dressed. I wasn't. I knocked at the door trying to get the guard's attention. She just ignored me.

Nine o'clock. What was going on? Court started at nine. Would the judge blame me for not being there on time? I was as nervous as hell.

Ten o'clock. A guard came, handcuffed me, and led me to another cell, the drunk tank. She told me I had to wait there for the next bus, for afternoon court. I asked about my clothes, and she said she would get them for me. She brusquely walked away, and I never saw her again—or my clothes.

There were no seats in the drunk tank, so I sat on the floor and began to contemplate my situation. On the down side, the drunk tank stank. It was smaller than my cell and made me claustrophobic. The floor was very uncomfortable, and my back hurt. On the up side, maybe I would be home that evening. I would see Victor and I would get a good meal. I sat there and wondered about my life after prison. What would it hold for me?

By this time, of course, I was very good at playing mind games to (a) relieve the boredom, (b) keep me from thinking about my anger, and (c) plan the future. Imagery is a great way to reshape your life, and I imagined all kinds of wonderful things—like finding a publisher for my book.

Another hour passed before another guard came. It was time for the bus, she told me. I protested that I hadn't been given my clothes and wasn't dressed for the cold weather, and a torn jail dress was definitely inappropriate for court. "Tough," she said. She told me I would have to get my clothes that evening when I was returned to Sybil Brand. I groaned. Instead of being released from the courthouse after the judge sentenced me, I would have to spend several more hours being returned to Sybil Brand, reprocessed, and then given my clothes and released. I wouldn't get home until the wee hours of the morning.

I knew this was totally unnecessary. Judy had told me the procedure. If the judge gave me probation, I could go home directly from court. But in prison clothes I couldn't.

When would this nightmare end? I shook my head and bit my lip. I followed the guard to the bus. The afternoon bus had several stops to make before it went to the courthouse. It wasn't very full, but for my own protection I was placed up front and shackled to my seat.

The bus stopped at the county jail, and we were all herded inside to the holding cells by the front door. After the other women were put in the inner cell, I was locked in the outer cell by myself. The inner cells had benches, but there were none where I was. It was either stand, or sit on the floor. I sat on the filthy floor. While I sat huddled on my haunches, looking with disgust at the dirt on the floor and at the passing cockroaches, a huge rat with something in his mouth scurried past me. He paused for a moment to look at me. I stuck my tongue out at him.

Time seemed to stop. I twitched and fidgeted, and couldn't think of a single mental game to play.

Once more I was shackled and loaded onto the bus. I couldn't have had more security if I had been a serial killer.

The bus toured the traffic court at the south end of Los Angeles—a familiar place for me. We picked up several prisoners, and everyone was given a sandwich for lunch—everyone but me. I was told I didn't need lunch since I was going home in a little while.

At last the bus pulled into the underground garage at the downtown courthouse. Although I was in the first seat, I was the last one taken off the bus. The guard took me to an elevator usually reserved for the most heinous criminals, and we went up to Division 32.

Bailiff Hart met me at the elevator. He looked at my face, turned around, sighed, "Oh, my God." He had a tear in his eye when he turned back. "What did they do to you, Norma Jean?" His voice was shaking with anger.

I was about to cry myself, but I tried to smile and said, "Nothing writing a book and selling a million copies won't fix!"

He asked me why I wasn't dressed in my own clothing. I explained the problem I had with the guards at Sybil Brand. He shook his head in disgust. He confirmed my suspicions that since I wasn't dressed, I was supposed to go back to Sybil Brand after court. But instead, as soon as Victor arrived, he promised to send him home to get me some clothes. He said it was his court, and he was going to let me go home if the judge granted me probation. I was touched by his concern. Throughout my trial he had been exceptionally kind to me and Victor. He could have made life hell, as some of the other bailiffs did, but instead he was decent and caring.

While I waited for court to reconvene, I was placed in a cell in back of the courtroom. A black woman with a broken leg was waiting with me, and we had quite a chat. Her incredible story entailed being in the wrong place at the wrong time, and with her broken leg, she couldn't get away when the police appeared to arrest her friend, who had a small amount of drugs on him. She was not well educated, and she certainly did not have the money for an attorney, so she was assigned a public defender. He was apparently too busy to be bothered with her, so he told her to plead guilty and do the thirty days. She was unemployed and had no money for food or rent, so she decided to do the time. At least she would have food to eat and a place to sleep over the Christmas holidays. The only problem was they didn't let her see the jail doctor for pain medication, and her leg was really bothering her. If the judge let her go today, she was planning to take the next bus to the nearest free clinic and get her leg treated.

When a person commits a crime against another human being that involves force, the threat of force, fraud, or coercion, the person should pay for that crime. I even believe that the death penalty is appropriate in some extreme cases. Some people should definitely be kept in prison and never let out again. But sometimes the justice system isn't just at all. People who don't belong in prison end up there because they are too innocent to know how to work the system, and the ones who do belong there are usually so clever and manipulative that they con the system and end up free. This woman was inarguably a victim—and will hopefully get justice someday.

The bailiff finally came for me. I walked out to face the judge. Victor had not yet returned with my clothes, so I stood before the entire court in my torn jail gown. I felt humiliated, naked. The following are excerpts from the transcript of the court proceedings.

THE COURT: I call the case of People vs. Norma Jean Almodovar, case no. A394853. This is the time set for probation and sentencing following her return from Frontera following the

Court's committing her to the custody of the Department of Corrections for an evaluation pursuant to the Penal Code Section 1203.03 . . . Counsel, do you waive further arraignment for judgment?

MR. CHIER: Yes, Your Honor. . . .

THE COURT: At this time criminal proceedings will be resumed. . . . Any legal cause why judgment should not now be pronounced?

MR. CHIER: No, Your Honor.. . . .

THE COURT: All right, Mr. Weber [the D.A.], you may proceed.

MR. WEBER: Yes, Your Honor. As the court has referred to the various cases, the court has not referred to *Tanner*, . . . also a mandate of the Supreme Court. And the *Dillon* case that the court referred to is distinguishable extremely from this case. The *Dillon* authority was used to reduce a life sentence from 25 to life into a second degree, 15 to life. This is not a reducible sentence here under 266(i). It is attempting to assert or insert something into the sentencing statutes which the legislature has removed from the court's discretion.

THE COURT: You're not comparing her acts in calling the lady to that of an armed robber going into a grocery store to rob somebody, are you?

MR. WEBER: Well, Your Honor, all these other cases . . . looks at those same crimes, so, yes, there is no distinction. . . . So in order to avoid the mandates provided by 1203 and in order to avoid *Tanner, Ross,* then this court has to insert something into the statute which is not there; and it is the People's position that the court does not have that authority or discretion to do such; and in order to do such, the court can only find that the statute is cruel and unconstitutional, at least as applied.

THE COURT: As applied to her, yes.

MR. WEBER: And as such—.

THE COURT: Counsel, a 33-year-old lady who has no prior history, no convictions, are you saying that she deserves to go into prison for three years for this offense?

MR. WEBER: I'm saying that the legislature has so spoken. That's correct, Your Honor. The legislature has said she does. Now you also take into consideration Miss Almodovar in her

particular status. You look at her background of ten years of
para-police, that she leaves for a stated purpose . . . because the
money was more enhancing. She could go out and make more
money and work less hours. And that's very true if what she says
to the press and to everybody else, that it's $200 an hour. I need
more money, too, but I don't go out and violate the law in order
to obtain that money.

MR. CHIER: Is this necessary, Your Honor? . . .

THE COURT: I have a question, though, for your client. Does
she understand if I place her on probation she is out of the prostitution business?

MR. CHIER: She understands, Your Honor.

THE COURT: Is she willing to do that?

MR. CHIER: Yes, she is.

THE COURT: Is that correct?

THE DEFENDANT: Yes, sir.

THE COURT: That means if you get busted at all for any reason
on prostitution, you'll go to the joint. I put you up there for a
reason. Number one, I wanted a report from the Department of
Corrections indicating whether or not they felt the same way the
probation department did, which was that you didn't really deserve to be in prison. The Department of Corrections . . . recommended I give you probation. They indicated . . . that you are a
suitable candidate for probation. And I also wanted to give you a
taste of what it's like to be up there. You've been up there around
sixty-five, seventy days, and if you violate probation, you'll do
another two years, eight months. . . . I think in this case it would
be unconstitutional to send this lady at the present stage of her life,
to say that she must do a minimum of three years in state prison.
I will note that . . . even robbers are given probation, and she is
in no way anyplace on the level of robbers. I think what happened
is obvious. The legislature intended to round up all the pimps and
the panderers, and they had the idea of—were thinking about
somebody on Hollywood Boulevard with a string of girls. So they
made a statute that tried to fit everybody in. As I indicated last
year, it is a procrustean statute that makes up for the shortcomings
by being draconian in nature. In this case the punishment is clearly
out of proportion to the actions of the defendant. I will suspend
proceedings. I place you on probation for three years.

I sighed with relief. The D.A. told the press he did not plan to appeal the sentence.

Victor arrived with my clothes, and I changed into some human garments. I thanked the bailiff for being so kind and rushed out to greet my husband. He hugged me so hard, I thought he would break my rib cage. I was free!

We left the courtroom before the judge could change his mind and went to our car. I wanted to drive but was in no condition to do so. Before getting to the courtroom, Victor had conferred with my therapist, who recommended some antidepressant medication. The therapist expected me to encounter some immediate depression, a reaction to being released from the stress I had been under. He was quite right. Although my first emotion was ecstasy, moments after we were in the car on the way home, I was overwhelmed with repressed anger. I started crying uncontrollably. It's a darn good thing I wasn't driving.

We didn't live very far from downtown. It took us less than ten minutes to get home. Our neighborhood never looked better to me, and our apartment could have been a palace, it looked so beautiful!

My legs were a bit unsteady as I got out of the car. Victor rushed over to help me walk. I don't know how I made it up the stairs, but eventually I was inside our home, safe at last . . . for a while anyway.

I didn't know what to do first. I was starved and thirsty for a soda (all I had in prison was water and Kool-Aid). I wanted a bath, and I desperately needed to shave my legs! I peeled off my clothes and jumped into the tub. I filled it so full with bubble bath, Victor couldn't find me when he brought me a diet Hire's root beer. I had submerged myself completely to get every bit of prison off my body. I scrubbed every inch of my skin until it was about to bleed.

When I didn't reek of prison anymore and was convinced I had no hairs left except those on my head and a few neatly trimmed pubic hairs, it was time to get out of the tub and face the next treat—pigging out!

Bless Victor's heart. He knew what I wanted to eat and had stocked the refrigerator with everything: ham, English muffins, a huge jar of Cheez Whiz, and even a bottle of Bailey's Irish Cream, the only alcohol I enjoyed because it tasted so rich and creamy.

I jumped into bed, and Victor brought me a tray with my favorite things. After I had my fill, it was time for a good night's sleep, a night uninterrupted by clanking gates, incessant ringing, and flashlights in the eyes. And with a nice, soft, comfortable bed with enough blankets to keep me warm.

It was early for sleep, but I was ready. Even though it was much too early for Victor to go to bed, I made him stay with me as I drifted off. Every time he tried to move, I grabbed him and held him tighter. I wasn't about to let him leave me that night!

Surprisingly, by the next day life was already beginning to return to normal. Everything was probably a little overdone, of course, because I had been deprived so long. I called all my friends to tell them I was home. I ate all day long, anything and everything I could think of. Over the next few months I put on almost fifteen pounds. What is truly amazing is that's *all* I put on!

Within a week Victor and I were on a plane to Boston to do "The Good Day Show." I had spoken to the producer of the talk show just before I went to prison, and he asked me to do the show the minute I got home. The producer gave me a copy of it, and in reviewing it later, I was quite surprised to see how well I functioned, considering what I had just gone through.

Over the next few months I was in and out of severe depression. There were days when I would stay in bed with the covers over my head, and cry and cry. I would be just fine one day, but the next I was suicidal. The healing process was slow. Some days I hated the whole world because no one had stopped the police from doing what they did to me.

Sometimes, while reading or watching TV, I would be overcome with rage. I screamed and yelled at Victor. When I could scream no more, I would crawl into bed, pull the covers over my head, and sob.

During this time I began to drink Bailey's Irish Cream regularly. I had always prided myself on the fact that I didn't need crutches the way other people did. Ha! This was one time in my life I felt I needed to escape, and escape I did. Fortunately, I have a very low tolerance for alcohol, and it would take only one or two glasses before I passed out. I put Victor through hell, blaming him for not protecting me. I knew there was nothing he could have done, but since I couldn't yell at the whole world, I took it out on him.

In several fits of rage I destroyed some of my artwork, including the first doll I had ever made. I swore no one in the world deserved to have anything I had created, and I would never again create anything that would give anyone pleasure. The doll was repairable, and when I was in a better frame of mind, I repaired it. But several weeks later, when I was consumed with fury again, I took the poor doll and this time used a hammer on her, smashing her beyond repair.

I got better as the months passed, and the periods between episodes of black anger grew longer and longer. I was able to function for weeks at a time without being overcome with indignation. One night, after an especially devastating attack, I decided it was going to be the last. I didn't need to do this to myself; I had to get on with my life. No more Bailey's Irish Cream. No more horrible, uncontrollable rages. I still got upset at times—particularly when I read about injustices in the newspapers or saw cops who got caught in the act being given a slap on the wrist—but I controlled my anger now.

I missed my clients, who had been supportive during my time of trouble. I was ordered by the court not to engage in prostitution, so even though they were friends as well as clients, I could not see them. And of course I missed the income. I had no financial support anymore and was living on what was left of my savings and the small disability settlement I had won from the city for my work-related accidents. Finances were tight. We were often forced to borrow money from friends to buy groceries and pay the rent. We lived on hamburger patties donated by an ex-client. I made a few dolls and sold them, but the time it took to make them was not nearly compensated by the little I was able to charge for them.

Victor did odd jobs for our friends, bringing in enough to pay for the car's gas. He also got some money from residuals. I did some consulting work for a movie producer on a film about prostitution, and the production company that optioned the rights to my story paid me another small sum to keep their option going. I don't know how we survived, but we did.

Our first wedding anniversary went well, and it seemed that since November 21 came and went without incident, Thanksgiving would be a piece of cake. But the day before Thanksgiving I went into a severe depression.

It's a good thing we had already done our grocery shopping because I was convinced that if Victor or I left the house, the police would show up and arrest us for something. Even if they released us on Friday, I reasoned, they would still have taken away my Thanksgiving again. I knew it was an irrational fear, but I felt powerless. The threat seemed so real to me that I wouldn't even let Victor take out the garbage.

As the day progressed I felt a little better. I fixed the stuffing and we cleaned the house, but every time I heard voices in the courtyard, I was sure they were coming for me. And I was prepared to fight until death to stay!

I burned vanilla and cinnamon incense late into the night and had a glass of Bailey's. Although it was only Thanksgiving, I listened to Handel's *Messiah* until even the angels must have grown tired of it. When I was finally convinced that Officers Fred Clapp and Alan Vanderpool must be off duty, I went to bed.

Thanksgiving dawned, and I got up early enough to watch Macy's Thanksgiving Day Parade and the encore presentation of *Miracle on 34th Street*. The turkey was delicious, and the stuffing was the best I ever made. Our friends were full and feeling fine when they left. I did everything I fantasized about the year before. The dishes were washed, the turkey was cut up for leftovers, and I was still at home with my husband, free of the shackles that bound me tightly the year before. For a change I felt wonderful.

21. STATE CERTIFIED—SAFE AND SANE

There are no words to express the pain that I feel,
No words
The whole damn thing doesn't even seem real
But then, it didn't from the start.

Now I am home, getting over the pain,
Trying to rebuild life anew.
The trouble is, now I've been declared sane,
What kind of work will I do?

"THE REVIEWING AND EVALUATING STAFF recommend probation with conditions. Subject does not have a prior arrest record and does not have a history of alcoholic or drug abuse. . . . She presently appears to be a cooperative person and is *not seen as* an antisocial personality or *a danger to the community* [emphases mine]. Probation is recommended." These were among the conclusions of the study that had taken a total of three and a half hours to conduct but fifty days of my freedom to determine.

After I came home from prison I was understandably angry. It was difficult for me to accept that I had done anything to anyone that called for removing me from society for fifty days and placing me in isolation and solitary confinement with women convicted of murder. If I had known then that I would be going back to prison for another eighteen months, I probably would have committed suicide. As it was, coping with the anger from one episode of incarceration was nearly enough to destroy me.

Therapy for me was not only rewriting the book but getting on as many talk shows as possible. It was important for me to let people know how their government wastes its time, money, and manpower while hundreds of thousands of truly violent criminals are walking the streets free.

First, I bought the *Talk Show Book* for advice on how to be a good guest. Then I put together a press kit and sent it to various media. I had little trouble getting booked. Everyone is curious about prostitutes, and to find one who was not only a call girl but a former traffic cop was apparently a talk show producer's dream.

I was unable to contain my anger on the first few shows I did. People responded to me but not nearly as well as when I'm happy. I tapped into my warped sense of humor (which I inherited from my mother) to help me through this difficult period.

Because of my controversial experiences, I expected to upset a lot of people, but the producers and bookers of the talk shows, both TV and radio, were very professional. I expected them to be civil but reserved since they were dealing with a hooker, but I was pleasantly mistaken. Almost without exception everyone I dealt with, from the host or hostess and show producer to the limousine driver, was warm, thoughtful, and considerate.

I can only recall one unpleasant experience during a show in Baltimore, Maryland. The show went well and the audience did not seem hostile. Afterward the security guards were waiting to rush me to the limousine outside, which was surrounded by police officers. I was petrified. Had I said something on TV that violated my probation? Was I now being hauled into the police station? Though it was nothing like that, it was rather serious. The show's producer called the hotel later and explained that they had received an anonymous phone call during the show saying a man in the audience had a gun and was going to kill that "bitch whore." Until they made sure I was taken to the hotel, my life was in danger. Though they did find a man with a gun, it turned out he was an off-duty security guard with a permit to carry it.

In October 1985 I went to the East Coast to do several talk shows. When I'm in the neighborhood, I always visit my mother. Mom had undergone many changes of her own since my childhood. When I was young, she would not allow a television in the house because she thought it was a tool of the devil. Now Mom not only has a television but also a VCR, and she has even watched a soap opera on occasion.

Her religious beliefs did not permit the girls in my family to wear slacks or short-sleeved blouses. But lately Mom has been caught wearing shorts, and she wears short-sleeved blouses regularly.

All things considered, Mom has accepted my life choices and changes quite well. I know she doesn't understand why I am what I am, nor does she approve, but she is always happy to see me when I come home.

One afternoon when I was home, Mom and I went downtown to visit my dad. Even though he had retired years earlier from his job at the factory, he continued to work as a janitor at Woolworth. Although my parents never divorced, they had been separated since my visit in 1973 when I had my father expelled from the house for sexually molesting one of my younger sisters. He had not spoken to me since then. A few years earlier, when I was downtown shopping with my sister, we ran into him on the street. Feeling some emotional stirrings similar to parental love, I said, "Hi, Pop." My father looked at me with bitterness and disdain and then, without a word, walked away.

It never occurred to me that he would ever forgive me, so I expected the same treatment when we stopped in Woolworth for coffee. I sat at the lunch counter while my mom looked in the back room for him. To my surprise the old man came up to me and gave me a hug. He offered to buy me a cup of hot chocolate. I joined him and Mom at a booth. Dad actually talked to me, and what's more, he told me he had seen all my talk shows.

While Mom was visiting the restroom, Dad, near tears, told me, "Honey, I'm proud of you."

Long ago I'd stopped hating him for the pain he'd caused me. He'd become such a poor, tired, pathetic creature. When he told me he was proud of me, I was deeply touched. Years of anger and bitterness had been reduced to a sad memory, and though I wanted to tell him I loved him, I didn't.

Many couch psychologists will probably wonder if I became a prostitute because my father molested me when I was young. He also molested my sisters, but none of them became prostitutes. Many teenage runaways who were molested became street prostitutes, but I didn't become a prostitute until my early thirties. And I didn't end up hating all men, either, because I realized all men were *not* my father, nor were they like him.

On September 5, 1985, I filed a $3 million lawsuit against the City of Los Angeles, the L.A.P.D., and Officers Fred Clapp, Alan Vanderpool, and Patricia Isgro. Among the charges were conspiracy (to violate my civil rights) and violation of civil rights.

When the City of Los Angeles was served with the lawsuit, I didn't expect them to take it lying down. I was certain they were not happy about my numerous talk show appearances. Each time I did one, the producers had to call the department and ask if Penny or Fred or Alan wanted to appear with me to rebut my allegations. They never did.

It did not come as a surprise, therefore, when the Los Angeles district attorney filed an appeal, on December 6, 1985, eleven months into my probation, demanding the revocation of my probation, after publicly stating they would not appeal my sentence. Among the reasons cited was that I was causing public ridicule of law enforcement! They accused me of "notoriously abandon[ing] my ten-year law enforcement career for a criminal one (as prostitute)."

Their thirty-one-page brief seemed to be filed in an attempt to silence me. After reading it, one of my friends contacted a friend of his in the D.A.'s office and asked why my probation was being appealed. He was told to stay out of it, and "If you can get the cunt to shut up on TV, we'll consider dropping the appeal."

There were not less than fifty-seven references to things other than the crime of pandering (which was my only charge) in that brief. Most referred to the book I was writing and the harm it would cause if it was published. I was accused of "magnifying my pandering by using literary means to sell prostitution as a glamorous career to a potentially vast readership, while commercially exploiting my law enforcement past to draw on scandalous escapades that undermine respect for the law."

References to Penny's physical characteristics were made. They invented a theory to cover the fact that she was unattractive and that it was highly unlikely I meant this date as anything other than a one-time occurrence. Among the statements made:

Prostitution could only be a part-time job for Isgro since not too many customers would go for a girl of her description (which sounded like your typical linebacker). . . .

Moreover, utilizing the victim as her personal secretary, respondent was also seeking to commercially exploit her own former career by writing a book about her many affairs, including with members of the police department (of which she was once herself a member) now to be exposed to public ridicule through her literary efforts. . . .

The consequences of respondent's acts go far beyond those ordinarily involved in a similar crime in that she was seeking to corrupt a member of a law enforcement agency which she was already exposing to public ridicule in a forthcoming book, thus lessening public respect for law enforcement.

In the brief, the district attorney claimed that even though there was no force or fraud involved, my crime was actually worse than other crimes such as rape and robbery. Among the district attorney's arguments:

> In holding the statutory punishment to be disproportionate to respondent's actions "in this case" . . . the trial court's rationale seemed to suggest that the act of pandering itself deserves less punishment than the crimes of robbery. . . .
> Nevertheless, in terms of impact upon the victim, whereas a robbery may have a traumatic effect on the victim lasting weeks or months, pandering can lead its victim to a lifetime of shame and degradation, robbing her of her bodily integrity, personal privacy, self-respect, and reputation. Whereas rape is accomplished by one act of force, pandering can cause a woman to be pressured into an endless series of indiscriminate sexual intercourse which progressively rape her spirit, character, and self-image. Unlike rape, pandering is a cold-blooded, calculating, profit-seeking criminal enterprise. It is clearly a "vicious practice". . . .
> As to state of mind, respondent is clearly unrepentant, having been motivated by years of bitterness against the police department as well as desire for notoriety and commercial gain. . . .
> It follows that the three-year mandatory minimum confinement condition of probation is not cruel or unusual punishment as applied to respondent.
> Wherefore, for the reasons stated above, the January 8, 1985, order of the Superior Court suspending proceedings and granting probation . . . should be reversed.
> Respectfully submitted,
> Ira Reiner, District Attorney of Los Angeles County . . . December 6, 1985

Here was another Christmas spoiled by the blue mafia! Undoubtedly appealing my probation was a political ploy by the new district attorney to make points with the police chief, who did not care for him.

In 1990 I dropped my lawsuit against the police "without prejudice" because I did not have money to pursue it further. My attorney, Don Cook, advised me that without another $10,000 we could not hire expert witnesses who were necessary to testify to the emotional and monetary damages caused by the confiscation of my unpublished manuscript.

If I had not been convicted of the crime of pandering and if I had found a publisher for the book prior to its confiscation, the damages would have been clearly established. (The fact that the original manuscript was never returned to me and I went to prison *should* have increased the amount of damages I could recover.)

Since I was a convicted felon and had not yet found a publisher, it was extremely difficult to establish a claim against the police. Even though it was obvious to me and to everyone else what the police had done, presenting my case before a jury without the expert witnesses would be futile.

When the government decides to destroy an individual, it has unlimited resources. For an individual without sufficient funds, it is difficult to fight back. Even if an individual wins in court, it can financially destroy him. It is easy to understand why so few people choose to take on the government.

22. TO CANDIDATE

Freedom—is there man born that lusts not after liberty?
Freedom—are there anywhere souls who crave not to be free?
Those who would not look up to the sky and to God vow
One has the right to live one's life the way one chooses how?

Freedom—man's noblest dream beset with well-intent restraints.
Freedom—is often lost midst "for your own good" refrains.
My freedom taken from me in the name of so-called moral right
But to what end am I enslaved for someone else's fight?

Liberty "adjusted" for whatever moral cause, and though they be,
If I have no right to choose, I have not liberty!
If I so choose the path to hell, I alone must so decide,
Else that we call our "liberty" mocks all those who ever died . . . for
freedom.

Freedom—our natural right and yet so new a concept to our human minds!
Freedom—each owns oneself, so simple an idea, so basic, it defines
All human interaction in that briefest, simple thought—
"To live one's life as each one decides the way one ought."

Freedom—it doesn't give the right to interfere by force or fraud.
Freedom—it is not reserved for those who say they're serving God!
Freedom—the very word, and all the word implies,
Does not assume the one that's free is good or pure or wise!

Liberty is for the brave and strong, the weak and coward, too,
And rich and poor alike, the fainthearted and the true—
All can huddle underneath the banner bought and paid for by our blood.
All are free to make a choice to live, be it bad or be it good.
It's freedom!

I WAS TWENTY-SEVEN YEARS OLD before I realized that politics affected every area of my life. Before then I was a political vegetable, blissfully ignoring elections and politicians. After Victor introduced me to Ayn

Rand's books, I was no longer a political innocent. When I realized how much politics affected me and everything I chose to do, I registered to vote. And I registered as a Libertarian.

There is a philosophical libertarian movement and also a political party, both of which are founded on the concept of liberty. Libertarians believe in self-ownership (autonomy) and that an individual is free to do whatever he or she chooses with his or her own life. Libertarians believe adults are better able to make choices for themselves than the government and that one has a moral right to do so, as long as it does not involve the use of force, the threat of force, fraud, or coercion.

These ideas made good sense to me and seemed to echo the very philosophy that our forefathers had in mind when they signed the Declaration of Independence and drafted the Constitution and the Bill of Rights.

When I went on the lecture circuit, it was only natural for me to speak to Libertarian Supper Club groups. Supper Clubs are places for active as well as nonparty Libertarians to meet, discuss philosophy, and socialize with people who also love their freedom passionately.

"You really should think about running for office," Larry Leathers told me after one of my Supper Club speeches. (He would later become one of my staunchest supporters.)

I laughed. I had enough to keep me busy: my lawsuits, rewriting the book, and now defending myself against the D.A.'s appeal.

But the more I thought about it, the more intriguing I found the idea of running for office. Perhaps it was a way to maintain a high profile and gain supporters while I fought the appeal. It would certainly give me a forum in which to tell people about the hideous pandering and prostitution laws.

Meanwhile in Oklahoma my brother Neil was also active in the Libertarian Party. He and a fellow Libertarian, John Robertson (J.R. for short), had been arrested for trespassing on public property while trying to get ballot access in Oklahoma City where Neil was a member of the Highway Patrol. My brother and J.R. became friends, and when J.R. was going to California, Neil told him to look up his sister, who was a call girl.

Shortly after his arrival, J.R. also proposed that I run for office. I had already given it a lot of thought. At his suggestion I agreed to run if he would be my campaign manager; he consented. My brother agreed to move to California to work on my campaign.

At first I thought about running for state attorney general, but one needed to be a lawyer for that position. Several people proposed that I run for United States senator and oppose the incumbent, Alan Cranston, who many believe later left office in disgrace after being involved with both the savings and loan scandal and Charles Keating. We learned there was a candidate running for that office who had financial backing.

Someone finally suggested that I run for lieutenant governor because it was a superfluous office; I could run for election without posing a threat to the rest of the state government. In fact, one of my campaign promises was to work to abolish the office and save the taxpayers of California over $2 million a year.

Once we decided on the office, the next step was to lobby for the endorsement of the Libertarian Party at its state convention. This was not easy. Surprisingly, quite a few Libertarians did not want a hooker representing the party in a state election. Many resented my decision to run for office since I had never been active in the party. Others felt certain that I would run a one-issue campaign.

To become a viable candidate for lieutenant governor, it was necessary to become knowledgeable on a variety of issues, including toxic waste and the deployment of California's National Guard in Central America. Even though I campaigned for the office from the perspective that the job was unimportant, I could not expect to be taken seriously by voters if I did not know or care about specific social and economic issues other than prostitution.

The Libertarian Party convention was held in February 1986 at the Viscount Hotel in Los Angeles. Neil, Larry, J.R., and I rented a suite for the weekend and stocked it with soda, champagne, and munchies.

As the delegates dropped by to view videos of the talk shows I had done, they questioned me about my motives for running. Slowly but surely I was able to persuade the majority of delegates to endorse me. When the vote was taken on Monday morning, I won the endorsement, with a 36-to-24 vote.

Next I needed to get fifteen hundred signatures or pay a fee to appear on the ballot. We collected the required number of signatures, and despite being a convicted felon, I officially became a candidate.

We decided to make a formal announcement of my candidacy at a Mardi Gras Ball in Newport Beach, sponsored by Bob McGinley's Lifestyles Organization.

Since I was running for office so that people with alternative lifestyles could continue making their own choices without harassment or interference from the government, it seemed appropriate to announce my candidacy at such a function.

Bob introduced me at the ball. I swallowed a sip of water and walked to the podium. I tried to smile, but my lips were dry and my mouth felt as if it were full of cotton.

I said I was the Libertarian candidate for the office of lieutenant governor of the State of California, and then I said:

> Many of you may be wondering why I feel qualified to seek public office. It is true that my past occupations might not seem politically oriented, even though prostitution and politics have more in common than one might think. It could even be said that since I have been prohibited from engaging in what I call "honest" prostitution, I am seeking to engage in legal prostitution—that is, politics.
>
> There is, however, a difference between a prostitute and a politician. There are some things a prostitute just won't do for money! Anyway, I am as qualified as anyone to run for public office. After all, I know how to screw the public. And, besides, we need some tits in Sacramento. We have enough asses. [The audience laughed, and I felt more confident.]
>
> Americans have been buying into a system that asserts they haven't the intelligence or self-control to govern themselves. I believe that if we remove the "victimless crime" laws, it would not only end the blatant violations of individual freedom of choice but would also lessen the resulting corruption that is inherent in the prohibition of any adult consensual activity. As former New York City Police Commissioner Patrick V. Murphy once said, "By charging our police with the responsibility to enforce the unenforceable, we subject them to disrespect and corrupt influences, and we provide the organized criminal syndicate with illicit industries upon which they thrive."
>
> And right now these "victimless crime" laws are being enforced at the negligence of serious, violent crime, which is the main reason that in many areas of our state people are afraid to go out of doors after dark.
>
> I am the only candidate for lieutenant governor who asserts that people have a right to own, use, and enjoy their bodies and should not have to worry that civil servants are peeking into their

bedrooms or extorting large sums of their money to pay for someone else's idea of utopia.

If I am elected, I do not promise to do anything for the people
who vote for me. I promise to let them do it themselves because
I think they can. Thank you.

In an effort to get endorsements from women's groups, I lobbied
before the National Women's Political Caucus, along with many other
women candidates running for public office. Because a television crew
was there to film my speech, the moderator chose to introduce me nearly
last so that other women who did not have the colorful past I did could
make some points on camera.

It was one of my most difficult speeches because not all the women
there favored my right to engage in prostitution. Many of them belonged
to the branch of feminists who believe all prostitutes are victims. My
comments were received with mixed reactions, but I couldn't imagine
that anyone leaving the meeting still believed I was a victim because I had
chosen to be a sex worker (the preferred term for prostitute).

March and April were spent writing more speeches and doing radio
talk shows all over the country. Reporters were dispatched from around
the world to interview me, and they were surprised to find that I wasn't
a gum-chewing airhead. Many interviewers reported that I was an artic-
ulate spokesperson for personal freedom. The interviewer for *Korea People's Magazine* was more interested in what I had to say about personal
freedom for women in American society than he was in my former career
as a prostitute.

In May my father passed away. As busy as we were, Neil and I went
to New York for his funeral. All fourteen children attended, something I
once thought impossible because of the way we felt about him.

When Mom called to tell us Dad was in the hospital, I knew he was
going to die. I sent him a get-well card. After he got out of the hospital,
he stayed with Mom so she could take care of him. He seemed to be
recovering. Then he went back to the hospital for tests because he couldn't
keep any food down. The doctors discovered cancer in his stomach as
well as in his esophagus, and told my mother he had a week to live.
Several of my sisters were with him when he died. For the first time in
their lives, he told them he loved them.

Maybe I can understand him a little better now, knowing that he had
never learned from his family how to express love. His children never
showed him any love, either. We picked on him and fought with him and

hated him without ever knowing who he was. In the bedroom at Mom's house where he stayed, he had posted all our get-well cards over his bed.

After he died my brothers cleaned out his apartment. They found boxes filled with Father's Day cards, letters, and school projects we had made for him during our childhood. All our pictures hung on his wall. He loved his children after all, but we never knew until it was too late.

His six daughters, some of whom he had molested as children, stood around his casket crying. All of us had wished him dead when we were young. Did he know that he could love his female children without sexually fondling them? I don't know. I wished I could tell him, "Daddy, wherever you are, I love you. For all the pain, I forgive you."

My father died the Thursday before Mother's Day, and his funeral was held on Saturday. Sunday, Mother's Day, was a dream come true for Mom. For the first time in twenty years all fourteen of her children were together for Sunday dinner. The group was so large, we had to eat outside. My brother Tim, who was a fireman, borrowed several long tables from the local fire station, and we set them up in the driveway.

Though I am one of the least domestic in the family, I ended up cooking dinner with my sister Ruth. Ham is still the all-around favorite of the Wright family, so we bought three huge hams and a ton of potatoes, asparagus, salad, and rolls. By the time Ruth and I finished cooking, sent everything to the table, and went outside to eat, the food was already gone! One serving apiece and there was nothing left. It was just like old times.

After the funeral I spent a few days visiting my friends and relatives, but then I had to get back to the campaign. Every Sunday afternoon the campaign staff and volunteers met to discuss new ideas. Once a month the other Libertarian candidates for state and local offices met with us. We had fun at those meetings. They were open to anyone who might have heard about my campaign. Everyone felt free to discuss all kinds of ideas. Some of our great one-line campaign slogans were born during those sessions.

We decided I would make a series of "cheesecake" posters that we could sell to raise money. Through a friend, Kay Parker, an adult movie actress, I found Suze Randall, a well-known photographer of erotica who was once a model. She volunteered her skills for the posters, and shooting was scheduled for May 28, the day after my thirty-fifth birthday. At eighteen I never would have imagined I'd be making sexy political posters at the ripe old age of thirty-five!

My campaign manager and I agreed that we would issue three different posters: Victory; Cut the Red Tape; and Whose Life Is It Anyway.

The first poster was unveiled on June 16 at the L.A. Press Club. After a brief introduction by my campaign manager, I gave a short speech:

> Sure, this is a rather unorthodox political poster, and we just might be accused of selling cheesecake to buy votes. Well that may be, but if we have the cheesecake, my opponents certainly have the beef. And it's all bull!
>
> Leo McCarthy and Mike Curb have both pledged to keep their clothes on for this election. For their sake and ours, I hope they keep that promise. I would hate to see either one of them get arrested for environmental pollution. But I have made no such promises.

The media was disappointed because I was not nude in the first poster. Nevertheless, the poster garnered great coverage, and its release was picked up by the media worldwide. We got calls from West Germany, Australia, England, and many other countries. Unfortunately, many people who knew about my posters and wanted to buy them didn't know how to contact me. Even though we had paid several hundred dollars to install a phone in our campaign headquarters, the phone company hadn't bothered to list us in information, so many people who wanted to call couldn't find us.

The media reported that sales of the unusual campaign posters were brisk. I only wish that had been true! It was our only fund-raising gimmick aside from straight contributions. We all hoped that the next poster would be an even bigger hit.

During late June and July, I spoke before such diverse groups as the Greater L.A. Mensa, Rotary Clubs, and gay and lesbian organizations. I rode in the annual L.A. Gay Pride Parade and manned a booth at the Gay Pride festival for two days.

Another female Libertarian candidate, Carol Newman, a lawyer running for state attorney general, accompanied me in the 1956 red Buick convertible that we rented for the parade. We both got unbelievably sunburned, but we did get good public exposure that day. There was a Victory poster on both sides of the car, and many people who had seen the media reports recognized me and cheered me on.

As the parade made its way down Santa Monica Boulevard, two West Hollywood deputy sheriffs stopped our car, to the dismay of the parade monitors, and asked if I would send them some of my posters. Laughing, I agreed.

My next poster, Cut the Red Tape, was scheduled to be released in mid-August at the annual Lifestyles Organization convention in Las Vegas. For the second year in a row I had been invited to be one of the speakers. Bob McGinley, himself a Libertarian, wanted his group to support my campaign. United States Attorney General Ed Meese's commission had just finished its report on pornography, and the Supreme Court had recently decided that private consensual adult sexual practices were the government's business, and upheld a Georgia law against sodomy.

The Las Vegas media attended my second unveiling. I signed and mailed posters to each of the other lieutenant governor candidates as well as the gubernatorial and attorney general candidates. This was my message to the bureaucrats: "Cut the red tape! Leave consenting adults alone!"

Every waking minute in Vegas was spent politicking. Even during the famous Erotic Masquerade Ball on the last night, I continued to campaign while Victor and the staff took the evening off to party. Ah, the lonely path of a driven crusader!

September was spent traveling throughout California, speaking to more colleges and basically to anyone who would listen. Our last poster, Whose Life Is It Anyway, was released in late September, just before I took time out from the campaign to attend the International Hookers convention in Brussels. At last the media was happy. I was really nude under the censored stamp.

My trip to Brussels gave me a very much needed rest from campaigning. However, my campaign fascinated the European press, and I didn't have much time to myself over there.

During the last week before the election, the crew from the Canadian Broadcasting Company arrived to film the campaign as part of a documentary they were making on democracy. Everyone on staff had to do interviews. The crew from the C.B.C. was wonderful, enthusiastic, and funny.

At five o'clock on election night, November 4, Victor and I walked to our polling place to vote. The C.B.C. was there to film me. There was my name, big as life, on the official ballot: Norma Jean Almodovar, Libertarian candidate for lieutenant governor. A convicted felon prostitute on the California ballot.

Later that night the campaign staff, volunteers, friends, and the C.B.C. crew joined Victor and me for a party at Catalina's, my favorite seafood restaurant in Hollywood. Victor and I met Catalina the first day of my campaign, which was also the day her restaurant opened. She offered us the use of her restaurant for election night and provided a magnificent feast for the end of the campaign celebration.

Mike Curb conceded defeat to Leo McCarthy early in the evening, but that didn't stop us from celebrating our own victory. I had made it through a long, hard battle that many people didn't think I would finish. I succeeded in staying public, visible, and alive.

I didn't win the election, nor did I get as many votes as I had hoped for, but for me the over one hundred thousand votes that I did get were proof that there are people who still care about their freedom. If the opportunity ever arises in the future, I will run for office again. Who knows, I just might win.

23. To Prison Again

No one would believe it,
I don't blame them, but then . . .
It's so hard to imagine
They could do it again!

Just when I'm getting over the pain
And starting to feel okay,
Just when I think they can't *do it again,*
They come back and take me away!

"IT's JUST NOT going to happen, Norma Jean. They wouldn't dare put you back in prison!'' my friends all told me as I shook my head. No one could or would believe the appellate court would rule against me. I knew better. My fight was far from over.

After running for office, I hoped the D.A.'s effort to overturn my probation would find its way to the round file where it belonged. Unfortunately, that was not to be.

A few weeks before Christmas my attorney called to tell me the oral arguments would be heard before the appellate court on December 15, 1986. Fortunately the court chose to postpone the decision until the holiday season was over, and so I spent a subdued Christmas and New Year's with Victor and my brother Neil. So much for yet another Christmas!

According to my attorney the appellate court had ninety days to make a decision, which meant the deadline was March 15, 1987. As that date grew closer, tension mounted. The three of us were grouchy, irritable, and irrational, and we fought over absolutely nothing.

A new movie about prostitution, *Working Girls,* had just been released and was causing quite a stir. Lizzie Borden, the film's producer, had upset some feminists who believed all prostitutes were victims. They did not like it that she portrayed the women as competent, nonvictimized, able-bodied people involved in the sex business because they chose to be.

To publicize the movie and draw attention to my case, the ''Donahue

Show'' producers arranged to have me on March 9, on a panel featuring another sex worker, Jennifer, and a female New York State Supreme Court Judge, Christen Booth Glen. The judge favored decriminalization of prostitution. Our only opposition was a representative of Covenant House in New York, an organization that helped young runaway street prostitutes get out of that life.

The show was very sympathetic to my cause, and it aired that day in every city but Los Angeles, which was the only place I cared about. The local N.B.C. station pulled the show and offered my supporters several contradictory reasons for doing so.

March 15 came and went, and I was a basket case. No decision had been reached. The black cloud still hung over my head, getting ever darker and more threatening. My attorney tried to reassure me that no news was good news. I didn't buy it.

Finally, ten days after it was due, the appellate court released its decision. They voted two to one to overturn my probation and ordered me to return to court for resentencing to the mandatory three- to six-year prison term. According to their twenty-nine-page opinion, it was not a cruel and unusual punishment to send me to prison. Judge Spencer, who disagreed with them, wrote a four-page opinion sharply condemning the mandatory sentence as it was applied to me.

My former campaign advisor, Larry Leathers, had been calling the court every day, and he gave me the bad news. I began planning my counterattack. I was not going to waltz back to prison without a fight. Thanks to writer Ellen Hawkes and chief editor Peter Block, the May 1987 issue of *Penthouse* carried my story. And according to the ''60 Minutes'' interview that aired in February 1988: ''Last summer, instead of trying to placate those she was annoying, she did the opposite. Norma Jean went back on the talk show circuit.''

I certainly did. I went on any and every talk show that would have me. The wonderful staff at the ''Joan Rivers Show'' scheduled me for another appearance, and the audience could not believe what I was facing. Joan Rivers, who lived in L.A. at the time, risked the ire of the police by allowing me on the show again.

I filed an appeal with the State Supreme Court, but unfortunately they decided not to hear my case. I read about their refusal in the newspapers on Friday, June 26. My attorney had not yet returned from Europe and did not know about it. I was reading the newspaper when suddenly there was my name and a reference to the Supreme Court. I realized it was *my* case the Supreme Court had refused to hear. The news hit me like a thunderbolt. Predictably, I got depressed since I knew I was one step closer to going to prison.

About a week later my former attorney, Richard Chier, called me with more bad news. The Court had sent the information about my resentencing date to him and not to my current attorney, Larry Teeter. He led me to believe the judge had options other than sending me to prison. I didn't think so.

I began calling my friends and the media to let them know when and where it was going to happen. I was able to reach a producer friend at the "Donahue Show" and told her my situation. She was shocked. Even though everyone knew it was a possibility, no one really believed it was going to happen. She was able to persuade the other program directors to have me back on the show even though I had already done their show earlier that year. Because of their booking schedule, it was not a live broadcast, and I was told it probably wouldn't air until after I was incarcerated. The mere thought of going back to prison made me shudder.

On Wednesday, July 22, I flew to New York. Of course I entertained the thought of not returning to California—only a fool wouldn't. Wouldn't it be easier to leave the country or just stay in New York? I could work as a call girl practically unnoticed and not worry about being extradited. As far as I knew, New York didn't extradite felonious book writers!

The flight to the East Coast was emotional and painful. When I said good-bye to Victor at the airport, I did not know if I would be seeing him again in a few days. And if I did, if I would be losing him anyway by going to prison. If I didn't come back, would he be able to join me wherever I went, or would he be arrested by the police in their attempt to lure me back? If he could join me, would it be in weeks, months, or years? There were so many loose ends for him to take care of for me. Leaving would mean leaving forever, and our lives were inextricably tied up with California.

I cried silently all the way to New York, but I kept thinking that if I returned to California after the show, I could never look back at what might have been. Whatever happened, I had to face it and deal with it. Easier said than done.

The "Donahue Show" was taped on Thursday in Connecticut instead

of New York City. On the panel this time was a D.A. from Minnesota
and a woman from Nevada who was on a one-woman crusade to close all
brothels.

On my side of the issue was *Penthouse* writer Emily Prager. While
the show was mainly about my case, we discussed the subject of prostitution. Even though I was a prostitute and my crime was pandering, the
issue, as always, was the book. That was why I was going to prison, and
everyone could see that, except the D.A. He insisted that since I had been
fairly convicted, I deserved to be punished. He wasn't concerned that
violent repeat offenders could receive probation while a telephone conversation discussing sex for money carried a mandatory three years in
prison on the first offense.

A fascinating part of the show was when Phil Donahue read the letter
the L.A.P.D. had sent to him in response to my appearance on his show
earlier that year. Although the L.A.P.D. was angry and upset by my use
of the term ''cop,'' they never once disputed the allegations of police
misconduct and corruption I had made on his show and many others.

After the ''Donahue Show'' I drove to my mother's house in Binghamton. During the drive I tried to think of what I would say to her. I was
facing actual prison time, not just a ninety-day study.

Mom was in tears when I told her it was fairly certain I'd be returning
to prison unless I made a run for it. I never thought my mom would
approve of that idea, but she was all for it! She knew why they were
sending me back to prison, and she was just as infuriated as I was. She
said she would do what she could to help me if I chose to go into hiding.

By then I was almost certain I would not return to California, but I
still hadn't made up my mind.

In the city I stayed with Lindsey, an old friend of mine. She favored
my running and offered to let me stay at her place indefinitely.

I called Victor every day from a pay phone. If my telephone in L.A.
was still being ''monitored,'' they couldn't trace the call to Lindsey's.
The last thing I needed was for her to get into trouble because of me,
although I really believed the police would be relieved if I did not return
to California. As a fugitive, I couldn't appear on talk shows anymore or
even publish my book. In any event, I was sure they would not bother to
hunt for me.

When I called Victor on Tuesday, he sounded extremely agitated.
''Honey, what's wrong?''

"I just spoke to Teeter [my attorney]. He wants you to come back. He thinks he can keep you out. He's filing a writ and will have it done by Thursday. He wants you to call him." I could hear the agony in his voice.

"Oh, my darling. What should I do? You and I both know there is nothing he or anyone else can do to keep me out of prison."

"I don't know what to tell you, sweetheart. It's something you'll have to decide." There was a brief silence on both ends. "Whatever you decide, I'm with you all the way."

It's sometimes the little decisions we make in life that have the most profound effect on our lives. Had I called Victor an hour earlier, before he spoke to Larry, I would not have been tempted to call my attorney. I hung up the phone and began to sob. I knew what the call would lead to, but with a heavy heart I dialed Larry's number. When he picked up the receiver, I was sobbing uncontrollably. Without my saying a word, he knew it was me.

"Norma Jean, listen to me. I am not going to let them put you in prison. You have to come back and let me make my motions before Judge Munoz. He doesn't want to put you in prison. After all, he was willing to stick his neck out the first time and give you probation, and he doesn't have to send you. I just know he will grant my motions."

I couldn't respond.

Larry continued, "I am going to tell him what Weber [the D.A.] said about you and the press. I am sure that will piss him off."

"What did Weber say?" I managed to say through clenched teeth.

"Didn't Victor tell you? Weber said that he didn't want to postpone this thing until he gets back from vacation because he wants you in prison now. He's sick of hearing you talk to the press."

"Oh, really? I thought I had a right to talk to the press!" My anger had returned, and with it my voice. "It shows what they're doing all of this for! And you really think you can keep me out of prison, Larry?"

"Norma Jean, you have to trust me. I know my motions are right, and if the judge has any integrity at all, he'll grant them."

"Even if he has integrity, why should he jeopardize his job on my behalf?"

"Because he is supposedly the most liberal judge on the bench. We couldn't have gotten a better one. Promise me you'll come back tomorrow. I'll get the case continued until Friday."

"Oh, God, Larry! How can you ask me to come back and go through hell? I don't care what motions you file or how right we are. If I come back, I'll go to prison. Nothing you or anyone else can do will stop them!'' I spit the words out in a torrent of rage as tears poured down my cheeks. This was my life we were talking about.

After a long pause Larry responded quietly, ''What can I say, Norma Jean? I think I can keep you out, and I am asking you to trust me. Please come back.''

I knew that nothing he or anyone else did would keep me out of prison. I knew I had ruffled too many feathers.

''Okay, Larry, I'll come back, but I have a strong feeling I'm going to regret this decision. I only hope you can live with yourself when I go to prison—''

''You're not going to prison, Norma Jean,'' Larry interrupted.

''Bullshit! Larry, you must know by now the judicial system is not in the least bit concerned about my constitutional rights, and they'll do whatever they have to do to cover their own asses. If that means sending me to prison for writing a book, then that's what they'll do. Freedom of speech, what a joke!''

I couldn't talk to him any longer, so I hung up the phone and called Victor. The phone rang several times before he finally answered.

''Darling . . .'' My voice choked up.

''Oh, sweetheart. Don't tell me. I don't want to hear it.'' Victor sounded desolate. ''I know what you're going to say. You're coming back, aren't you?'' Victor knew that as much as I wanted to run, it went against everything I believed in.

''Yes, my love, I am. Don't ask me why. Larry really thinks he can keep me out of prison.''

''Honey, we both know he can't.''

I sighed again. ''I know. Believe me, this is the hardest decision I've ever had to make. Please don't make it any harder.''

''I will stand by you no matter what you decide. If you feel you can trust Larry and you want to come back, I'll go along with it. I love you, Norma Jean, with all my heart. I just don't want to see you go through what you went through before. I don't know if I can take it. But you do what you have to.''

I hung up and then dialed American Airlines. I explained to the agent I had missed the flight on Sunday, and she informed me that the flight had been canceled anyway. I made a reservation for early afternoon, with an L.A. arrival time of 6 P.M. I called Victor and gave him the information. Then, slowly, I walked back to Lindsey's apartment.

After I packed and got ready for bed, I was once again overwhelmed with despair, and I started crying. I remained in a state of deep depression and anger all night long. I tossed and turned, and never slept. In the morning I got up tired, miserable, and despondent.

The only way for me to cope with profound anger, pain, and bitterness is to first get to the point where I am suicidal—the point where I feel I can no longer take the kind of pain I am experiencing. Then my rational mind takes over, and I again become determined to win this war against the cops. Only then am I able to find a place in my mind to store my anguish while I continue my life.

I look out of my eyes as though they're not my eyes, and mechanically I do the things that must be done. I tell myself, "That's just what you have to do, so just get on with it." It doesn't mean I don't feel the pain anymore, I just don't let it stop me from doing what I have to do.

At the airport I felt so forlorn as I waited for the plane. Everything around me looked so much clearer than it had before, and yet I was in a daze. I wanted to memorize every detail of my journey back to hell so that someday, if I survived, I could tell the world about it.

In Los Angeles, Victor met me. When I had been doing talk shows and lectures, he picked me up in front of baggage claim so he didn't have to park and walk a distance with the luggage. But this time he was waiting at the gate with open arms. We both began to weep as we embraced.

Larry Teeter was waiting at our apartment. "I'm glad you came back, Norma Jean. I don't think you'll regret it."

I hugged him woodenly. "Yeah, yeah, Larry. I hope not."

"I want you to look at the motion I am going to file in the morning. I'm also going to bring up Richard Weber's remark about being tired of hearing you talk to the press. I am sure Judge Munoz will not be thrilled about that. I think we have a real good chance with this motion. After all, we have truth on our side." The motion brought up several important points, including the fact that I had already served most of the probation sentence. If that time was applied to any new sentence, I would not have to go to prison.

He talked with us for another hour, then left us alone for our last evening together. My brother Neil was still living with us, and the three of us sat around and commiserated until the wee hours of the morning.

I was exhausted from lack of sleep the night before, but I knew we'd never fall asleep that night.

I packed an extra set of clothes—a pair of jeans, a T-shirt, and some sneakers—to change into just in case. I did not want to wear my high heels to prison. I also took along a small plastic bag for my jewelry so Victor could take it home.

At five in the morning Victor and I went over a few last-minute details of what to do with everything in case I was sent to prison and in case I didn't come home.

Copies of the computer disks containing the chapters of my book had been distributed to several close friends and one to my attorney. One had also been placed in a safe deposit box, so the book was safe. No matter what happened to either one of us, I knew the book would find its way to a publishing house someday. I was determined that publication of the book, for which I had paid such a high price, would not be stopped.

"Honey, if I go to prison this morning—" I started to say, but Victor put his hand over my mouth.

"Hush now. You are not going to prison," he said grimly.

"Okay, well, but if I do, please promise me you'll write every day. I don't care what you say—write the alphabet if you have to, or copy a poem or something, anything—just write me something from you, that you sign and put a hug and kiss on the bottom. I will need that more than anything I can think of."

He kissed the top of my head. With tears in his voice as well as in his eyes, he said, "Darling, of course I will. You know that. And I want you to call me every day. Okay?"

"Yes, my love. I will if they let me. If I am in solitary again, I won't be able to call, remember?"

"Larry promised us that if they put you in, they won't put you in solitary again."

It was already very warm in our apartment, so I knew it was going to be a scorcher. I looked in my closet for a summery and comfortable outfit to wear for my last appearance in court. The media would be there, I knew, so I wanted to wear something that would not be the focus of their report. I could envision the news story: "Ms. Almodovar appeared in court today, with her long purple hair hanging down over her green silk ensemble. Her three-inch hot pink nails dug deeply into the wooden podium as she stood uncomfortably on her green five-inch heels." In their effort to sell the story to the public, they would probably miss the real issue, that my First Amendment rights were being violated by the police and the D.A. With this scenario in mind, I chose a soft pink cotton sundress that went well past my knees. It wasn't tight or low-cut, but I had very little in my wardrobe that fits that description anyway.

By 7:45 we were ready to go. As we left the apartment, I turned and looked carefully at everything in our home for what might be the last time. The early morning sun was streaming through the big picture window in the living room, casting its radiance on the furniture. I wanted to remember the warmth of the home we had created over the years, to comfort me in the weeks, months, and perhaps years of emptiness that lay ahead. Suddenly I panicked. Shouldn't I have vacuumed, washed the dishes in the kitchen sink, or cleaned the bathtub?

As Victor helped me down the stairs, I thought about how soldiers must feel when they leave their homes and families to go off to war, not knowing if or when they'll return. I wondered if weird thoughts like repairing broken furniture or tending the lawn ever entered their minds as they left to fight.

We took a cab. That way we could hold each other all the way downtown. It was a beautiful, warm summer morning in L.A. The sky was a clear, dazzling blue that enhanced the green fronds of the palm trees that lined the streets. It was bewildering that anything so beautiful could be so painful to look at.

The cab let us out in front of the superior court building. Victor paid the fare and then took my arm and escorted me past the court groupies who are always hanging around. We stood quietly waiting for the elevator, both of us lost in thought. Victor was behind me, embracing my shoulders and kissing my hair tenderly.

The elevator was a bit crowded, and we barely squeezed in between a cop and a lawyer. I recognized the cop from my days in Hollywood, and he recognized me.

"What's happening, Norma Jean?" he asked politely. "How's your case going? You off probation yet?"

I shook my head negatively. "Not hardly. I guess I'm going to prison today. Your old boss, Daryl baby, can't stand the things I say about you boys on TV."

He looked surprised. "Really? They're going to do that to you? Unbelievable! I'm sorry to hear it. If it's any consolation to you, a lot of us think you're getting the shaft."

"Thanks. I think so, too."

The elevator reached the eleventh floor, and we stepped out and were greeted by an avalanche of reporters. Many of them were there to see if I would show up. I think they had placed bets, and those who bet against it were disappointed.

"Norma Jean, you came back! You think they're going to send you to prison?"

"I don't know. I hope not, but you know these guys can't take a joke. I guess they didn't like what I said on TV about their sexual incompetence." I tried to smile and at least look brave.

"What's going to happen to the book if you go to prison? Are you still going to publish it?"

"Absolutely. Why would going to prison stop me?"

"Well, maybe the police figure this would make you change your mind."

"Don't bet on it!" I walked into the same courtroom I had originally been sentenced in. It was difficult to breathe. The thought occurred to me that I would probably not be going out through that door. I wanted to vomit. My stomach was in knots. It's hard to be a caped crusader.

Larry Leathers, looking bedraggled and distraught, and my brother Neil, along with several other Libertarian supporters, were already at the courthouse when we arrived. They were talking to the press. I had a press release ready to hand out, and I gave it to Neil to distribute.

The *Los Angeles Times* didn't bother to print any of my statement. Part of my media release was quoted in the *Herald Examiner:* "A corrupt system has decided I am a threat to society because I talk about the abuses of power and authority that I have witnessed. I am not a threat to society, but I am a threat to the system. Because I thought I could influence people and bring about change, I have stepped on a lot of toes, and now certain members of the police department, with the help of the district attorney's office, are engaging in a blatant vendetta."

Victor and I found a seat near the back of the courtroom while the press interviewed Neil and Larry. Several reporters who had covered my trial since the beginning wanted to talk to me, but I just couldn't answer. I didn't want to disappoint them or go on record sounding like a case of sour grapes.

I sat there and sighed, struggling to keep calm. What they were about to do to me was just so wrong, so unbelievably wrong. Anger filled me, turning to deep, unfathomable rage. There were so many people to blame. Why was no one stopping this charade?

Please, Norma Jean, stop it. Don't think. Don't feel. Just get through this. You have to make it. Show Victor you're strong. If he thinks you'll break, so will he.

The court disposed of a few other cases on the docket before they got to mine. Victor and I sat holding each other, our fingers locked together tightly. Finally, at about 8:30 on Friday, July 31, 1987, Judge Munoz called the case of The People *vs.* Norma Jean Almodovar. I kissed Victor hard and looked deep in his eyes before I made my way to the front of the courtroom.

Looking straight ahead at Judge Munoz, I stood silently while Larry Teeter made his motions. The TV cameras captured the moment for me because I was too dazed to hear what was being said. I do remember the judge saying ''Motion denied'' several times.

Larry mentioned Richard Weber's outrageous statement about wanting me in prison because ''he was tired of hearing me talk to the press.'' It fell like water off a duck's back. Judge Munoz and Mr. Weber snickered at each other.

In less than five minutes it was all over. All of Larry Teeter's motions were denied. Without looking at me, Judge Munoz resentenced me to state prison for a period of three years. Out of that three years I could expect to be incarcerated for at least eighteen months *if* I was allowed to be in the general population. If not, I would be there for three years, minus the credit I was given for the original time I had spent in state prison in 1984–85. No credit was given to me for the two years and seven months of violation-free probation I had served.

I turned around and looked at Victor. His face was contorted with anger and anguish. He walked toward me but was stopped by the court deputy. The other deputy, a female, grabbed my arm.

I pleaded with her. ''Please. Can't I kiss my husband good-bye?'' My voice sounded so distant.

''No, miss. You can't do that. You're in custody now. Come along.'' She jerked me toward the holding tank door.

''Oh, Norma Jean,'' Victor moaned across the courtroom, his arm raised toward me over the head of the deputy.

With one hand tightly on my arm, the female deputy unlocked the heavy door and then shoved me inside. I strained to look over my shoulder at my husband. ''Oh, Victor.'' I choked. The door closed behind us, separating me from my husband, from my life. I was in prison—again.

EPILOGUE

THIS TIME, my attorney managed to keep me from being housed in isolation. It took a while to convince the lieutenant, but after being processed I was allowed to be placed with the other inmates. At least I could have access to the "rights and privileges" inmates attain after a minimum time in custody.

I was first taken to Sybil Brand Institute where the incarceration process begins. The "Donahue Show," which I had taped a week earlier, aired on Thursday, a week after my incarceration. I was in the visiting area when it came on, and by the time my fifteen-minute visit was up and I had been escorted back to the dorm, the program was almost over. The inmates in the dayroom were wildly applauding me through the window.

The officer with the keys stopped short and had me stand back against the wall. "Stay right there, Almodovar." He walked rapidly down the hall. I could see the TV through the window, and the program was still going on. I saw my face as I told the audience that "my body belongs to me, not the state." My fellow inmates cheered loudly.

"What are you saying that is causing those women to behave like that, Almodovar?" I was so busy trying to see the show that I hadn't noticed I had been joined by a sergeant. He grabbed me by the arm roughly.

"I really don't know, sir."

"Well, you're going to have to be moved. We can't have you inciting a riot here. Get your things. You're going upstairs."

He unlocked the door and shoved me inside with the other women. My bunk was in the dayroom—overcrowding in the jail necessitated unusual sleeping arrangements. I was one of the lucky ones. I could have been issued a mattress on the floor.

I walked through the dayroom to my bed, deliberately keeping my face from the window. An inmate whom I had befriended, Patricia Baldwin, came up to me and patted me on the back. "Hey, Norma Jean, you were great! You really told them!"

"Thanks, Pat. Listen, they are sending me up to solitary. Could you call my husband and let him know?" The guard outside tapped on the window, motioning me to hurry. I smiled as though nothing was wrong.

Pat quickly got the sense of what was happening and immediately got the other women involved. They surrounded me while someone wrote down Victor's phone number so that the guard couldn't tell what was going on. Then she helped me carry my meager belongings to the door. "Don't worry, honey. I'll call your husband right now. We'll have you out of there in no time. I don't see how they can do this to you just because you went on TV and told it like it is!"

I was marched up to the same unit that I had been in years earlier. This time I got a cell at the end of the block on the other side of the corridor.

Pat must have reached Victor right away because no sooner had I been locked in when a lieutenant arrived, informing me that a television station had just called, wanting to know why I was in lockdown. "We have a problem here, miss. Somebody from Channel 4 wants to interview you because we have you up here in solitary. You aren't in solitary. This is administrative custody. How'd they know you were up here anyway?"

I shook my head. "I have no idea, sir!"

They would not allow me to be interviewed by the television reporter unless it was over the telephone. The next morning arrangements were made to use the pay phone to make a collect call to my home, where the reporter was interviewing Victor and Neil. While I was being interviewed, a sergeant stood outside the bars, listening to every word I said. I chose my words carefully.

After returning to my cell, I was staring at the wall when the sergeant returned to get me. "Your husband is here for a visit." He was very cordial. I wondered why I was getting a special escort to the visiting room and how it was that Victor had been admitted so quickly.

Later that day I was taken in a special van to the California Institute for Women. After completing the initiation process, which took four weeks, I graduated to the yard and moved into Miller A Cottage. My first roommate, Isabel, was serving a life sentence for murdering her wealthy husband.

After the process of classification, when it was determined that I was a minimum custody case, I was transferred to a lower security prison,

California Rehabilitation Center. Before I was transferred in October 1987, Ed Bradley from "60 Minutes" came to interview me.

Each day I expected my attorney to have good news about a new trial. It never came, although he kept reassuring me that we would win the appeal soon. In my heart I knew it would never happen. Prostitutes are just not high up on the Supreme Court's list of priorities.

After being transferred to C.R.C., I was assigned to a job in order to be eligible for the "day for day" release program. For each day an inmate works at an assigned job, the sentence is reduced by a day. My first job was as a dorm porter, scrubbing toilets, and so forth.

Yet another classification took place, and I was given my permanent work assignment as a clerk in the art studio. Also, after being in custody for five months, I was allowed my first conjugal visit with Victor during Christmas season in 1987.

In February 1988 the "60 Minutes" interview aired, which brought me much publicity but no new trial. However, the publicity I received while in prison kept me from harm.

In July 1988 I was eligible for a work furlough or a halfway house. It was questionable that I would be allowed to go because mine was a high-notoriety case, which was unwelcome at any work-furlough establishment. With a little pressure from my friends outside, though, I was allowed to go. Four and a half months before my release date I had my first little taste of semi-freedom.

The van was late on the morning of my transfer. I had already gone to R&R, turned in my sheets, and was checked out. When count time came I was told to go back to my dorm until after lunch. The van finally arrived. As my box of belongings was loaded into the back, I waved good-bye to the few friends I had made.

The corrections officer driving the van was unaware of how traumatic it was to ride in a vehicle for the first time in over a year. Even though she was only maintaining the speed limit, it felt as though we were speeding along recklessly. We arrived at the halfway house just in time for dinner. The work-furlough house was a converted apartment building in a shabby neighborhood south of downtown Los Angeles, near the Coliseum. The rooms on the ground floor were the women's quarters, but the rest of the building was occupied by men—men who, in some cases, hadn't seen women in years.

During the entire time I spent behind prison walls I never had any problems with any of the officers, at least not in the form of physical assault. On my first day at work furlough, however, I was sexually accosted by the male corrections officer who gave the orientation to the new inhabitants. I was in my room alone when he came in and began fondling my breast as he fondled his groin. He used sexually explicit language to explain that some of the female drug users exchanged sex with him for a clean drug test. He made me the same offer, not knowing that I didn't use drugs. (In the real world, had I not been a criminal and he an officer, he could have been charged with sexual assault.) I didn't dare report him for fear of being transferred back to prison. I did tell my friends, however, in case something further happened to me. Thankfully, it did not.

Since work-furlough rules allowed me to have possessions from home, my husband brought me my computer. I was also allowed to have my vibrator, although I wasn't ready to use it.

A temporary agency was willing to hire me, and I was placed for the duration of my confinement at a job with the Southern California Gas Company. I asked only that I receive nothing more than minimum wage because most of my salary went to the work-furlough house to pay for my room and board. The less I made, the less they got from me.

During this time I began to gather notes for a second book about the prison experience. When the administrator learned that I was using my computer to write a book about prison, I was ordered to get rid of the computer.

I was released from work furlough on December 14, 1988. I completed parole on January 26, 1989. After nearly seven years I was finally a free woman again.

POSTSCRIPT

◇

I ATTENDED the Second World Whores Congress in Brussels in October 1986. Our conference was attended by male and female sex workers from seventeen countries as well as doctors from New York, London, and Amsterdam.

The doctors, who had been working with different groups of prostitutes, confirmed what most sex workers already knew: Prostitutes are not spreading AIDS. The prostitutes who have tested positive are IV drug users, and if they are transmitting the disease, they do so through shared needles.

One of the most memorable moments of the conference was a graphic demonstration of safe sex, using a condom on a cucumber. There is a way for someone to put a condom on an unwilling man while performing oral sex. Place it under your tongue; it is like having a piece of gum and not chewing it. When you start to orally stimulate the man, put the condom over your tongue and work it down his penis with your mouth. Most men are oblivious by this time. We are quite certain this works. So far there are no known cases of cucumbers coming down with any sexually transmitted disease.

Out of that conference came a book entitled *A Vindication of the Rights of Whores,* edited by Gail Pheterson and Margo St. James, and published in 1989. For anyone interested in learning what issues prostitutes discuss when they get together, I highly recommend it.

In the years since becoming a prostitute I have been interviewed on hundreds of radio and television talk shows, and I have lectured at colleges, universities, and before many other organizations. The following are some of the most frequently asked questions about prostitution:

Do you think men are silly for paying a woman to fulfill their sexual fantasy?

No. I think men who see prostitutes are more honest about who they are and what they want because they admit to having a need and are willing to pay someone to help them fulfill it, rather than asking someone who does not want to participate. If you ask me if I think some men are silly, yes. But so are some women.

What kind of men see prostitutes? Married? Single? Blue-color workers? Politicians? Preachers?

All of the above. Any living man with a penis is a candidate for seeking the services of a prostitute, and a growing number of women see (male and/or female) prostitutes, too. Sex is the second basic human drive, and everyone who engages in it is eligible to use the services.

Weren't you afraid of catching a venereal disease?

Frankly, I was in more danger of catching a disease when I was having sex (for free) with the cops. Until I became a prostitute, I did not even know what venereal diseases there were to catch, nor did I know what the symptoms were. When I started working as a professional, I learned about safe sex practices and how to take care of myself. That doesn't mean that one is completely safe from the threat of disease, of course, but as I always say, sexually transmitted diseases don't acknowledge cash transactions. They spread with or without the exchange of money.

The issues concerning the spread of sexually transmitted diseases were addressed in a 1967 report for the President's Commission on Crime called "The Challenge of Crime in a Free Society." It included an article that argued:

> Of course a state has an interest in protecting the health of its citizens, and the spread of venereal diseases is a serious health problem. In light of the statistics which show that prostitution contributes very little to the problem, however, a general prohibition of prostitution on that basis is overbroad to achieve the legislative purpose, and should be reevaluated.

In 1972, Dr. Charles Winnick, a member of the American Social Health Association and professor of sociology, City College of the City

University of New York, stated, "We know from many different studies that the amount of VD attributable to prostitution is remaining fairly constant at a little under 5 percent, which is a negligible proportion compared to the amount of VD that we have."

Later studies indicate that VD from prostitutes is now about 3 percent. The majority of sexually transmitted diseases comes from non-commercial sexual encounters, particularly among high school and college-age people.

Prostitutes make a lot of money, but never save any of it.

It's true that prostitutes can make very good money. Not all of them do, however. As for saving their money, some do and some don't. But then, some waitresses and actresses and secretaries and even traffic officers don't save their money. The wise ones that do usually invest it for their later years.

It's really a short-term career for women. What happens when your looks fade and your clients won't see you anymore?

A career in sports is also a short-term career. No one ever promised that life was fair. When a woman gets too old, she cannot work as a prostitute anymore, but neither can a baseball player or a football player or a tennis player. Like others in short-term careers, prostitutes should make long-term financial goals and alternative career plans.

Isn't it dangerous to be a prostitute? Aren't you afraid of getting hurt by one of your clients?

Some levels of prostitution are not as safe as being a call girl. One of the reasons women might be in danger is that in an illegal profession they are not able to go to the police to report crimes, such as abuse inflicted on them by either their johns or pimps.

Some people use the argument that since prostitution might be dangerous to women, we should keep it illegal. This makes as much sense as making police work illegal. I was in far more danger when I worked alone in Hollywood in the wee hours of the morning. While in uniform I was once attacked by a businessman. No one wanted to arrest and imprison me then "for my own protection."

There are some very violent and abusive husbands and even some abusive wives, which makes marriage a potentially dangerous arrangement. There are parents who molest and/or brutalize their children, making childhood hazardous for many children, some of whom don't survive. However, no one would consider or suggest outlawing marriage or prohibiting people from having children.

As an adult I chose to become a prostitute. I did not suddenly regress to childhood again, nor did I need some kind of perverse protection that included arrest and imprisonment. What prostitutes really need is to be able to work in an environment where they can get the same police protection as a man or woman employed in any other profession.

When a police officer is killed, the police rightfully spend their time and energy looking for the killer. When several prostitutes are murdered by a serial killer, the public responds by suggesting that the police arrest more girls and get them off the streets.

I worked as a call girl, and the madam for whom I worked knew most of the clients she referred to me. These men had been seeing prostitutes for many years, and as far as I knew wouldn't think of abusing a woman.

Don't some prostitutes rob their johns?

Prostitutes engage in sex or lewd acts for money or other consideration. Thieves rob people. Sometimes a man or a woman pretending to be a prostitute robs a man. He or she may even have sex with the victim first, but that person is not a prostitute. He or she is a thief.

In California, jail sentences for theft and robbery are not as severe as sentences for prostitution. If it is argued that prostitution should be prohibited because a prostitute *may* steal, then if that crime occurs, by all means arrest and punish the person for theft.

Isn't the mob involved in prostitution?

Organized crime has been involved in some forms of prostitution in a limited way because of the illegal status of prostitution. The Mafia was able to gain control over the sale and distribution of alcohol during prohibition because of the corruptible nature of human beings, not because of the nature of alcohol. Similarly the illegality of prostitution allows any element of organized crime to move in and gain control over some areas of it. But for the most part prostitutes are highly independent and are very hard to organize. Most men and women operate independently of organized crime, although many end up paying for police protection, which in my view is racketeering even if it is extortion done by a governmental agency.

In a memorandum filed by the Honorable Gerald Adler in the case of

Cherry vs. Koch, et al., Kings County, New York, the Honorable Adler says, "It has long been recognized that commercial sex has many attendant evils." Quoting from *Commonwealth vs. Dodge,* he asserts, "Prostitution is a source of profit and power for criminal groups who commonly combine it with illicit trade in drugs and liquor, illegal gambling, and even robbery and extortion. Prostitution is also a corrupt influence on government and law enforcement machinery. Its promoters are willing and able to pay for police protection; unscrupulous officials and politicians find them an easy mark for extortion."

Examining every issue raised in that statement, it's clear the illegal status of prostitution causes these problems, not the act of prostitution itself. Almost all the problems involving police corruption and extortion could be eliminated if prostitution were decriminalized.

I read that women who become prostitutes have low self-esteem. Is that true?

Robert Karen, in the January 1987 issue of *Cosmopolitan* magazine, wrote, "A crippled self-esteem, profound anger toward men, reckless disregard for danger, and desire for easy cash—such is the sickness and the need that drives educated women into a profession that ravages body and soul."

Well, I can't speak for all men and women who become prostitutes, but no one has ever accused me of having low or a crippled self-esteem. Besides a few select cops, I have no profound anger toward men since all men are not cops. If I have a reckless disregard for danger, perhaps that same attitude impels people into law enforcement. A desire for easy cash? Probably, since cash is what pays the rent and for other necessities of life. Since everyone who is not independently wealthy has the same need to earn a living, I don't see that the desire for an above-average living, working fewer hours, is a sickness.

Isn't prostitution a degrading and demeaning activity?

That really depends on the individual involved or how one views sex. It was not degrading to me because I think that sex is a positive, nurturing act, and whether it is given out of love or rendered as a service, as long as it is consensual it is still positive.

On a scale of the pain or pleasure human beings can inflict on each other, if murder, rape, and torture are the worst, certainly giving another person an orgasm must be among the best. I cannot fathom how one could think that making another human being feel good for a fee could be degrading or demeaning unless it is degrading to make other people feel good.

There are plenty of jobs that I think are degrading, but plenty of people are in those professions. And in many cases they earn a great deal of money. Garbage collecting, sewer service cleaning, and so forth, are jobs that I would not want to do, but they pay well. No one attempts to prohibit those professions because they're degrading.

If the reason society continues to arrest men and women who engage in prostitution is that it is degrading, then perhaps someone could explain how going to jail, being strip-searched, checked for lice, and asked to undress in front of dozens of insensitive guards and inmates somehow resolves this problem. Jail and prison were degrading to me, not prostitution.

Isn't it immoral to sell one's body?

Morality is the belief of the person. I don't consider it immoral. Everyone who works "sells" one or more parts of his or her body. Athletes, actors, actresses, and construction workers "sell" their body. The body is what is needed to engage in physical work. It would be difficult to engage in any profession without the use and therefore "sale" of one's body.

Perhaps because the genitalia is involved, people object to prostitution. In a free society people should be able to engage in behavior that others find immoral or objectionable as long as no force or fraud is involved. As an adult I feel confident that I can make my own moral judgments. For me it is not immoral to make other people feel good in a sexual way and receive payment for providing the service.

Aren't all prostitutes hooked on drugs?

No. That's another myth. There are men and women in the profession who use drugs, and certainly there are people who go into prostitution to support their drug habit. But the percentage of prostitutes who use controlled substances and abuse them is about the same as people in other professions with above-average incomes, such as baseball players, football players and other athletes, rock stars, actors and actresses, singers, musicians, writers, movie producers, stockbrokers, lawyers, doctors, judges, and even police officers.

If society desires to cite drug use among prostitutes as a reason to prohibit prostitution, then perhaps society ought to consider outlawing professional sports, theater, music, and so on.

What's the difference between legalization and decriminalization?

Legalizing prostitution might mean that the government would enact laws to license prostitution and put the control of prostitution in the hands of the police or the state, much as it has done in certain areas of Nevada—and in some other countries. In my view, the police department has no business running or regulating prostitution any more than it should run restaurants or grocery stores or the movie industry. Prostitution is a business, a service industry. It should not be subject to special rules and regulations enforced by the local police or sheriff.

Decriminalization would remove all criminal penalties from non-coercive adult commercial sex activity and permit prostitution to be run as a business, subject to the same kinds of regulations as other service industries. To protect women from being coerced into prostitution, laws already exist that prohibit the use of force and fraud. Those laws could be enforced against anyone who violated them, as they are now when force or fraud is used against a customer or a practitioner in any other profession.

If prostitution was decriminalized or legalized, wouldn't young women be forced into the life?

There is already a law that makes it illegal to engage in sexual activities with minors. Decriminalization of prostitution would not affect those laws. Because the laws against prostitution and related activity make no distinction between coercive and noncoercive activity, a person who is willing to use force is no more at risk than a person who does not use force. The result is that law enforcement is spread thin, trying to entrap men and women who are engaging in consensual adult behavior rather than going after those who are using force against others, including minors.

Decriminalization would leave the police with more time and manpower to go after those who hire underage girls and boys. Men and women in the profession would be able to report acts of violence or force used against them to the police without being subjected to ridicule or the threat of imprisonment themselves.

If prostitution is legal in Nevada, why don't you go there to ply your trade?

Prostitution is legal only inside a brothel, and only in certain remote counties of Nevada. In addition, prostitutes are subject to rules and regulations that are devised and imposed (often arbitrarily) by the local authorities, even though the brothels are privately owned and operated.

In Nevada a woman cannot ply her trade independently. She must work inside the brothel, be on duty the hours it is open, take the days off she is given, and see any of the clients who might choose her. In many instances she is not allowed to have her boyfriend or spouse live in the town where she works, she cannot attend a restaurant or other public facility without the madam from the brothel, and she is not allowed on the streets of the town after a certain hour; a prostitute in Nevada is virtually under house arrest during the three weeks a month she is working. That's just not for me! As a call girl I worked independently. I made my own hours and was my own boss. If I didn't like a client, I didn't have to see him. There is a world of difference between the life of a call girl and a brothel worker!

If you like the good life and having money, instead of becoming a prostitute, why didn't you find a rich man to marry?

The law defining prostitution as a lewd act for money or other consideration does not limit the act to singles. A woman or man who marries for money is just as much a prostitute as a person who sees many people in exchange for money or other consideration. I would rather see a variety of clients, openly admitting what and who I am, than lie to one man, tell him I love him, and marry him for his money.

It would certainly have been easier to marry a wealthy man. I would not have been arrested and would not be facing all my financial problems. There is no shortage of available rich men, if one is looking.

I myself had several offers of marriage from very wealthy men. But it was not really an option because I was and still am in love with Victor. Without him to share my life, all the money in the world would not make me happy.

The following questions are most often asked about the police department:

Are all police officers corrupt?

No, of course not. Not even the majority of them are corrupt. Unfortunately for those who are good, hardworking, honest law enforcement officers, the bad ones seem to have most of the power and make it necessary for the good ones to look the other way. Sadly, when you give men and women a badge and a gun, you can not expect they will all be heroes.

You say that the police often force prostitutes to become informants. Since prostitutes are committing a crime anyway, shouldn't the police be able to do this?

When police arrest a suspect, they often bargain with the person to "give up" someone else who may have committed a more serious offense than the person arrested. But after cooperating with the police, the arrestee is not at liberty to go out and continue committing criminal acts. In the case of prostitution, however, not only is the prostitute allowed to continue committing acts of prostitution, she is actually encouraged by the police to do so. Without her continued illegal activity, she has no information to offer the police. If she continues to cooperate with the police by turning in other women or giving the police the names of her clients, she can work without fear of being arrested. In other types of businesses, forcing ongoing cooperation in exchange for protection is called extortion.

In many cities the police also use the law to extort the prostitute for sex and/or money. Since prostitution laws were intended to protect women from being exploited, it seems inappropriate to allow the police to use the laws for this purpose. In a decriminalized system of prostitution, women in the sex industry could report acts of extortion against them without fear of reprisal.

Why didn't you try to do something about the corruption while you were still employed by the police department?

It is almost impossible for anyone to change something while in the situation. Only after one leaves can one make a significant difference. Attempting to do anything about illegal activity committed by one's peers and supervisors can result in harassment, transfers, unemployment, and even death. Faced with such powerful incentives to keep one's mouth shut, it is no wonder that the Code of Silence thrives.

The only way to minimize this temptation among police is to eliminate the prohibition against private consenting adult activity. Until then, unfortunately, police corruption will continue to be a way of life.

Our justice system is often too soft on real criminals and terribly unjust to people who make personal moral choices that are not condoned by some members of society. It's a shame that some people feel the need to have their personal religious or moral convictions backed by a gun. The courts and jails are clogged with people being prosecuted for their personal choices, while real criminals are being set free. And we wonder why our justice system is not working, why our cops become corrupt, and why no one has any respect for the law.

It is important that people question the power that is given to the politicians, bureaucrats, and other government employees to make moral choices for us. We need to remember that these people are not our masters but our servants. They have no right to make moral choices for anyone but themselves. When we allow them to do so, a lot of good, honest people are forced to look the other way, while a few powerful, corrupt, dishonest civil servants (police officers included) get away with murder—sometimes literally.

In a free society everyone has the right to make his or her own moral decisions. No matter how immoral, self-destructive, repulsive, or wrong it may seem to others, private adult consensual behavior that does not involve force, the threat of force, fraud, or coercion should not be the concern of government. After all, everyone has a right to his or her own life.

When you become weary of having your tax money wasted on the regulation of private consensual adult behavior, contact your legislators. While it probably won't put the dollar back in your pocket, you will at least know it's not being wasted on this.

ORGANIZATIONS FOR THE RIGHTS OF PROSTITUTES

United States

National Task Force on Prostitution
P. O. Box 26354
San Francisco, CA 94126

C.O.Y.O.T.E. (Call Off Your Old Tired Ethics)
1626 N. Wilcox Avenue, #580
Hollywood, CA 90028
Director: Norma Jean Almodovar, (213) 738-8028

C.O.Y.O.T.E.
2269 Chestnut Street, #452
San Francisco, CA 94123
Director: Samantha Miller, (415) 474-3037

C.O.Y.O.T.E.
P. O. Box 621
Astor Station
Boston, MA 02123-0621
(617) 783-3572

P.O.N.Y. (Prostitutes of New York)
25 West 45th Street, #1401
New York, NY 10036
Veronica Vera, (212) 713-5678

H.I.R.E. (Hooking Is Real Employment)
P. O. Box 7781
Atlanta, GA 30309
President: Dolores French, (404) 876-1212

International

I.C.P.R. (International Congress for Prostitutes' Rights)
Postbus 725
1000 AS Amsterdam, Netherlands
Phone (in Netherlands) 31-20-168597/594

C.O.R.P. (Canadian Organization for the Rights of Prostitutes)
P. O. Box 1143
Station F
Toronto, Canada M4Y 2T8
(416) 964-0150

HYDRA
Kantstrasse, 54, D. 1000
Berlin 12, Germany
Phone 49-303-3128061

P.L.A.N. (Prostitution Laws Are Nonsense)
42, Thornhillsquare
London, N1, England

THE RED THREAD (Rode Draad)
Postbus 16422
1001 RM Amsterdam, Netherlands
Phone 31-20-243366

Centre de Documentation International sur la Prostitution
24, rue de Neuchâtel
CH. 1201
Geneva, Switzerland
Phone 41-22-328276

Australian Prostitutes Collective
P. O. Box 470
Kings Cross 2011
Sydney NSW, Australia
Phone 61-2-357-1300

ISER National Network of Prostitutes
Largo Do Marchado 21. Co.
Rio de Janeiro 22211, Brazil
Phone 55-21-205-4796

ACKNOWLEDGMENTS

THERE ARE SO MANY wonderful people whose contributions to my life during the past ten years made it possible for me to endure the unendurable. I must take this opportunity to thank those people, and to those of you whom I may fail to mention, thank you, too.

Victor, the love of my life, who stood by me through it all, held my hand, and refused to let me give up. My mother, who never disowned me or stopped loving me, even though our philosophies are worlds apart. Frank Esposito and Rochelle Bell who stood by to bail me out during the appeal. Shae, Jaime, and the writer's group—we did it! My agent, Luise Healey, for having faith in the book after all the others became discouraged and gave up. My editor, Fred Hills, who had the courage to say yes after so many rejections. Laureen C. who helped me birth the baby. R. N. Bullard for being more than a friend. Ann, Val, Foxy, and Ginger for their friendship and hospitality. For their support during my campaign: John Robertson, Larry Leathers, my brother Neil, Chris Rud, Terry R. S., and all my campaign staff and volunteers—Jack Dean and those who talked me into running for office. Our good friends Ric, Margaret, and Monica; Jax and Debbie; Richard and Patty B.; Cynthia M. and Aurora, Cynthia C., Cheri, Lucy, Scarlot Harlot, Sydney B. B., Margo St. James, Priscilla Alexander, Richard Chier, Charlie, Fred C., Larry C., Carol L., Selma and Paul Lewin, John D., Charles T., Ephraim Margolin, Larry Teeter, Suze Randall, Mona Coates, Jeffrey Bruce and Wayne, Frank Almodovar, Sandy O., Budd Moss, Larry A., Gordon Arnold, Bob C., Gerhardt, Roger and Paul, Medea and Millie E., Libertarian Party of California, Karl Hess, Mike Holmes, Bernie B., Mike Acree, Hester, Katie, Beth, Liz and Syd, Ted and Ethel H., Geoff and Nancy N., Bailiff Hart, Jim Morris, Catalina, Nicky, Irwin Zucker, Sam Perlmutter, Sandy W., Tosh A., Carol S., Bobby Littman, Dr. Bob McGinley, the Lifestyles Organization, P.I.P.'s, Oliver, Ed's Copy Service, all the people who supported my campaign: my brothers Doug, Phil, Dave, Neil, K., John, T., Joe, sisters Ruth, G. E., Virginia, M. and E. J. My work-furlough roommate Bobby T., Carol Michals from the art studio. Special thanks to Patricia Baldwin, the inmate who contacted my husband when the guards threw me in solitary confinement after the "Donahue Show" aired.

The media, all so wonderful to me: Ed Bradley and "60 Minutes" (Marley Klaus, Grace Deikhaus), Phil Donahue, Joan Rivers, Oprah Winfrey, Sally Jessy Raphael, Michael Jackson, Larry King, Morton Downey, Jr., Richard Shanks, Paul

Gonzalez, Peter Anderson, Ben Stein, Ellen Hawkes, Bob Stewart, Jeff Snyder, Greg Roberts, Glen Costin, Michael Hoffman, Linda Deutsch, Malchom Boyes, *Playboy, Penthouse,* Peter Block, Alan Boch, Peter Brennan, Dave Rossie, Kelly and Co., "Current Affair," and the many journalists, producers, radio and television hosts who were so gracious to me.

In memory of John Dentinger, who passed away in 1992.

PHOTO CREDITS